T3-BPD-615

Literature and Journalism

Also by Mark Canada

Literature and Journalism in Antebellum America (2011)

Literature and Journalism

Inspirations, Intersections, and Inventions from Ben Franklin to Stephen Colbert

Edited by Mark Canada

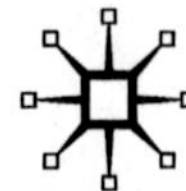

Figure I.1, *The York Family at Home* by Joseph H. Davis (1837) is reproduced by kind permission of the Abby Aldrich Rockefeller Folk Museum, The Colonial Williamsburg Foundation. From the collection of Abby Aldrich Rockefeller; gift of the Museum of Modern Art

First published in 2013 by PALGRAVE MACMILLAN® in the United States—a division of St. Martin's Press LLC, 175 Fifth Avenue, New York, NY 10010.

Where this book is distributed in the UK, Europe and the rest of the world, this is by Palgrave Macmillan, a division of Macmillan Publishers Limited, registered in England, company number 785998, of Houndmills, Basingstoke, Hampshire RG21 6XS.

Palgrave Macmillan is the global academic imprint of the above companies and has companies and representatives throughout the world.

Palgrave® and Macmillan® are registered trademarks in the United States, the United Kingdom, Europe and other countries.

ISBN: 978-1-137-30062-1

Library of Congress Cataloging-in-Publication Data

Canada, Mark
Literature and journalism : inspirations, intersections, and inventions from Ben Franklin to Stephen Colbert / Mark Canada, Editor.
p. cm.
Includes index.
ISBN 978-1-137-30062-1 (alk. paper)
1. Journalism and literature—United States—History. 2. Literature and society—United States—History. 3. American literature—History and criticism. I. Canada, Mark, editor of compilation.
PS121.L55 2013
810.9'39—dc23 2012040884

A catalogue record of the book is available from the British Library.

Design by Scribe Inc.

First edition: April 2013

10 9 8 7 6 5 4 3 2 1

Contents

Illustrations

Acknowledgments

When I set out to put together a collection of essays on literature and journalism in the United States, I set my sights high, approaching many of the leading scholars in the field. Readers need only glance at the list of contributors for this volume to see how fortunate I was. When they turn to the essays themselves, readers will find fresh, revealing, and intriguing studies of the long-lasting and ongoing relationship between literature and journalism. What they won't see is the remarkable level of professionalism these scholars showed me in our interactions. I can't imagine many—or even any—editors have had the good fortune of working with a more dependable, punctual, and congenial group of scholars. I am deeply grateful for all they have done to make my work a joy.

In the later stages of production, I also had the good fortune of working with other consummate professionals: Brigitte Shull and Maia Woolner at Palgrave have patiently and punctually replied to my questions; Michael Alewine at my institution's academic library has been helpful, as always; and Nami Montgomery has been an able, conscientious, and reliable graduate assistant. Thank you all for being the ideal partners for this project.

Finally, I thank my wife, Lisa, and our children, Essie and Will, for their patience and support, as well as their help with the cover art.

INTRODUCTION

A Brief History of Literature and Journalism in the United States

Mark Canada

ON HIS WAY TO COVER A STORY overseas, a young reporter learns that his ship is in trouble. In the midst of this once-in-a-lifetime—possibly end-of-a-lifetime—story, he observes the scenes around him: a young oiler bailing water in the ship's fire room, the oiler and others (with help from the reporter himself) struggling to lower a lifeboat, the chief engineer jumping onto a raft, the first mate diving into the sea, and at last the ship going down. A full day later, after a harrowing journey in a ten-foot dinghy with three other men, he finds himself back on terra firma, the rich details of the story still fresh in his brain.

Now what?

For Stephen Crane, the answer must have been obvious: write the story. Within days, the *New York Press* ran Crane's account of the ship's launch, its demise, and the fate of the oiler but, curiously, no details concerning the adventures of the four men in the dinghy. "The history of life in an open boat for thirty hours would no doubt be very instructive for the young," the article teases, "but none is to be told here now." Six months later, Crane would tell this history in the form of a short story in the June issue of *Scribner's Magazine*. Today, after the lapse of a century and more, few people have even heard of Crane's news story, but countless readers know "The Open Boat."[1]

Crane's dual accounts of his adventures at sea point to an important, longstanding, productive, and fascinating relationship in American letters. Over the past three centuries and more, thousands of American men and women have sought to capture truth in words. Many have published their accounts in newspapers and magazines aimed at mass audiences, usually following the conventions of something that has come to be called journalism. Although these conventions have evolved since the appearance of the first American newspaper, the *Boston News-Letter*, in 1704, journalism has largely consisted of factual accounts of recent events deemed newsworthy. Reporters and other journalists have frequently chosen material based on accepted news values, such as timeliness and impact, and packaged this material in conventional ways. Particularly in more recent times, for instance, reporters have commonly written summary leads that hit at least some of the five *W*s and an *H*—who, what, when, where, why, and how—and followed up with additional details in an "inverted pyramid" style, moving from the most important to the least important information.[2] Other American writers, equally concerned with reporting truths to their readers, have published their writing in books and literary magazines, where journalistic criteria and conventions did not apply. *Literature*, a loose term for this kind of writing, shows signs of other sorts of conventions—those of plot, character, rhyme, and rhythm, for instance—but displays a great deal of freedom, as well. Writers of novels, short stories, plays, and poems generally do not have to write about timely subjects or present their information in any defined order. They don't even have to stick to facts. Even the authors of nonfiction writing, such as essays and autobiographical narratives, have wide latitude when it comes to language and approach. Their audiences, which tend to be smaller than those of newspapers and general-interest magazines, expect and prefer a much looser approach to truth telling. In short, we might say that journalism reports timely facts in prescribed formats for mass audiences, while literature explores timeless truths in a variety of artistic ways for select readers.

If "Stephen Crane's Own Story" and "The Open Boat" roughly illustrate these two approaches to the same event, the first journalistic and the second literary, the bigger picture of Crane's career as a writer points to the various ways that these two forms of truth telling have intersected over the past three centuries. Indeed, the experience of Crane is a kind of microcosm of the ongoing relationship between literature and journalism in American letters. Consider, for example, that Crane published some of his work in Sunday newspaper supplements, which amounted to mixed bags of fact and fiction. In this sense, these publications resemble the newspapers of the eighteenth century, when newspapers featured literary satires and poetry along with presumably factual news items. During this era, we might say, journalism and literature were in a state of peaceful coexistence. Later, after the rise of the mass media in the 1830s, there came not only a separation between these two brands of writing but a sibling rivalry between journalists and authors, as Crane's own experience demonstrates: when he tried to write journalism after publishing his first few novels, he drew angry and sarcastic responses from some newspapers, which ridiculed or dismissed him and his dispatches.[3] During this same era, but particularly in the latter half of the nineteenth century, many writers were both journalists and authors. Indeed, Crane, who both wrote for various New York papers and published several books of fiction and poetry, is one of numerous American writers—including Walt Whitman, Frederick Douglass, Mark Twain, Theodore Dreiser, Ambrose Bierce, Willa Cather, Jack London, Ernest Hemingway, Dorothy Parker, Tom Wolfe, and others—who produced both journalism and literature in their careers as writers. Indeed, some scholars argue that journalism provided a kind of "apprenticeship" for literary authors such as Twain, Dreiser, and Hemingway. Finally, perhaps because of his experience as a crossover writer, Crane combined elements of literature and journalism to create "An Experiment in Misery" and other blended works. In this respect, he anticipated Tom Wolfe's "New Journalism," Truman Capcte's nonfiction novel *In Cold Blood*, and Jon Stewart's "fake news."

Although they can be found here and there throughout the history of journalism and literature in the United States, these four kinds of intersections roughly correspond to four major eras: "Colonial Coexistence," "Antebellum Rivalry," "Postbellum Apprenticeships," and "Modern Hybrids." A brief history of these four eras shows how the relationship between literature and journalism has evolved over the past three centuries.

COLONIAL COEXISTENCE

For much of the eighteenth century, literature and journalism lived side by side in American newspapers. Essays, satires, and poetry frequently appeared in the pages of papers such as the *New-England Courant* and the *Pennsylvania Gazette*. Connecticut's *New-London Gazette* carried a feature called "Poets Corner," and the final page of the *Farmer's Weekly Museum* sometimes featured poems, essays, literary criticism, and anecdotes under the heading of "The Dessert." Although publications of the era featured the kinds of reports of fires, war, mutiny, deaths, and politics that one would expect in a *news*paper, much of their contents could and sometimes did come under the heading of "Miscellany." Like the appropriately named "magazine," which also emerged in the colonies during this era, the colonial newspaper was a storehouse of various forms: reports, essays, poems, and other reading matter designed to inform, educate, delight, and titillate.[4]

In light of the conditions under which the colonial newspaper emerged and evolved, such a coexistence of literature and journalism was only natural. For one thing, the newspaper was a new phenomenon in the American colonies—and not all that common anywhere else in the world. Some two centuries after Johann Gutenberg's development of movable type made a mass medium possible, Londoners saw the founding of the *Oxford Gazette*, the first English newspaper, in 1665. When John Campbell launched his *Boston News-Letter*, the first American newspaper, in 1704, there were only a handful of other papers in the major cities of the world. Journalism was not yet a discipline or a profession with its own rigid set of principles or conventions. For nearly a century, furthermore, the publishers of America's newspapers typically were printers. The contents of their newspapers naturally resembled the miscellany of other items they printed and sold as part of their trade—that is, government documents, pamphlets, and broadside ballads, along with books of fiction, history, theology, and more. The notion of a reporter, who through education or experience could learn specific skills and develop an identity and a mission, was still unknown. Instead, printers wrote some of their articles themselves, relied on local intellectuals for essays, and printed items from the exchanges, speeches, proclamations, shipping reports, and items collected from foreign correspondents—literally, letter writers in other places.[5]

If these printers did not have a firm sense of the journalistic criteria and conventions that would evolve later, they did have some rudimentary appreciation of "news." Their small publications, some of them consisting of only four pages, contained accounts of foreign wars—and eventually, of course, the American Revolution—along with reports of crimes, diseases, shipwrecks, natural disasters, births, and deaths. Still, the lack of a reporting staff or any other kind of highly effective newsgathering mechanism, coupled with limitations on communication and transportation, meant that it was often difficult to collect enough news to fill even their small papers. Eventually, the Committees of Correspondence, a crude form of a reporting cooperative, would help collect news about the Revolution, but the Associated Press, telegraphs, steamships, and railroads were still decades away. An elegy or a fictional anecdote could help editors fill their columns. Indeed, Elizabeth Christine Cook argues, "the small colonial weekly was often forced to become literary or cease to exist." Noting the editors' own explanations for the material in their papers, Cook explains, "Over and over again 'the present scarcity of news' is pleaded as the excuse for publishing 'what . . . may be useful to Mankind in general.'" It may be no mere coincidence that, as Cook has noted, the *New-England Courant* and *New England Weekly Journal*, the first two colonial newspapers "with literary pretensions," were published by men who were not postmasters and thus lacked easy access to news via the mail.[6]

For some printers, however, such literary material was more than "filler." Both the Franklins, for example, clearly conceived of their newspapers as venues for enrichment and diversion. Indeed, as Norman Grabo has noted, Franklin conceived of the role of the journalist as a kind of "man of letters" responsible for enlightening readers. Franklin was not alone in this conception. Even Samuel Keimer, his one-time eccentric employer and founder of the *Pennsylvania Gazette*, apparently breathed the Enlightenment atmosphere—for he reproduced text from the *Cyclopaedia: or, an Universal Dictionary of Arts and Sciences* of Ephraim Chambers in the *Gazette*. Indeed, Grabo argues that individual incidents—the substance of modern journalism—were, in the eyes of colonial journalists, secondary to "statements." He explains, "Events are seen at best as anecdotes, statements taking precedence over events themselves, assuming that statements—sermons, laws, proclamations, addresses, even opinions, in prose essays and in poems—have about them a greater permanence, and with that a greater authority."[7]

Perhaps partly because of this reverence for permanent "statements," factuality was not a given in the colonial press. Modern readers of newspapers from this era may struggle to determine whether some of the items in them are accounts of actual events, works of fiction, or conflations of the two. In some cases, in fact, contemporary readers would have had the same difficulty, although they seem to have been less fastidious about—or even conscious of—the distinction. In his study of the world of British letters in the sixteenth and seventeenth centuries, Lennard Davis argues for the existence of what he terms a "news/novel discourse," which "seems to make no real distinction between what we would call fact and fiction." Commenting on the eighteenth century, Doug Underwood has made a similar observation, suggesting that "the line between the real and the imagined was very much blurred." Both Davis and Underwood focus on British writing or writers, but there is no reason to think that the situation was much different in America, which was for most of the eighteenth century an extension of Britain in both political and cultural terms. Much of what appeared in American newspapers, in fact, came from the Mother Country. Given these conditions, it perhaps should come as no great surprise that two of the most famous works of colonial American literature—namely, "A Witch Trial at Mount Holly" and "The Speech of Polly Baker"—were published first in newspapers, where they read like news items, even though they apparently were partly or entirely fictional. Because of this apparent conflict, modern readers conventionally refer to such works as *hoaxes*—a term that reflects a modern appreciation for the distinction between factual reporting and fictional telling. We may assume, of course, that colonial Americans knew the difference between something that actually happened and something that a writer invented, but they apparently did not feel that they *needed* to know which was which when they read their newspapers. After all, if Grabo is correct, what mattered was the "statement," not the details.[8]

Literature and journalism, then, were intimate companions in these early years. This coexistence would continue, though eventually in a more limited way, well into the next century, but dramatic changes in journalism would introduce a new chapter in the intersections of the two fields.

Antebellum Rivalry

More than a century after its founding, American journalism was born again, this time as a true mass medium. In 1833, Benjamin Day ushered in the age of the penny press by launching his *New York Sun*. One-sixth the price of current mercantile papers such as the *Journal of Commerce* and the *Courier and Enquirer*, this new penny paper was affordable to the masses. Thanks in part to the news judgment of Day and the particularly savvy James Gordon Bennett, who followed Day's example with his own penny paper in 1835, the masses responded. By the following year, Bennett's *Herald* was reaching some 20,000 readers—a far cry from the circulations of a few hundred or a few thousand in the eighteenth century.[9]

Bennett and his contemporaries put a new face on the American newspaper. Literature continued to appear in the newspapers of this era, but the main attraction was the news. During this period, facts assumed new importance in newspapers, as both Michael Schudson and Hazel Dicken-Garcia have noted.[10] As journalists quickly realized, facts could be every bit as entertaining as fiction. "If a Shakspeare could have taken a stroll in the morning or afternoon through the Police [Office]," Bennett asked in the pages of his *Herald*, "does any one imagine he could not have picked up half a dozen of dramas and some original character?" He added, "The bee extracts from the lowliest flower—so shall we in the Police Office." In the police station—and courthouses and resorts—Bennett found plenty to titillate the New York masses. If colonial journalists sometimes catered to their readers' appetites for salacious material about murderers and "wonders," Bennett, Day, and their fellow editors took sensationalism and "human interest" to new heights. Contemporary Horace Greeley, editor of the *New York Tribune*, notes that Bennett "knew how to pick out of the events of the day the subject which engrossed the interest of the greatest number of people, and to give them about that subject all they could read." In a typical issue of the *Herald*, readers might find news of a murder, a fight, or a trial, along with a quip, an anecdote, or a generous helping of rich or spicy self-promotion. Perhaps the greatest innovator in the history of American journalism, Bennett also introduced new means of newsgathering and

Figure I.1 *The York Family at Home* by Joseph H. Davis, 1837.

Courtesy of Abby Aldrich Rockefeller Folk Art Museum, The Colonial Williamsburg Foundation. From the collection of Abby Aldrich Rockefeller; gift of the Museum of Modern Art.

pioneered the coverage of business, sports, and society news. If they appreciated the value of news, the journalists of the penny press era were not above—or below—the appeal of literature. One of the most famous stories to appear in a newspaper of the 1830s was actually a fiction: the *New York Sun*'s sensational "Moon Hoax," which claimed to report on the existence of winged creatures on the moon. Furthermore, as William Huntzicker and Isabelle Lehuu have noted, even actual news stories resembled works of fiction, such as morality plays.[11]

No one—including the nation's literary class—could overlook the rising prominence and power of this sensational new force on the American scene. Newspapers were everywhere—in homes, in stores, on trains, and in the hands of newsboys, who sold them on the streets. Henry David Thoreau put it this way: "The newspaper is a Bible which we read every morning and every afternoon, standing and sitting, riding and walking. It is a Bible which every man carries in his pocket, which lies on every table and counter, and which the mail, and thousands of missionaries, are continually dispensing. It is, in short, the only book which America has printed, and which America reads. So wide is its influence."[12] Such a presence was perhaps certain to provoke a response from Thoreau and his fellow authors, who were themselves mounting a revolution in letters. In an age that would come to be known as the American Renaissance, Thoreau, Ralph Waldo Emerson, Herman Melville, Edgar Allan Poe, Nathaniel Hawthorne, James Fenimore Cooper, Frederick Douglass, Walt Whitman, Harriet Beecher Stowe, and countless other novelists, poets, and essayists were producing their own written accounts of reality, or "truth," and had to compete with the ubiquitous newspaper.

Responses varied. Douglass, who learned to read partly through the use of newspapers and had become enamored of William Lloyd Garrison's *Liberator*, praised journalism as an agent of reform and even started his own paper: the *North Star*. Whitman used his position as a newspaper editor in the 1840s as a platform from which to argue for political reform. Many of these authors, however, attacked journalism as an inferior medium for telling the truth. Thoreau blasted some Boston papers' failure to speak the truth about slavery, and Stowe and Rebecca Harding Davis called attention to the inadequate coverage of slaves and the working classes. Emerson suggested that Americans were wasting their time on newspapers, time they could have spent more productively with books. Cooper likened the press to a tyrant, and Poe ridiculed journalists, accusing them of incompetence, bias, and more. Taken together, these critiques reveal the anxiety that was troubling many authors as newspapers tugged at their own potential readers. These authors' specific complaints, moreover, point to their own conceptions of truth telling. When Thoreau announced that he "never read any memorable news in a newspaper," he was questioning journalists' news judgment. He continued, "If we read of one man robbed, or murdered, or killed by accident, or one house burned, or one vessel wrecked, or one steamboat blown up, or one cow run over on the Western Railroad, or one mad dog killed, or one lot of grasshoppers in the winter,—we never need read of another. One is enough. If you are acquainted with the principle, what do you care for a myriad instances and applications?" Here is an argument for reporting on deeper, more important truths—an argument that resounds throughout *Walden*. In critiques such as this one, we see an implicit argument for a different form of truth telling—one that exposes underlying principles and examines nontraditional "news."[13]

In a still more important response to journalism, several of these same authors produced poetry, fiction, and nonfiction that amounted to alternative forms of journalism, or "news of their own." Thoreau and Dickinson "reported" on the news of the natural and spiritual worlds in works such as *Walden* and "The Largest Fire Ever Known," often while also explicitly or implicitly critiquing the approaches or values of their counterparts in journalism. Poe, in "The Unparalleled Adventure of One Hans Pfaall" and other works, endorsed the value of the hoax, arguing that it could tell a kind of truth not reported in newspapers. Finally, Poe, Stowe, and Davis all crafted their own versions of what we might call "investigative fiction," in which they used the devices of fiction to solve a mystery or reveal hidden truths.[14]

These writings point to the influential role that journalism played in shaping both the attitudes and the products of America's antebellum authors. Journalism moved from an intimate companion of literature to an uppity younger sibling, whose new power and different values threatened the appeal and sway of literature with American readers.

Postbellum Apprenticeships

The literary attacks on it notwithstanding, journalism continued its ascent after the Civil War. Indeed, the war itself drew even more attention to the newspapers. "Since everyone had a stake in the war and thus a driving need to know about events," Dicken-Garcia explains, "the newspaper became primary reading material as never before." Hundreds of correspondents and illustrators sent their stories and images to papers in New

Figure I.2 *Newsroom at the* New York World, January 1890.
Courtesy of Newseum.

York, Boston, Richmond, Chicago, and other cities. Circulations reached new heights. Bennett's *Herald*, which claimed a circulation of 77,000 in 1860, had more than 100,000 readers the following year. By century's end, the media moguls William Randolph Hearst and Joseph Pulitzer were seeing the circulations of their newspapers approach or top one million. No longer a 4-page miscellany of news, anecdotes, and advertisements, the postbellum newspaper was, in many cases, a 16-, 24-, even a 72-page index to all that was happening in America and the world, as well as a major source of entertainment.[15]

In their famous newspaper wars, Hearst and Pulitzer competed for New Yorkers' attention by offering seductive news and features. Hearst's *New York Journal* and Pulitzer's *New York World* published lurid stories of crime, sex, and scandal and sent celebrities such as Stephen Crane, Richard Harding Davis, and Frederic Remington to cover wars in Europe and the Caribbean. On the entertainment side, Hearst, Pulitzer, and some of their contemporaries served up gossip, comics, fiction, the syndicated columns of Bill Nye and others, and accounts of stunts by reporters such as Nellie Bly, who faked her way into an insane asylum and later traveled around the world in an attempt to beat the "record" of eighty days set by novelist Jules Verne's fictional traveler, Phileas Fogg. Hearst and Pulitzer also wrangled over star writers and artists, including Richard Outcault, creator of the wildly popular comic strip "The Yellow Kid." The color of this kid provided a name for the sensational news coverage that characterized Hearst's and Pulitzer's newspapers: *yellow press*.[16]

The flourishing world of newspapers meant that there were more opportunities than ever before for a young writer to earn a living with a pen. Many writers, in fact, did. This phenomenon predated the Civil War—Walt Whitman, for example, worked for several newspapers before publishing *Leaves of Grass*—but it was remarkably widespread in the postbellum era, when nearly every major author could claim an apprenticeship in journalism. The list includes Mark Twain and William Dean Howells, who worked for newspapers before the war while they were still young men, as well as Crane, Willa Cather, Frank Norris, Jack London, Henry James, Bret Harte, Ambrose Bierce, Theodore Dreiser, H. L. Mencken, Carl Sandburg, and Ernest Hemingway.[17]

For some of these writers, a start in journalism was just that, and they were happy to move on, if they could. Twain referred to his work on the *Sacramento Call* as "fearful drudgery, soulless drudgery" and eventually, after writing thousands of articles for the *Call* and other papers, bowed out of journalism, saying he would "simply write books." Howells worked for his father, an editor of rural papers in Ohio, and became a successful editor of magazines—notably the *Atlantic Monthly*—in his own right, but preferred writing fiction. "I hate criticism. . . . I never did a piece of it that satisfied me; and to write fiction on the other hand, is a delight," he wrote. "Yet in my old age, I seem doomed (on a fat salary) to do criticism and essays. I am ending where I began, in a sort of journalism." He may not have known it, but Howells was echoing another author "doomed" to work in journalism. William Cullen Bryant, the poet who became editor of the *New York Evening Post* in the 1820s and spent approximately half a century in the position, once compared himself to a "draft horse harnessed to the wain of a daily paper."[18]

Other "crossover writers" returned to journalism even after they achieved literary success. The most notable example is Crane, who cut his teeth as a reporter for his brother's New Jersey Coast News Bureau and newspapers such as the *New York Tribune*, became a literary celebrity after the publication of *The Red Badge of Courage* in 1895, returned to journalism as a war reporter for Hearst's *Journal* and other papers, and produced still more fiction, as well as poetry, after returning from the front. In *Stephen Crane, Journalism, and the Making of Modern American Literature*,

Michael Robertson argues that Crane's experience is evidence of a "shift from an antagonistic to a symbiotic relationship between journalistic and literary careers."[19] One of the authors who followed in Crane's footsteps was Ernest Hemingway, who, after a stint as a reporter for the *Kansas City Star* and the *Toronto Star*, produced a stream of classic short stories and novels, including *The Sun Also Rises* and *A Farewell to Arms*, but then returned to journalism, contributing several articles to *Esquire* in the 1930s. His book *Death in the Afternoon*, published in 1932, is itself a kind of journalism—a nonfiction study of bullfighting.

It is easy to imagine that the experience of observing events firsthand, interviewing participants, and trying to transform these events and people into a piece of prose that conforms to journalistic conventions of structure and style would have an impact on a writer's literary style or outlook. In her study of Whitman, Twain, Dreiser, Hemingway, and Dos Passos, Shelley Fisher Fishkin has suggested a crucial connection between journalism and what Philip Rahv termed "the cult of experience in American writing." In the case of Twain, Fishkin finds other kinds of influence, as well: "His apprenticeship in the West taught him how to transcribe dialect, manipulate vocational jargon, and puncture verbal pomposity. It taught him how to paint a vivid picture with the written word, how to communicate a visceral sensation, how to evoke a noxious smell. It exposed him to a wide range of people, practices, and policies. As he would comment in later years, 'Reporting is the best school in the world to get a knowledge of human beings, human nature, and human ways.'" Furthermore, Fishkin observes that this experience in journalism "educated his eye and ear to be suspicious." Edgar M. Branch notes Twain's experience, among other things, expanded his knowledge of people, as well as "civic processes and social tensions." Similar observations have been made of Twain's younger contemporaries Crane and Dresier. Their experience in journalism, Joseph J. Kwiat argues, "was invaluable in formulating many of their unconventional attitudes toward life, their selection of subject matter, even their techniques." Hemingway's work as a reporter provided him with a stock of material for his fiction, as William White has observed. Hemingway himself famously acknowledged his debt to the style sheet of the *Kansas City Star*, which called for "short sentences" and "vigorous English," discouraged the use of adjectives and clichés, and offered various tips for using language deliberately. "Those were the best rules I ever learned for the business of writing," Hemingway said. "I've never forgotten them. No man with any talent, who feels and writes truly about the thing he is trying to say, can fail to write well if he abides with them."[20]

If their journalistic experiences helped to shape some writers' own literature, they may also have helped to set a tone or expectations for later writers. In fact, the image of the journalist secretly pecking away to write the Great American Novel has become something of a motif in American culture. Eventually, in one of the major literary trends of the twentieth century, some journalists would produce not only novels but also groundbreaking hybrids of journalism and literature.

Modern Hybrids

Journalism remained a central American institution throughout the twentieth century and into the twenty-first, although the ubiquitous newspaper was sharing the stage with more and more rivals. Magazines, which had their beginnings in the United States in Franklin's day and exploded during the antebellum print revolution, thrived in the twentieth century. In the first decade or so, "muckrakers" such as Ida Tarbell and Lincoln Steffens published exposés of corruption and more in *McClure's* and other magazines. Later, newsweeklies such as *Time*, photography organs such as *Life*, and literary magazines such as the *New Yorker* and *Esquire* all became staples in American life. Meanwhile, a series of technological innovations provided alternatives to print journalism. Following on the heels of some lesser-known predecessors, the National Broadcasting Company, or NBC, and the Columbia Broadcasting System, or CBS, began broadcasting in the 1920s, eventually becoming leading news outlets. In the middle of the century, Edward R. Murrow and his colleagues helped turn television into a major news medium, and by the 1970s, CBS news anchor Walter Cronkite was widely known as "The Most Trusted Man in America." Another chapter in the history of news began in the 1980s with the founding of the Cable News Network, or CNN, which would make news available around the clock. Finally, with the explosion of the Internet in the next two decades came the most revolutionary media development since the introduction of movable type in the fifteenth century. Today, Americans, along with people all over the world, can not only read, hear, and watch news and other content from countless professional and amateur outlets on their computers or smart phones, usually without paying a cent, but also report their own news to others through tweets, blogs, and posts on social media sites. The new millennium is indeed a new age for journalism and, if some observers are correct, the end of the newspaper as we know it.

The age of innovation in journalism also has been a time of experimentation in literature, as any reader of Faulkner's novels or e. e. cummings's poetry is acutely aware. Perhaps inspired by this spirit of innovation, coupled with their own backgrounds in newspapers or magazines, a number of American writers sought to combine journalism and literature in a variety of hybrid genres. The idea was not exactly new. Even after journalism and literature began to develop along distinctive tracks, antebellum and postbellum authors used their fiction as a kind of alternative journalism. Modern authors of hybrid genres, however, brought a new awareness and deliberation to their craft. Whereas Poe, Davis, and later Upton Sinclair had more or less casually reported on current events in their stories and novels, their successors crowed about their innovations and christened their creations with terms such as the "nonfiction novel" and "The New Journalism." In one of the many interviews he gave after the publication of his "nonfiction novel," *In Cold Blood*, Capote explained, "The interest of the book is in how it sets out to explore what I consider an unexplored literary medium and what one does with it." Wolfe, recollecting his own early experimentation with literary technique in his journalistic pieces for the Sunday supplement called *New York*, says, "I had the feeling, rightly or wrongly, that I was doing things no one had ever done before in journalism." Capote, Wolfe, Norman Mailer, Joan Didion, Hunter Thompson, and a host of other modern writers took both journalism and literature in hand and made them new. It is surely no accident that today, in the wake of these innovations, the American literary scene is awash with an old genre bearing a new name: "creative nonfiction."[21]

Various factors may have helped to drive and shape this new trend toward hybrid genres. In "The New Journalism," Wolfe points to a competition among New York columnists and feature writers in the early 1960s to tell the best stories. Meanwhile, Wolfe explains, novelists turned away from the society novel, leaving a vast panorama of material to other writers: "The—New Journalists—Parajournalists—had the whole crazed obscene uproarious Mammon-faced drug-soaked mau-mau lust-oozing Sixties in America all to themselves." Taking a broader view, John Hollowell argues that "the economics of publishing life and the financial plight of struggling newspapers and magazines also gave new impetus to experimentation." Hollowell suggests that new attitudes—skepticism about authority, for instance—helped to shape the new journalism as well. "The usual news article often reflects, unwittingly, the official attitudes of those with vested interests in how the news gets reported," Hollowell writes. "The new journalist, in contrast, strives to reveal the story hidden beneath the surface facts."[22]

Whatever the complex combination of literary impulses, economic factors, and cultural trends, the world of American letters underwent something of a revolution in the 1960s and 1970s, leading some observers to wonder whether the day of the novel—the traditional one anyway—had come to an end. Much of the best-known—and, some might say, most important—books to come out of this era were not works of pure fiction, but factual narratives that could, in Wolfe's words, "read like a novel." These books, as well as shorter pieces in magazines, reported on real events or real people with techniques that had long been common in fiction and in literature in general: dialogue, the use of revealing details of habit or dress, reconstructions of individuals' thoughts, composite characters, and more. Wolfe explains:

> What interested me was not simply the discovery that it was possible to write accurate non-fiction with techniques usually associated with novels and short stories. It was that—plus. It was the discovery that it was possible in non-fiction, in journalism, to use any literary device, from the traditional dialogisms of the essay to stream-of-consciousness, and to use many different kinds simultaneously, or within a relatively short space . . . to excite the reader both intellectually and emotionally.

Often, the writers of these hybrid genres used journalistic techniques, such as interviews and research, to collect the material on which to build their books or articles. Before coming out with *In Cold Blood*, Capote famously spent years talking with countless people who knew the victims or perpetrators of a mass murder in Holcomb, Kansas, as well as the murderers themselves. He also conducted "months of comparative research on murder, murderers, the criminal mentality," eventually boasting that few people knew more about the psychology of murder than he. Wolfe has used the term "Saturation Reporting" to describe the process he and others have used to immerse themselves in a subject before producing a work of nonfiction about it. Some writers have gone so far as to become participants in the events or culture they were reporting. Two famous examples are Hunter Thompson, who rode with a motorcycle gang and lived (barely) to tell about it in *Hell's Angels: The Strange and Terrible Saga of the Outlaw Motorcycle Gang*, and George Plimpton, who worked out with a professional football team before publishing *Paper Lion*.[23]

More recently, two prominent comedians have combined journalism and imaginative writing in another way. In the television programs *The Daily Show* and *The Colbert Report,* Jon Stewart and Stephen Colbert combine facts and images with commentary and interviews, ultimately producing a genre known as "fake news." In his study of *The Daily Show,* Geoffrey Baym notes that the program's position outside the mainstream news media frees it from certain news conventions—the use of the sound bite and the expectation of objectivity, for example—and ultimately enables it to do what these mainstream outlets are not doing well enough: report the whole truth. Indeed, in Baym's view, *The Daily Show* is an "alternative kind of journalism, one that turned to satire to achieve that which a postmodern media had all but abandoned." As early as the 1960s and 1970s, *Laugh In* and *Saturday Night Live* featured comedians such as Dan Rowan and Bill Murray reporting news events that never happened or twisting actual news accounts for comic effect. Stewart and Colbert, however, have become more influential figures. Although Stewart steadfastly insists he is a comedian, not a journalist, some Americans have come to prefer his brand of reporting to the kind found on CBS or CNN. A poll conducted by *Time* magazine in 2009, in fact, showed that Stewart had inherited Cronkite's title as "The Most Trusted Man in America." For some, this attitude points to a crisis in American journalism. On another level, it is simply one more chapter in the long and fascinating history of the parallels and intersections of literature and journalism in the United States.[24]

***

These parallels and intersections have been the subjects of a variety of books and articles by scholars of both literature and journalism. In what may be the first book on literature and journalism in American letters, *Literary Influences in Colonial Newspapers, 1704–1750* (1912), Elizabeth Christine Cook examines the coexistence of the two disciplines in the colonial press, noting the presence of both British and homegrown literature in newspapers such as the *Virginia Gazette* and the *Maryland Gazette.* Cook suggests that nearly all the secular literature of the time appeared on the pages of newspapers and calls the colonial paper "a vastly more important channel of literary influence" than literary clubs, bookshops, or libraries. After modern writers such as Tom Wolfe and Truman Capote began creating hybrid forms in the latter half of the twentieth century, John Hollowell responded with *Fact and Fiction: The New Journalism and the Nonfiction Novel* (1977), which presents possible causes behind the turn to new forms of truth telling, an anatomy of the new journalism, and case studies of Capote, Mailer, and Wolfe. Fishkin produced a major study of journalistic apprenticeships in *From Fact to Fiction: Journalism & Imaginative Writing in America* (1985), where she argues that many writers' experiences in journalism help to explain the "cult of experience" in American letters. Furthermore, such experiences, Fishkin suggests, had the effect of introducing new people, subjects, and styles into American literature. Andie Tucher takes up a different kind of interaction of literature and journalism in *Froth and Scum: Truth, Beauty, Goodness, and the Ax Murder in America's First Mass Medium* (1994). In her study of the penny press, Tucher examines what might be considered literary elements in newspapers, noting not only the use of archetypes such as the "Poor Unfortunate" and the "Siren" but also outright fabrication in the tradition of P. T. Barnum's "humbug." In *Stephen Crane, Journalism, and the Making of Modern American Literature* (1997), Michael Robertson examines one of America's best-known crossover writers, arguing that Stephen Crane's experience exemplifies a transition in American writers' attitudes toward journalism—from hostility, as expressed by Howells and James, to appreciation, as seen in the experiences of Dreiser and Hemingway. Indeed, much of Crane's own writing, in Robertson's view, should be recognized as a brand of literary journalism. Whatever their attitudes toward journalism, Howells, James, and Crane—along with many other American authors—were connected to newspaper syndicates, the subject of Charles Johanningsmeier's *Fiction and the American Literary Marketplace: The Role of Newspaper Syndicates, 1860–1900* (1997). As Johanningsmeier shows, readyprint, plate service, and galley-proof syndicates, such as those operated by Irving Bacheller and S. S. McClure, acted as intermediaries between authors and newspaper editors, helping both major and minor authors find a market while giving millions of readers, particularly rural Americans, access to fiction. The influence of literature on journalism is the subject of Karen Roggenkamp's *Narrating the News: New Journalism and Literary Genre in Late Nineteenth-Century American Newspapers* (2005). Roggenkamp argues that the writers behind the new journalism of the nineteenth century adapted literary genres such as detective stories and historical romances when packaging their news stories. Doug Underwood revisits the apprenticeship model in *Journalism and the Novel: Truth and Fiction* (2008), examining numerous writers and arguing for the role of journalism in shaping the directions of both British and American literature. One of the newest products of the relationship between literature and journalism receives extensive treatment in Baym's *From Cronkite to Colbert: The Evolution of Broadcast News* (2010). Although commonly known as "fake news," the work of Jon Stewart and Stephen Colbert is, in Baym's view, an alternative form of journalism—one that fits in a "still-developing neo-modern paradigm of news" and hearkens back to the "high-modern ideals" of the network age. Finally, my *Literature and Journalism in Antebellum America: Thoreau, Stowe, and Their Contemporaries Respond to the Rise of the Commercial Press* (2011) examines the "sibling rivalry" between antebellum journalists and authors, as well as attempts by Poe, Dickinson, and other authors to craft "news of their own." These book-length treatments amount to only a fraction of the scholarship on literature and journalism—a body of work that also includes numerous essays and chapters by David Reynolds, Thomas Leonard, Tom Wolfe, Nancy Barrineau, and others.[25]

This collection of new essays builds on this foundation, providing fresh insights into the various inspirations, intersections, and inventions that have developed as literature and journalism have shared the stage of American letters. First, Carla Mulford sheds light on one form of the colonial coexistence of literature and journalism, focusing on the work of a man who was both the leading author and the leading journalist of his age. For Benjamin Franklin, Mulford argues, literary journalism was a political instrument, one he used to portray the American colonists as Britain's "true and loyal subjects." In the next essay, David Reynolds examines Walt Whitman's early career in journalism as a form of apprenticeship, one that left its stamp on *Leaves of Grass* in the form of themes, imagery, and "a new kind of poetic persona, a loving, democratic 'I' who embraced not only Southerners and Northerners but people of all ethnicities and nationalities." Although Whitman published his great poems in the form of a book, many of his lesser-known contemporaries regularly placed their verse in newspapers. In her essay, Elizabeth Lorang examines a particular group of these papers, the now-forgotten hospital newspapers, where patients and caregivers alike gave voice to their experiences and, Lorang argues, framed the war for their readers. Poetry continued to appear in newspapers after the war, but so did a less conspicuous form of "literature." As Andie Tucher shows, even while some Americans were preoccupied with the "real thing," some journalists were reveling in the widespread practice of "faking": producing news that was actually, in some part anyway, fiction. In her essay, she examines the contemporary discussion about this practice and its meaning for the world of truth telling. A different form of newspaper fiction—that is, short stories *about* reporters and journalism—was appearing in the 1890s, as Karen Roggenkamp shows. Focusing on one of the authors of this genre, Elizabeth

Jordan, and her "True Stories of the News," Roggenkamp examines "the shifting—and shifty—nature of how 'true stories' could unfold in journalism and literature alike at the turn of the twentieth century." In light of the intimate relationship of literature and journalism during this time, literary scholars would do well to mine more of the newspapers published in the late nineteenth and early twentieth centuries. As Charles Johanningsmeier shows, these publications hold secrets to biographical information about authors, the publication histories of their works, their true audiences, and more. During and after this era, journalism was more than a training ground, an inspiration, and a vehicle for literature. As Doug Underwood argues, it also could be a means to literary celebrity, which often comes with a price. One writer whose reputation owes much to journalism is Ernest Hemingway. In particular, *Esquire* publisher Arnold Gingrich played a significant role in publicizing this most celebrated of celebrity authors, both during his career and after his death, as John Fenstermaker shows in his essay. In the final essay of this collection, Geoffrey Baym examines a modern hybrid genre, arguing that Stephen Colbert's satirical *Harvest of Shame* constitutes "an alternative mode of public voice," one that combines rational-critical and aesthetic-expressive discourse.

As the example of Colbert shows, the intersections of literature and journalism are by no means old news. As both forms of truth telling continue to evolve, we can expect them to continue to inform, challenge, and inspire each other. The essays in this volume not only shed light on the fruitful and the toxic in their relationship over the last three centuries but also promise to illuminate the potential and the threats in the centuries to come.

NOTES

1. Stephen Crane, "Stephen Crane's Own Story," in *Prose and Poetry* (New York: Literary Classics of the United States, 1984), 875–84; Stephen Crane, "The Open Boat," in *Prose and Poetry*, 885–909.
2. For discussions of the nature of journalism, the development of news criteria, and the evolution of the structure of news articles, see Mark Canada, *Literature and Journalism in Antebellum America: Thoreau, Stowe, and Their Contemporaries Respond to the Rise of the Commercial Press* (New York: Palgrave Macmillan, 2011), 20–22; Norma Green, "Concepts of News," in *American Journalism*, ed. W. David Sloan and Lisa Mullikin Purcell (Jefferson, NC: McFarland, 2002),

34–43; Tim P. Vos, "New Writing Structure and Style," in *American Journalism*, 296–305.

3. A writer for the *Los Angeles Express* observed, "Stephen Crane, the novelist, badly disguised as a newspaper war correspondent at Athens, has published a letter chiefly made up of abuse of a western newspaper man who succeeded in getting an interview with King George. . . . Mr. Crane's dispatches, by the way, are pretty specimens of fair English, but as far as their information-values go, have the disadvantage of being one or two days behind the news dispatches sent from the seat of war." For other attacks on Crane, see Mark Canada, *Literature and Journalism*, 54–56.
4. Luther Mott, *American Journalism: A History: 1690–1960* (New York: Macmillan, 1962), 55, 114–15; Christine Cook, *Literary Influences in Colonial Newspapers, 1704–1750* (Port Washington, NY: Kennikat, 1966), 175–76, 178, 213, 235. For examples of the coexistence of literature and news in early newspapers, see the July 24, 1732, issue of *The Pennsylvania Gazette*; the September 12, 1732, issue of *The Pennsylvania Gazette*; the April 4, 1797, issue of *The Farmer's Weekly Museum*; and the June 19, 1797, issue of *The Farmer's Weekly Museum*. The last of these publications, for instance, contains, among other items, "Proceedings of the Federal Congress," an account of the Battle of Casasola, death notices, and poems.
5. Edwin Emery and Michael Emery, *The Press and America* (Englewood Cliffs, NJ: Prentice-Hall, 1984), 12; Mott, *American Journalism*, 47, 50–51, 103, 155.
6. Mott, *American Journalism*, 48, 52, 55; Cook, *Literary Influences in Colonial Newspapers*, 3, 6, 32–33. For examples of the contents of colonial newspapers, see the March 16, 1732, issue of the *Pennsylvania Gazette*, which features an edict by the Portuguese king, news from Amsterdam and other European cities, brief items about a local fire and a suicide, shipping news, and several advertisements.
7. Wm. David Sloan and Julie Hedgepeth Williams, *The Early American Press, 1690–1783* (Westport, CT: Greenwood Press, 1994), 59–60; Norman S. Grabo, "The Journalist as Man of Letters," in *Reappraising Benjamin Franklin: A Bicentennial Perspective*, ed. J. A. Leo Lemay (Newark: University of Delaware Press, 1993), 34.
8. Lennard Davis, *Factual Fictions: The Origins of the English Novel* (New York: Columbia University Press, 1983), 51; Doug Underwood, *Journalism and the Novel: Truth and Fiction*, 1700–2000 (Cambridge: Cambridge University Press, 2008), 34.

9. Emery and Emery, *The Press and America*, 140, 144; Mott, *American Journalism*, 104, 159.
10. Michael Schudson, *Discovering the News: A Social History of American Newspapers* (New York: Basic, 1978), 77; Hazel Dicken-Garcia, *Journalistic Standards in Nineteenth-Century America* (Madison: University of Wisconsin Press, 1989), 82.
11. "Police Office," *New York Herald*, August 31, 1835; James L. Crouthamel, *Bennett's New York Herald and the Rise of the Popular Press* (Syracuse, NY: Syracuse University Press, 1989), 33; Mott, *American Journalism*, 156; Greeley is quoted in Crouthamel, *Bennett's New York Herald and the Rise of the Popular Press*, 156; Emery and Emery, *The Press and America*, 144; Mott, *American Journalism*, 233–35; Crouthamel, *Bennett's New York Herald and the Rise of the Popular Press*, 45; "Harrington's Great Lunar Panorama," *New York Sun*, September 28, 1835, 2; "Herschel's Great Discoveries," *New York Sun*, September 1, 1835, 2; William Huntzicker, *The Popular Press, 1833–1865* (Westport, CT: Greenwood Press, 1999), 20; Isabelle Lehuu, *Carnival on the Page: Popular Print Media in Antebellum America* (Chapel Hill: University of North Carolina Press, 2000), 50; Karen Roggenkamp, *Narrating the News: New Journalism and Literary Genre in Late Nineteenth-Century American Newspapers and Fiction* (Kent, Ohio: Kent State University Press, 2005), 7. For examples of the *Herald*'s contents, see the October 24, 1835, and April 12, 1836, issues of the *Herald*, which feature, among other things, coverage of the grisly murder of Helen Jewett, news of a fatal steamboat accident, stories of a stabbing and the death of a prodigal heir, and a brief item with this taunt of a rival paper: "THE SUN is alarmed (and very justly too) at the rapid progress of the Herald in popularity, patronage, and circulation. It begins to call in the aid of its low, vulgar editors and police reporters."
12. Henry David Thoreau, "Slavery in Massachusetts," in *Reform Papers*, ed. Wendell Glick (Princeton: Princeton University Press, 1973), 100.
13. Frederick Douglass, *Narrative of the Life of Frederick Douglass*, in *Slave Narratives* (New York: Literary Classics of the United States, 2000), 362; Frederick Douglass, "Our Paper and Its Prospects," Dec. 3, 1847, The Papers of Frederick Douglass, Container 21, Reel 13, Library of Congress; Canada, *Literature and Journalism*, 52; Thoreau, "Slavery in Massachusetts"; Harriet Beecher Stowe, *Uncle Tom's Cabin*, ed. Mary R. Reichardt (San Francisco: Ignatius, 2009), 259; Rebecca Harding Davis, "Life in the Iron-Mills," in *A*

Rebecca Harding Davis Reader, ed. Jean Pfaelzer (Pittsburgh: University of Pittsburgh Press, 1995), 25–26; Lehuu, *Carnival on the Page*, 126; James Fenimore Cooper, *The American Democrat*, in *Representative Selections*, ed. Robert E. Spiller (Westport, CT: Greenwood Press, 1936), 215; Edgar Allan Poe, "The Mystery of Marie Roget," in *Collected Works of Edgar Allan Poe*, ed. Thomas Ollive Mabbott (Cambridge, MA: Belknap Press of Harvard University Press, 1978), 723–74; Henry David Thoreau, *Walden*, ed. J. Lyndon Shanley (Princeton: Princeton University Press, 1971), 94.

14. For a complete study of these authors' responses to newspapers, see Canada, *Literature and Journalism*.
15. Dicken-Garcia, *Journalistic Standards in Nineteenth-Century America*, 51; Emery and Emery, *The Press and America*, 194, 197–98; Mott, *American Journalism*, 332, 546; Huntzicker, *The Popular Press*, 139.
16. Mott, *American Journalism*, 436–37, 442, 482, 524–26.
17. For discussions of several of these writers, see Doug Underwood, *Journalism and the Novel*.
18. Mark Twain, *Mark Twain in Eruption: Hitherto Unpublished Pages about Men and Events*, ed. Bernard DeVoto (New York: Harper, 1940), 255–56; Twain is quoted in Edgar M. Branch, "Introduction," in *Early Tales and Sketches* (Berkley: University of California Press, 1979), I: 50; Howells is quoted in A. J. Kaul, "William Dean Howells," in *American Magazine Journalists, 1850–1900*, ed. Sam G. Riley (Detroit: Gale, 1989), 202; Bryant is quoted in James Boylan, "William Cullen Bryant," in *American Newspaper Journalists, 1690–1872*, ed. Perry J. Ashley (Detroit: Gale, 1985), 84.
19. Michael Robertson, *Stephen Crane, Journalism, and the Making of Modern American Literature* (New York: Columbia University Press, 1997), 4.
20. Shelley Fisher Fishkin, *From Fact to Fiction: Journalism and Imaginative Writing in America* (Baltimore: Johns Hopkins University Press, 1985), 5–6, 59–60, 66; Edgar M. Branch, *The Literary Apprenticeship of Mark Twain* (New York: Russell & Russell, 1950), 151; Joseph J. Kwiat, "The Newspaper Experience: Crane, Norris, and Dreiser," *Nineteenth-Century Fiction* 8 (September 1953): 99; William White, "Hemingway Needs No Introduction . . . ," in *By-Line: Ernest Hemingway: Selected Articles and Dispatches of Four Decades* (New York: Touchstone, 1967), xii; "The Star Copy Sheet," *Kansas City Star*, http://www.kansascity.com/static/pdfs/Hemingway_style_sheet.pdf; Hemingway is quoted in Matthew Bruccoli, ed.,

"Back to His First Field," in *Conversations with Ernest Hemingway* (Jackson: University Press of Mississippi, 1986), 21.

21. Truman Capote, interview on "The Public Eye," May 24, 1966, CBC; Tom Wolfe, "The New Journalism," in *The New Journalism* (New York: Harper & Row, 1973), 20.
22. Wolfe, "The New Journalism," 3–9, 31; John Hollowell, *Fact and Fiction: The New Journalism and the Nonfiction Novel* (Chapel Hill: University of North Carolina Press, 1977), 38, 23. See also George Plimpton, "The Story Behind a Nonfiction Novel," *New York Times*, January 16, 1966, http://www.nytimes.com/books/97/12/28/home/capote-interview.html.
23. Plimpton, "The Story Behind a Nonfiction Novel"; Capote, interview on "The Public Eye"; Wolfe, "The New Journalism," 9, 15, 31–33; Hollowell, *Fact and Fiction*, 26–31. Both Wolfe and Hollowell enumerate specific features of the new journalism.
24. Geoffrey Baym, *From Cronkite to Colbert: The Evolution of Broadcast News* (Boulder: Paradigm, 2010), 106–7, 110, 112.
25. Cook, *Literary Influences in Colonial Newspapers, 1704–1750*, 2, 6; John Hollowell, *Fact and Fiction*; Fishkin, *From Fact to Fiction*, 6–7; Andie Tucher, *Froth and Scum: Truth, Beauty, Goodness, and the Ax Murder in America's First Mass Medium* (Chapel Hill: University of North Carolina Press, 1994); Robertson, *Stephen Crane, Journalism, and the Making of Modern American Literature*; Charles Johanningsmeier, *Fiction and the Literary Marketplace: The Role of Newspaper Syndicates, 1860–1900* (Cambridge: Cambridge University Press, 1997); Roggenkamp, *Narrating the News*; Doug Underwood, *Journalism and the Novel*; Baym, *From Cronkite to Colbert*, 20; Canada, *Literature and Journalism in Antebellum America*; Wolfe, "The New Journalism," 1–52; David S. Reynolds, "Public Poison: Sensationalism and Sexuality," in *Beneath the American Renaissance: The Subversive Imagination in the Age of Emerson and Melville* (Cambridge: Harvard University Press, 1988), 167–333; Thomas B. Connery, "A Third Way to Tell the Story: American Literary Journalism at the Turn of the Century," in *Literary Journalism in the Twentieth Century*, ed. Norman Sims (New York: Oxford University Press, 1990), 3–18; Thomas L. Leonard, "News at Walden Pond" in *News for All: America's Coming-of-Age with the Press* (New York: Oxford University Press, 1995), 93–100; Nancy Warner Barrineau, "Introduction" to *Theodore Dreiser's Ev'ry Month* (Athens: Univ. of Georgia Press, 1996), xv-xl; Mark Canada, "The Critique of Journalism in *Sister Carrie*," *American Literary Realism* 42.3 (Spring 2010): 227–42.

CHAPTER 1

BENJAMIN FRANKLIN, LITERARY JOURNALISM, AND FINDING A NATIONAL SUBJECT

CARLA MULFORD

SOME OF THE MOST MEMORABLE STORIES FOUND in Benjamin Franklin's autobiography are those related to his youth, when he taught himself to enter the world of words by working his way through the literary journalism of his day. Franklin's recollections in the autobiography tell of Franklin's hard work at his brother's press and his having taught himself to write literary journalism by imitating *The Spectator* by Joseph Addison and Richard Steele. He became so skilled at such writing that he was able to dupe his brother into publishing his artful sketches, the inventive periodical series of "letters" by "Silence Dogood." When Franklin established his own press in Philadelphia, his literary journalism found its maturity in his writings for his *Pennsylvania Gazette* and his Poor Richard almanacs. Such a literary apprenticeship suited Franklin's creative talents and served the colonies well when Franklin traveled to England and France to negotiate on the colonies' behalf during and then after the war against Britain.

Examining Benjamin Franklin's literary journalism enables us to observe that through much of his career Franklin attempted to use the press—and literary journalism in particular—to craft a version of British national identity that featured British North Americans as the ideal "true and loyal subjects" of Great Britain. As America's "Creole pioneer" (as Benedict Anderson labeled him), Franklin saw, by the end of his life, that the liberal identity embraced by Britons in England—an identity that he had spent much of his writing and printing career attempting to establish—had greater viability in North America than it ever had in Britain.[1] This chapter will examine the threads of early modern liberalism interwoven with the history of literary journalism by looking into the career of Benjamin Franklin. For the sake of simplicity, I'll consider four different moments in Franklin's writing career: his early contributions (the "Silence Dogood" essays), which featured many of the positions we might associate with the Whig liberalism available in *Cato's Letters* (by John Trenchard and Thomas Gordon), which Franklin admired; his middle years, when, as chief negotiator for the colonies in England, Franklin sought to find a middle course for the Empire that would be acceptable to Britons in North America and Britain (periodical writings in the *London Chronicle*, among other newspapers); his later years as peace negotiator working strenuously to negotiate the lasting peace that became the Treaty of Paris of 1783 (a hoax newssheet); and his last years, when Franklin, an elder statesman, served the Constitutional Convention and the Pennsylvania Abolition Society. In most ways, Franklin's literary journalism contributed in major ways to the fostering of American national identity.

Literary Journalism in British North America

The impact of literary journalism in the colonies can best be assessed if we consider the print media available to most readers prior to the appearance of literary journalism in the newspapers and magazines in North America. Books were scarce in British North America, because they were printed elsewhere and imported and thus were expensive. In the late seventeenth and early eighteenth centuries, books were imported by those in elite circles, but, except for the Bible, they were not frequently available for common people, unless they had been brought over in the initial crossing. Few American publishers attempted to publish books because publication was expensive and the reading market uncertain. There were no lending libraries for the general circulation of books. In the absence of newspapers, then, most people in the colonies would have had little or nothing to read. In fact, the newspaper was the medium most frequently read, after the Bible.

In North America, rates of literacy were relatively high—higher, in fact, than in many parts of Europe. Richard Brown has noted that in some regions, literacy levels were at 90 percent by the year 1800.[2] Given the high rate of literacy, it is likely that newspapers were read by both women and men and by people of all stations and backgrounds. But few received formal training in reading and writing, and few attended the few colleges (Harvard, Yale, and William and Mary) that were originally established. Until Benjamin Franklin devised a different educational agenda for a college in Philadelphia in the mid-eighteenth century, university culture was expressly designed in behalf of classical training. Young men were taught to read Greek and Latin, and they were trained primarily for the ministry. In life outside university, by contrast, newspapers, especially those employing literary journalism, became the medium of exchange of news and cultural values for most people. They formed the center of community activity, from the largely government-oriented, commercial endeavors of the first newspapers to the more elaborate literary journalistic endeavors of the press of James Franklin and others who followed his lead in printing journalism more like that available in London and European centers of learning. The rise of literary journalism promoted the formation of literate cultures in North America. Beginning in 1691 in Anglophone North America, newspapers numbered well over 2,100 by 1820; 461 of them lasted longer than ten years.[3] Such printing numbers indicate that newspapers were the central vehicles for the circulation of vernacular culture.

Most newspaper publishers were their own writers of text, as well. Success in the trade meant that the publisher would have to be an informed and able writer. As Benedict Anderson, following Lucien Febvre and Henri-Jean Martin, has reminded us, it was in colonial North America that publishers first hit on the newspaper as a primary vehicle for making money in the absence of a market for and the materials to produce a significant book trade. In Anderson's words, "Printers starting new presses always included a newspaper in their productions, to which they were usually the main, even the sole, contributor. Thus the printer-journalist was initially an essentially North American phenomenon."[4]

Printers relied on postmasters for the circulation of the latest news, both incoming and outgoing, so ties between the postmaster's office and the printer's store helped foster business. In Anderson's words, "Since the main problem facing the printer-journalist was reaching readers, there developed an alliance with the post-master so intimate that often each became the other. Hence, the printer's office emerged as the key to North American communications and community intellectual life."[5] When Benjamin Franklin succeeded in establishing his own admired newspaper, the *Pennsylvania Gazette*, and then became the Pennsylvania government's printer and the postmaster of Philadelphia, he was well on his way to having a significant monopoly over the circulation of news (and thus of culture) in the middle colonies of North America at precisely the time when intellectual and mercantile commercial power shifted away from the port cities of Boston, Massachusetts, and Newport, Rhode Island, to Philadelphia. Yet Franklin's idea of using the press to consolidate colonial Britons was ultimately premature, as signaled by the failure of his attempt to develop a news magazine—the *General Magazine and Historical Chronicle, for All the British Plantations in America* (1741)—that he hoped would circulate through the various printers in the printing network he had set up from Rhode Island and Massachusetts through New York, Pennsylvania, and Maryland, to South Carolina and the Caribbean.[6] Even though Franklin's *General Magazine* ultimately failed, it reveals his acute understanding of the extent to which periodicals—and in particular, literary journalism—might be used to sway public opinion, so that imperial subjects, however dispersed around the Atlantic Ocean, might conceive of themselves as having a common interest and common destiny.

The Idea of a Free and Informed Citizenry and Franklin's Early Literary Journalism

Political consolidation, especially with regard to the North American colonies, was important to Britain during the eighteenth century, yet the interest politics that dominated the ministry and court life worked against the very possibility of forming a system of common values that those in power would acknowledge as viable. The political situation tended to pit wealthy and powerful groups (i.e., the aristocracy and growing mercantile classes) against laboring people. Tory interests sought to overpower Whig interests, and out of the fray between the two groups emerged *Cato's Letters*. For fostering the idea of political consolidation under the notion of British "liberties," while propagandizing French and Spanish oppression, no greater vehicle was available than *Cato's Letters*. These were printed and reprinted in Britain and the colonies in the early eighteenth century. Written by John Trenchard (1662–1723), an Irish Commonwealthman and Whig propagandist educated at Trinity College, Dublin, and Thomas Gordon (c. 1692–1750), a Scot trained for the bar perhaps at Edinburgh, *Cato's Letters* were published in the *London Journal* and later in the *British Journal* from 1720 to 1723.[7] The initial letters were a response to the South Sea Bubble (an investment banking scheme that nearly bankrupted Britain's major shareholders and thus the Commonwealth), but the 144 letters eventually covered most of the central tenets of liberal thought. Written under the pseudonym *Cato*, the name of a Roman statesman

(95–46 BCE) who had defended individual rights against the tyranny of Julius Caesar, the letters supported political and civil liberties such as individual and constitutional liberties, the freedom of the press, and freedom of conscience and denigrated the idea of standing armies and the powers associated with the established church. They reveal how literary journalism was used as political propaganda, and their impress marked a liberal tendency in political discourse for Britons globally situated.

Even a cursory search for *Cato's Letters* in eighteenth-century newspapers reveals their wide circulation throughout the British Commonwealth. Ireland, Scotland, North America, and England all printed and reprinted the letters, sometimes with editorial glosses indicating the importance of the letters to this or that local social or political matter but frequently with no editorial gloss whatsoever. The *Letters* were especially popular in the colonies, where trade restrictions and local problems over church and town governance caused fiscal instability, ecclesiastical power contests, and political rancor. They were first published in British North America (by Benjamin Franklin) in James Franklin's *New-England Courant* in 1721 and then reprinted throughout the eighteenth century in Massachusetts, Rhode Island, Vermont, New Hampshire, Connecticut, New York, Pennsylvania, New Jersey, Maryland, Virginia, and South Carolina. The *Letters'* appeal to the colonists is understandable, given the colonies' political subordination to England. Colonial administration and the Navigation Acts affected matters of trade and manufacture, local self-governance, military funding, and taxation. *Cato's Letters* on individual liberties and freedom of conscience were particularly important to the colonists, fostering a liberal republican message that the colonists absorbed through the medium of journalistic prose. Through the open exchanges of ideas available in *Cato's Letters* and other writings on society and politics in the journalistic media, Britons in North America came to understand the fractures in the supposedly common political discourse, especially the discourse of civil and religious liberty, of the British commonwealth.

Some have argued, following Clinton Rossiter, that *Cato's Letters* more than any other texts were the central reading matter of the American revolutionary generation. As Rossiter famously phrased it, "no one can spend any time in the newspapers, library inventories, and pamphlets of colonial America without realizing that *Cato's Letters* rather than Locke's *Civil Government* was the most popular, quotable, esteemed source of political ideas in the colonial period."[8] This statement assumes that newspaper media had so permeated the cultural fabric that a fundamental shift in the circulation of ideas had occurred, from manuscript to print and from books and pamphlets to serial publication. Serial production enabled readers to participate more widely in what Benedict Anderson called an "imagined community": an idealized formative relationship between the self and one's community that laid the basis for nationalism. *Cato's Letters* could be taken as a pre-eminent vehicle for assisting the formation of national values that would later facilitate the state formation of British North America as the United States. Jefferson's language in the Declaration of Independence—"We hold these Truths to be self-evident, that all Men are created equal, that they are endowed by their Creator with certain inalienable Rights, that among these are Life, Liberty, and the Pursuit of Happiness"—has resonance with Cato's letter No. 45, "Of the Equality and Inequality of Men," which opens, "Men are naturally equal, and none ever rose above the rest but by force or consent: No man was ever born above all the rest, nor below them all."[9] This exemplifies the extent to which individuals could call into being a nation, based on a presumably common cultural and political link to others in the same imagined community that was initially consolidated by the serialized circulation of print.

When James Franklin started his newspaper, *The New-England Courant*, in 1721, he was launching a new kind of journal in North America. Benjamin Franklin, apprenticed in his brother's print shop, was on the proverbial ground floor, finding type and working the presses, finding material for newspaper filler, and listening in on the literate conversations of James and his friends as they critiqued local and London government. They must have been reading *Cato's Letters* from the start of their publication in London in 1720, and just as soon as the newspapers offering them reached Boston. Indeed, it seems as if James Franklin's continued challenging of the government's high-handed approach to governance arose partly from a sense that it was time for individual and press liberty to be tested in New England as well as old.

The opening numbers of James Franklin's paper, likely set to press by his brother Benjamin, called into question the government's authority in handling smallpox inoculations.[10] The newspaper then went on to criticize members of the General Court and the means by which the court sought to protect its own interests against all critics. James Franklin would later be found guilty of malfeasance in printing criticisms against the town for not providing the proper protection for its citizens. Legal actions against James Franklin prompted local authorities to call for his arrest. James Franklin went into hiding to avoid jail. The authorities' goal was clear: they wanted the newspaper to be shut down. Young Benjamin Franklin took over the publication of the newspaper.[11]

In taking over the newspaper in his brother's absence, Benjamin Franklin proved just as fearless as James had been.[12] Benjamin Franklin's earlier "letters" by Silence Dogood, his pseudonym for a middle-aged matron, had criticized social hypocrisy, the folly of hankering after fashion when practical apparel was more useful, and the quality of learning taking place at Harvard, where parents essentially bought their sons seats at the throne of indolence. Once his brother James had to go into hiding, however, Benjamin Franklin took a different approach: he reprinted *Cato's Letters*—the first printing of the *Letters* in the colonies—on the topics of freedom of speech in a purportedly free country and on religious hypocrisy and its deleterious effects when political leaders are also religious leaders. Benjamin Franklin's "Silence Dogood" letter No. 8, published July 9, 1722, reprinted Trenchard and Gordon's *Cato's Letter* No. 15 from the *London Journal* (No. 80), originally printed on February 4, 1721. Full of references to Charles I's proclamations abolishing parliaments, "Cato," quoted by Silence Dogood, observed, "Without Freedom of Thought, there can be no such Thing as Wisdom; and no such Thing as publick Liberty, without Freedom of Speech; which is the Right of every Man, as far as by it, he does not hurt or controul the Right of another: And this is the only Check it ought to suffer, and the only Bounds it ought to know." In addition to reprising the assertions by "Cato" that linked freedom of thought with freedom of speech and general civil liberties, "Silence" also quoted a portion associating freedom of speech with the security of property. This part related directly to the government's effort to seize James Franklin's presses. Speaking of the "natural right" of freedom of speech, Cato wrote, "This sacred Privilege is so essential to free Governments, that the Security of Property, and the Freedom of Speech always go together; and in those wretched Countries where a Man cannot call his Tongue his own, he can scarce call any Thing else his own. Whoever would overthrow the Liberty of a Nation, must begin by subduing the Freeness of Speech; a *Thing* terrible to Publick Traytors."[13] The linking of freedom of speech with natural rights, a rhetorical method typical in some of Trenchard and Gordon's *Cato's Letters*, aptly suited the situation of James Franklin's press. The language of liberty that the entry offers is a central premise of the Commonwealth tradition that Benjamin Franklin already admired. Calling liberty of person and liberty of speech "sacred Privilege[s]" assured *New-England Courant* readers, without speaking the statement explicitly, that the meddlesome government was usurping the rights of the printer and, in so doing, was encroaching on the rights of every citizen. By implying that an ideological attachment obtained between the Massachusetts government and the court of King Charles I, which New Englanders had, of course, originally escaped by removing to North America, Silence Dogood (and her erstwhile publisher/author) could effectively evoke the living memory of the Commonwealth without making charges directly against the local government.

Silence Dogood No. 9 reprinted another of *Cato's Letters*, this time No. 31 from the *London Journal* of May 27, 1721. Silence was reproducing the materials "from an ingenious Political Writer in the London Journal, the better to convince . . . Readers, that Publick Destruction may be easily carry'd on by *hypocritical Pretenders to Religion.*"[14] This letter by Thomas Gordon, a pseudophilosophical diatribe against weaknesses and inconsistencies in human nature and aimed at the South Sea debacle, is used by Silence Dogood in answer to her rhetorical question opening her essay, "Whether a Commonwealth suffers more by hypocritical Pretenders to Religion, or by the openly Profane?" Silence Dogood's point is that those in state offices, "publick Hypocrite[s]," can deceive people into thinking them great, public-spirited men, whereas they are knaves, in reality. Silence uses her platform to argue that "we cannot better manifest our Love to Religion and the Country, than by setting the Deceivers in a true Light, and undeceiving the Deceived, however such Discoveries may be represented by the ignorant or designing Enemies of our Peace and Safety."[15]

Silence Dogood No. 9 has been understood (by the editors of Franklin's papers, among others) as a specific remark about the Massachusetts governor, Joseph Dudley, who studied for the ministry but entered political life. More recently, J. A. Leo Lemay argued that the letter is a diatribe against Samuel Sewall, who was serving as Chief Justice overseeing the court actions taken against James Franklin.[16] While these hypotheses bear up under examination, I believe they miss the larger point: Silence Dogood's No. 9 essay criticizes all those who would argue that they serve the people when they are primarily serving themselves. Its point is especially directed against those who hypocritically serve others under the guise of religion, but the essay speaks more fully to all "Political" hypocrites. Such a challenge to authority was as relevant in the days of Oliver Cromwell as it might have been in Franklin's Boston.

Indeed, if we remove ourselves from the local concerns and consider Silence Dogood No. 9 in a broader context of liberalism and its foundations, we discover that Franklin is making a significant philosophical comment on the human condition and on the nature of power—that power corrupts even the best of people and even those who claim to profess a higher calling of serving their God. Take, for example, the epigraph Franklin employed, "*Corruptio optimi est pessima*" ("The best, when corrupted, are the worst"), which seems to have been proverbial, in Franklin's day, for speaking about the misuse of religion. Silence Dogood No. 9 is a critique of anyone who engages self-love to the exclusion of societal betterment, and it finds that those especially heinous in this offence are those who hide behind the surplice. The letter clearly separates goodness and justice (qualities with which, in early modern liberal thinking, an uncorrupted natural man is born) from deception and fraud (qualities that occur when society has fallen to a corrupted state) that masquerade under the countenance of religion. This line of liberal argument is worth underscoring as belonging to Benjamin Franklin's canon from his earliest years, and it is one he employed throughout his life.

FRANKLIN'S LONDON YEARS: TESTING THE LIMITS OF THE COMMONWEALTH

Franklin's ideas of liberalism were inherited from an early modern tradition that impugned the majesty of the monarchy by questioning the legitimacy of the divine right of English kingship. Turning to notions of presumed ancient liberties of English peoples, writers in the Commonwealth tradition worked to disentangle ideas of personal liberty (including liberty of conscience) from the figure of the British monarch (purportedly free because not owing allegiance to the Pope). Franklin adhered to the stance of the Commonwealth tradition—the stance espoused by Trenchard and Gordon and others—for most of his years of first maturity. He eventually shifted his ideas about Parliament and the monarchy when he faced, as agent for Pennsylvania and then as agent for all the colonies, an obdurate Parliament that insisted on its right to tax Britons in North America without allowing legal or representative standing in Parliament. Under these circumstances, Franklin went from assuming the liberal position that Parliament's rule was superior to the monarch's (because members of Parliament were elected) to a nearly opposite position that the king in council was the ultimate authority over all Britons and British landholdings. He finally concluded that Parliament ought to have no authority over the colonists—that only the king in council deserved obeisance.

Franklin conceived that colonists in North America held, like subjects in the English mainland, the same political status as equal and free subjects in an imperial system. His conceptions were consonant with some of the earliest writings on Anglo-American colonialism. He began articulating his liberal political philosophy in literary journalism published in his *Pennsylvania Gazette*. In "A Dialogue between X, Y, and Z" (*Pennsylvania Gazette*, December 18, 1755), Franklin wrote that "British Subjects, by removing to America, cultivating a Wilderness, extending the Dominion, and increasing the Wealth, Commerce and Power of their Mother Country, at the Hazard of their Lives and Fortunes, ought not, and in Fact do not thereby lose their native Rights."[17] Such remarks are of a piece with his comments under the pseudonym "The Colonist's Advocate" in 1770, when he published No. 7 in the *Public Advertiser* (February 1, 1770): "Government must depend for it's Efficacy," he wrote, "either on Force or Opinion." He created a summary history, for British readers, of the attitudes of Britons in North America:

> We have been taught by our Forefathers to look upon the British Government as free. What our Sons may call it is not yet certain. Free Government depends on Opinion, not on the brutal Force of a Standing Army. What then are we to think of a British Statesman who could find in his Heart to run the desperate Hazard of shaking and overturning that on which Government depends, for the Sake of obtaining by authoritative, not to say arbitrary, Means, what might have been had more abundantly, with a good Grace, in the good old Way, and nothing moved out of it's Place.[18]

And he concluded that members of Parliament, who were—like all other people—fallible, did not act properly regarding their attitudes about the colonies. Taking the tone of an elder British statesman, Franklin wrote that "our Laws for regulating our Colonies, and their Commerce, have not always been framed according to the purest Principles of Wisdom, Justice, and Humanity. These Errors ought to convince us, that our Parliaments (what are P——s but Assemblies of fallible Men?) are but incompetent Judges of the State and Abilities of our remote Fellow-Subjects[.]"[19] These were positions he would articulate again and again for British readers, from the time of the Stamp Act controversy to the time when he finally, having been denounced in the "Cockpit" by Alexander Wedderburn, left England. The king—and the king alone—had the right to rule over all subjects in lands under British dominion and the King's crown, according to this position.

Franklin emphasized the presumably common natural rights of all Britons, wherever they were situated globally. These were ancient rights, in the Commonwealth tradition, extending back to the charter rights in the Magna Carta. In a statement published in the *London Chronicle* (January 5–7, 1768), Franklin insisted that Americans, as British citizens, had a "natural right" to develop, manufacture, and use their own goods, form their own assemblies, and expect to contribute to their own law making: "There cannot be a stronger natural right than that of a man's making the best profit he can of the natural produce of his lands[.] . . . It is of no importance to the common welfare of the empire, whether a subject of the King's gets his living by making hats on this or that side of the water."[20] American colonists, as Britons, deserved to be "Masters of the Fruits of their own Industry," he argued in another place in 1770.[21] According to the theory of the dominion of the British Crown, then, the colonists were British subjects, and they should be held accountable to the King for their actions. But only the King held dominion over them ultimately. Any other laws regulating colonial activities should emanate from the colonists' own elected assemblies, not from those Franklin called king's subjects. In a statement printed in the *Gentleman's Magazine* (January 1768), the position is phrased most clearly:

> The British state or empire consists of several islands and other distant countries, asunder in different parts of the globe, *but all united in allegiance to one Prince*, and to the *common law* (Scotland excepted) as it existed in the old provinces or mother country, before the colonies or new provinces, were formed. . . . [N]otwithstanding this state of separate assemblies, the allegiance of the distant provinces to the crown will remain for ever unshaken, while they enjoy the rights of Englishmen; that is, with the consent of their sovereign, the right of legislation each for themselves; for this puts them on an exact level, in this respect, with their fellow subjects in the old provinces, and better than this they could not be by any change in their power. But if the old provinces should often exercize the right of making laws for the new, they would probably grow as restless as the Corsicans, when they perceived they were no longer fellow subjects, but the subjects of subjects.[22]

But colonists were not "subjects of subjects." The colonists were subjects of the king of England. Such were the arguments that Franklin boldly offered British readers, in an effort to insist on the equal rights because of common heritage of the Britons in North America with Britons closer to the seat of power in London.

The imperialist views Franklin developed were, for the most part, classic ones developed around what has been called a consensual model of political relations.[23] For Franklin, British subjects in Britain were attempting to interfere with the rights of British subjects in the colonies. They were negatively affecting the English nation in their selfish attempts to achieve local and personal gain at the expense of the English nation around the globe. This view of empire, in then-burgeoning eighteenth-century fashion, links imperialism with nationalism. Franklin and political theorists like him were imagining a community of people subject to the British crown all around the globe. In imagining that a group of people could relate together under one flag of commonwealth, they were envisioning what Benedict Anderson in *Imagined Communities* has characterized as a sort of "horizontal comradeship," where difference would be eased if not erased in the imagined common citizenship. Under the banner of nationhood, their imagined community would exist as a visionary and potential reality "regardless of the actual inequality and exploitation that [might have] prevail[ed]."[24]

Yet Franklin was tilting at windmills, imagining a community of equals, despite what he knew to be the fact—that interest politics, where individuals in Parliament and the ministry held both political and financial power, drove the British state. There were limits to "common" wealth, as Franklin was forced, again and again, to have to recognize. It was here that Franklin's apprenticeship in literary journalism in Boston and then Philadelphia served as his outlet during these years of difficult diplomacy. If he had proven unsuccessful with those in power, perhaps he might persuade the people reading newspapers. Thus, in essay after essay, published pseudonymously, Franklin wrote about the wrongheadedness of Parliament to assume it could tax the colonists, about the unfounded fears of the mercantile sector that worried that the colonies would take jobs from and sap the population of Great Britain, and about the equal rights of all Britons, wherever geographically located, to the classic liberties of speech, conscience, and labor.

The best known of Franklin's more "literary" writings about the political and fiscal impasse he was facing are his "Rules by Which a Great Empire May Be Reduced to a Small One," published in *The Public Advertiser* (September 11, 1773), followed by "An Edict by the King of Prussia" (September 22). In both satires, Franklin mocked the pretensions of Britons in Great Britain. In "Rules," Franklin adopted the stance of a "Simpleton" seeking to show how Britons in England appear to the colonists in North America. In the "Edict," Franklin composed a fictitious story about Prussia's oppression and a military takeover of England to illustrate what it might feel like to have one's lands, goods, and persons overtaken by a foreign power that was, presumably, a friend. The pieces are different. In the first, Franklin employed a trenchantly mocking tone that clearly and straightforwardly framed the colonists' grievances. In the second, Franklin employed satire. Adopting a tone of reportage, he pretended to reproduce an edict issued by the Prussian king and, in accompanying remarks, suggested that the king intended a "Quarrel with England." Franklin placed in the supposed king's mouth many of the assertions the British ministry made against the rights of the colonists. While Franklin preferred the "Rules" for the clarity of its position, most who admire his ability at literary hoaxing admire the satire of the "Edict." In fact, Franklin took great pleasure in seeing that the supposed "Edict" was taken seriously by his readers: his satire had hit its mark. The satire encapsulated the claims of the colonists by creating a reverse situation for people in Britain: the King of Prussia claimed that as the lands had been settled by Germans, and as its defense against France in England and North America had been made, by extension, through the use of German men and financial support, then it was time the King of Prussia exacted the taxes due him. Ironic reversals were common fare in eighteenth-century literary journalism, but few writers of satire could—as did Franklin and Swift—succeed so cleverly in duping their targeted readers so completely.

In Franklin's "Edict" and his "Rules," we find his tactics shifted, as did his usually diplomatic tone. In Britain, North Americans were no longer, even for the sake of argument, perceived as Britons. North Americans ought, most Britons argued, to be subject to British interests, held accountable by Parliament and, in effect, ruled. This was not Franklin's view, and the commonwealth he had imagined for Great Britain was just that—an imagined community, not a real political entity. Having to face such a reality was difficult for Franklin. It took him nearly two years to accept that his diplomatic mission in England had reached its conclusion. And so it was with dismay and a feeling of defeat—he had tried, and failed, to secure a peaceful solution to the problems between Britain and North America—that he packed up his bags and on March 20, 1775, left London for Portsmouth, to set sail for America.

DIPLOMACY IN FRANCE: FRANKLIN'S SAVAGE ELOQUENCE

Franklin's "Rules by Which a Great Empire May Be Reduced to a Small One" included very clear statements justifying rebellion against tyranny, many of them hearkening back to his views of liberalism from his earliest years as a journalist. When Franklin set sail from Liverpool, England, for America in 1775, he was setting sail for a revolution that he had warned both sides against and sought legal redress to prevent. When the Declaration of Independence was written with his assistance, it made clear to Britain that the ties of common heritage were, at his signature, broken. During the years of the war, Franklin worked to secure funding from France and finally became the diplomat with the most significant power in the French court. His reputation had been secured by his scientific achievements, but he was far better known in France as a genial man, a natural philosopher with a homespun moral conscience. At the time of his arrival, he was celebrated throughout France as America's new world ambassador—a role Franklin knew he had to play well.

Franklin was still struggling with the British ministry, however, as he sought to create an enduring peace once Cornwallis had surrendered in 1781. To secure such a peace, equal partners needed to be at the negotiating table. Thus Franklin had to insist that Britain acknowledge the independence of the colonies as confederated states *at the time Britain attacked them.* This was, of course, a different view from the view of Britons geographically dispersed that he had spent many years arguing, but it was the only condition that could, legally speaking, procure a lasting peace at the bargaining table. In effect, Franklin was insisting that the colonies had developed their own sense of confederated identity, one that bound the disparate colonial groups established along the Atlantic seaboard. In addition to working on a resolution that the colonies were their own legal entities, Franklin was attempting to resolve political and financial disputes. He believed that because Britain had been the original aggressor, Great Britain owed reparations to the colonists for the destruction of the American cities and estates of leaders, townspeople, and rural dwellers. He also believed that, while the peace was in the process of negotiation, Britain ought to engage in a fair exchange of prisoners, so that Americans taken prisoner could return home to their families and begin to get their lives back in order.

As he had in the past, Franklin turned to anonymously published literary journalism to make his views known to the general population. He created two elaborate satires, hoaxes he printed on his own press at Passy, as if they had come as an "extra," a "Supplement" from Boston's *Independent*

Chronicle.[25] On one side of this two-sided news sheet, he presented a purported letter from a Capt. Samuel Gerrish about scalps the British troops had acquired from Indians who slew colonists. On the other, he offered a hoax letter supposedly written by John Paul Jones to Sir Joseph Yorke, Britain's ambassador to the State General (the Netherlands). Both satires evince Franklin's rhetorical skill of satirical inversion, where the tables are turned on the aggressors, their transgressions exposed. Both, too, bespeak (by reverse example) the liberal views of humanitarianism, justice, and freedom that were Franklin's trademarks.

In the case of the hoax typically called the "scalping letter," Franklin, posing as Gerrish, explains that the Seneca chiefs in Britain's employ were sending "eight Packs of [colonists'] Scalps, cured, dried, hooped and painted, with all the Indian triumphal Marks." The supposed letter describes the means by which the scalps were supposedly taken, whether by nighttime surprise or by their method of killing (by bullet, hatchet, and so forth). The cool detail of the letter is jarring, even today. By creating such a grisly representation of the achievements of the Indians, whose work was fostered by the British military, Franklin revealed for European and British readers a shocking portrait couched as if it were on-the-ground reportage. The situation was fictitious, but Franklin knew well enough from his own firsthand knowledge of war in North America that this is what was going on as far back as the days of Indian wars in New England and going on presently in underprotected borderlands. Such real wartime outcomes were a far cry from the high-minded political rhetoric bandied about by aristocratic politicians, members of Parliament, and even the British merchant class, who had not faced a civil war in more than a century and who thus had little to no real understanding of a war's impact on those on the ground.

The purported letter by John Paul Jones touched another situation unfamiliar to most British people. Yorke, to whom Jones's "letter" was written, was the key figure who prevented the appropriate exchange of prisoners of war. Franklin had been deeply touched by firsthand accounts of the mistreatment of American prisoners held in squalid conditions in England, Ireland, and Scotland. His British friend David Hartley had attempted to assist the Americans by subsidizing their food and raiment, but the amount of money and goods given the Americans fell far short of the imprisoned Americans' need. So Franklin decided it would be worthwhile to fund privateering raids on British ships running the coastline of Britain and Europe and running the channel. He hired John Paul Jones, Luke Ryan, and some others, fitted out their ships, and sent them sailing with the high hope that they would bring back prisoners of war who could be exchanged for American prisoners. The problem was that Franklin had no location where the prisoners could be housed, so he gave each man a parole paper indicating he might be called back to prison or used for exchange in future. Yorke took advantage of the situation by saying that the prisoners Franklin's privateers had taken, if not held in jails on land, did not count as prisoners of war.

Franklin, outraged, turned to his pen to articulate his mockery of British subterfuge and pretention. In Franklin's hands, "John Paul Jones" mocked Yorke's pretentious representations of the situation and mocked the very core sets of values on which British notions of liberty and liberalism had been founded. In truth, the actions of the British administration were more piratical than those of Jones: under the offices of Yorke, Britain was holding American prisoners and denying them the rights of British citizens. As Franklin paints him, Yorke comes off as illiberal, ungenerous, inhumane, priggish, and selfish. Recollecting the era of the wars of the four kingdoms, when early modern liberal values were formed, Franklin's Jones remarks to Yorke:

> Have you then forgot the incontestable principle, which was the foundation of Hambden's glorious lawsuit with Charles the first, that "what an English king has no right to demand, an English subject has a right to refuse?" But you cannot so soon have forgotten the instructions of your late honourable father [Lord Chancellor Philip Yorke, Earl of Hardwicke] who, being himself a sound Whig, taught you certainly the principles of the [English] Revolution, and that "if subjects might in some cases forfeit their property, kings also might forfeit their title, and all claims to the allegiance of their subjects."

Franklin placed into Jones's mouth a series of rhetorical questions that had formed the centerpiece of the American peace commissioners' negotiations, all problems associated with the legal conception of the king in council. The Jones letter drew attention to two subjects, then—the baseness of Yorke's duplicitous dealings over the prisoner exchange and the brutalizing falseness of the British ministry's vaunted views of liberty and liberalism.

Franklin had the satisfaction of seeing his hoaxes read as if they were true reportage, even by his friends, so he had a full sense that the newssheet would hit its mark in England. This was his strategy: if he could get the general population in England interested in the situation of Britons in

North America, then he might finally see pressure against the ministry and members of Parliament who had been promoting the war and preventing a fair peace. Franklin worked fast to get his hoax into print on his press at Passy because he was attempting to foment concern among Britons at precisely the time that the chief negotiators in England would be considering their final decisions about the peace with the North Americans. At the time he was creating the Supplement to the Boston *Independent Chronicle*, Franklin was engaging in protracted and difficult negotiations with several state powers, including France, Britain, the States-General (Netherlands), and Spain. The fate of the confederated states and their independence—indeed, the whole liberal enterprise of liberty in political self-determination in British North America—lay in Franklin's negotiating hands. The quality of these pieces as satires is extraordinary, matching the extraordinary circumstances Franklin was facing.

FINDING A NATIONAL SUBJECT

Investigating Franklin's literary journalism for its liberal agenda, we can see the extent to which Franklin's ideas about civic and political freedoms, which he began to formulate while still quite young, prompted a series of openly cautionary and/or satirical expressions about the nature of liberty and oppression. Franklin's views are those typically associated with early modern liberal discourse. The freedoms he gave voice to were those freedoms held dear in the civic memory of the Whig tradition: freedom of conscience, freedom of person and labor, freedom of the press, freedom of association, freedom from social and political oppression.

When he returned to Philadelphia after securing the Treaty of Paris of 1783, Franklin took part in the various conventions associated with forming the confederated colonies into states under one Constitution. He knew there were flaws in the Constitution they constructed, but he also understood the importance of presenting a united front to the American people and to Britain and Europe. On the floor of the Constitutional Convention, as it concluded its deliberations on September 17, 1787, Franklin said, "I confess that I do not entirely approve of this Constitution at present," but he went on to say, "I agree to this Constitution, with all its Faults, if they are such; because I think a General Government necessary for us, there is no *Form* of Government but what may be a Blessing to the People if well administred; and I believe farther that this is likely to be well adminstred for a Course of Years, and can only end in Despotism as other Forms have done before it, when the People shall become so corrupted as to need Despotic Government, being incapable of any other[.]"[26] Franklin understood that it was better to appear unanimous in their decisions, in order to "astonish our Enemies, who are waiting with Confidence to hear that our Councils are confounded" than to leave the convention speaking about the differences that emerged therein. He concluded that "[o]n the whole, Sir, I cannot help expressing a Wish, that every Member of the Convention, who may still have Objections to it, would with me on this Occasion doubt a little of his own Infallibility, and to make *manifest* our *Unanimity*" about the document, given that this would probably be the best system they could come up with.

Yet Franklin saw discrepancies in American social and political practices. As he had in London, Franklin became profoundly distressed by the ironic distance he witnessed between Americans' professions about civil liberties, especially the liberties of person and property, and their actual practices. Franklin's last public writings, and his last literary journalism, spoke to the problem of Americans' professing a belief in liberty while condoning slavery. We gain a sense of Franklin's disquietude about the matter in the very fact that he spoke out about slavery at a time when he conceived a united public front was essential to the wellbeing of the new American State. But speak out, Franklin did.

Franklin had been elected president (an honorary title) of the Pennsylvania Abolition Society in 1789, and as the society's titular head, he drafted memoranda related to slavery. Franklin's memorial to Congress of February 3, 1790, written two months before his death, speaks to the inalienable right of freedom and the destructive practice of slavery in a purportedly free country. He wrote, "From a persuasion that equal liberty was originally the Portion, and is still the Birthright of all Men, and influenced by the strong ties of Humanity and the Principles of their Institution," the Pennsylvania Abolition Society members "conceive themselves bound to use all justifiable endeavors to loosen the bands of Slavery and promote a general Enjoyment of the blessings of Freedom." He remarked that they "earnestly entreat[ed]" the "serious attention" of Congress "to the subject of Slavery," hoping that Congress "will be pleased to countenance the Restoration of liberty to those unhappy Men, who alone in this land of Freedom are degraded into perpetual Bondage, and who amidst the general Joy of Surrounding Free men are groaning in servile Subjection, that you will devise means for removing this Inconsistency from the Character of the American People, that you will promote Mercy and Justice towards the distressed Race, and that you will step to the very verge of the Powers vested in you, for discouraging every Species of Traffick in the

Persons of our fellow Men."[27] Franklin's views on slavery were humanitarian, to be sure, but they also were driven by a lifelong concern that political practices ought to support the potential of each human being to fulfill certain social roles for the good of the majority of the people. Anything else, and especially anything as dehumanizing as legalized slavery in a free state, was oppression, and oppression deserved rebellion. Along with Franklin's memorial to Congress are several other pieces written during the years 1789 and 1790 that reveal Franklin's efforts to improve the living conditions and welfare of both enslaved and free blacks.

The discrepancy between American representations about freedom and the practice of slavery was galling to Franklin—so much so that he turned, yet again, to literary journalism in an effort to bring home to his American readers the striking prejudices under which they operated. His letter under the pseudonym "Historicus" to the editor of the *Federal Gazette*, published March 23, 1790, less than a month before his death, shows that Franklin's skill at satire had not diminished from its heyday use in London and Paris during the negotiations against war and then in behalf of peace.[28] The letter reports on the remarks of one Sidi Mehemet Ibrahim on the slave trade taking place in Algiers, where Christians held in captivity were required to perform all kinds of labor. Franklin's "Ibrahim" concluded that too many problems would emerge were the Christian slaves freed. His conclusions were strikingly reminiscent of the contentions employed by Congress in defense of the slave trade: What would become of the freed slaves? Who would be the laborers in the fields and homes? How would Americans make money? Who would protect Americans from the freed slaves' thieving? Who would train them in a foundational education and in religion? Aren't slaves safer in the enslaved condition than they would be if set free and turned loose in a world where they would be unwelcome? These reasons for continuing the slave trade—and others—Franklin mimicked and thus ridiculed by using ironic reversal in the satire. As he had in his youth, Franklin was denouncing pretension and hypocrisy, social stratification based on false premises, and the absence of humanitarian values among self-professing Christians. Franklin was thus using the ideals of early modern liberalism in an effort to configure a national identity based in the liberal freedoms he believed in and had argued for throughout his long life.

Franklin's literary journalism was of many kinds, sometimes serious and sometimes frivolous. But his journalism based in liberal values of the Commonwealth tradition is memorable for its adaptive use of values associated with early modern liberalism to justify a new American cause.

No printer-publisher-shopkeeper in eighteenth-century North America was more successful than Benjamin Franklin, who began printing while a youth, working in his brother James Franklin's print shop and who essentially (although he eventually sold his Philadelphia print shop to his partner, David Hall, and "retired") never stopped printing and writing for the press. Franklin made of printing a distinctive trade, a vocation and avocation both, and his success accrued in large measure to his achievements as a writer of literary journalism who knew how to adjust his prose style to capture the interest of people, whether they were the tradesmen and townspeople of his youth, members of the intelligentsia in the republic of letters in Britain and Europe, or common people in a transatlantic network of literary exchange.

Notes

1. In a chapter entitled "Creole Pioneers," Anderson writes, "The figure of Benjamin Franklin is indelibly associated with Creole nationalism in the northern Americas." See Benedict Anderson, *Imagined Communities: Reflections on the Origin and Spread of Nationalism*, New Edition (London: Verso, 2006[1983]), 63.
2. Richard D. Brown, *Knowledge Is Power, 1700–1865* (New York: Oxford University Press, 1989), 12.
3. Lucien Febvre and Henri-Jean Martin, *The Coming of the Book*, ed. Geoffrey Nowell-Smith and David Wootton (London: Verso, 1984), 209–11, data offered at 211.
4. Anderson, *Imagined Communities*, 63.
5. Anderson, *Imagined Communities*, 63–64. See also Charles E. Clark, "Boston and the Nurturing of Newspapers: Dimensions of the Cradle, 1690–1741," *New England Quarterly* 64 (1991): 243–71, and *The Public Prints: The Newspaper in Anglo-American Culture, 1665–1740* (New York: Oxford University Press, 1994).
6. Franklin's *General Magazine* lasted for only six issues: the January 1741 issue was published in February, and Franklin had difficulty keeping ahead of the publishing schedule.
7. The "letters" were collected and published in four volumes as *Cato's Letters, Essays on Liberty, Civil and Religious and Other Important Subjects* in 1724. By 1755, six editions had appeared. See Ronald Hamowy's useful introduction to his edition of John Trenchard and Thomas Gordon, *Cato's Letters: Or, Essays on Liberty, Civil and Religious, and Other Important Subjects*, 2 vols. (Indianapolis: Liberty Fund, 1995).

8. Clinton Rossiter, *Seedtime of the Republic* (New York: Harcourt, Brace, 1953), 141.
9. Text of the Declaration of Independence is from the original broadside printed by John Dunlap, *In Congress, July 4, 1776, a declaration by the representatives of the United States of America, in General Congress assembled* (Philadelphia: John Dunlap, 1776). Text of Cato's Letter No. 45 was written by Thomas Gordon and originally published as a letter to the editor, signed "Cato," in *The London Journal*, September 16, 1721, the source of this quotation.
10. Carla Mulford, "Pox and 'Hell-Fire': Boston's Smallpox Controversy, the New Science, and Early Modern Liberalism," in *Periodical Literature in Eighteenth-Century America*, ed. Mark L. Kamrath and Sharon M. Harris (Knoxville: University of Tennessee Press, 2005), 7–27.
11. J. A. Leo Lemay's summary and evaluation of the situation of *The New-England Courant* and James Franklin's challenges to authority constitute the most complete study of the Franklins' tribulations over the newspaper. See Lemay's *The Life of Benjamin Franklin: Vol. 1, Journalist, 1706–1730* (Philadelphia: University of Pennsylvania Press, 2006), 109–206. David Paul Nord called James Franklin's *New-England Courant* "the first overtly heretical newspaper in America" in "Teleology and News: The Religious Roots of American Journalism, 1630–1730," *Journal of American History* 77 (1990): 9–38, quotation at 35. An additional important assessment of the debates about James Franklin's paper appears in Clark, "Boston and the Nurturing of Newspapers."
12. J. A. Leo Lemay considered the Franklin brothers fearless in their efforts to insist on freedom of speech and the press. See Lemay, *Life, Vol. 1*, 186.
13. *The Papers of Benjamin Franklin*, 40 vols. to date, ed. Leonard W. Labaree et al. (New Haven: Yale University Press, 1959—), 1:27. Hereafter, this magisterial edition of Franklin's papers will be cited simply as "BF *Papers*" with the volume number and page number(s). Because this edition of Franklin's papers is incomplete at this time, for materials published by Franklin after 1782, the valuable, compact edition of Franklin's writings, edited by J. A. Leo Lemay, will be used.
14. BF *Papers* 1:31.
15. BF *Papers* 1:33.
16. Lemay, *Life, Vol. 1*, 109–206.
17. BF *Papers* 6:299.

18. BF *Papers* 7:53.
19. BF *Papers* 7:53–54. For background and analysis of Franklin's many letters to the British press during his years of negotiation and for a fine collection of these pieces, see Verner W. Crane, *Benjamin Franklin's Letters to the Press, 1758–1775* (Chapel Hill: University of North Carolina Press, 1950).
20. Franklin to the *London Chronicle*, January 5–7, 1768, BF *Papers* 15:10.
21. Franklin to the *Public Advertiser*, January 4, 1770, BF *Papers* 17:7.
22. Franklin in *The Gentleman's Magazine* 38 (1768): 6–7, printed as "Subjects of Subjects," BF *Papers* 15:36–37.
23. According to Verner Crane, "By 1774, Franklin's formula for empire had become the American formula of John Adams, James Wilson, and Thomas Jefferson. It was the formula implied in the Declaration of Independence." *Benjamin Franklin's Letters to the Press, 1758–1775* (Chapel Hill: University of North Carolina Press, 1950), 128. My book in progress, *Benjamin Franklin and the Ends of Empire*, explores Franklin's imperial writings.
24. Anderson, *Imagined Communities*, 7.
25. For a complete analysis of the Supplement, see Carla Mulford, "Benjamin Franklin's Savage Eloquence: Hoaxes from the Press at Passy, 1782," *Proceedings of the American Philosophical Society* 152.4 (December 2008): 490–520. Text of the Supplement is taken from the two-sided copy available at the American Philosophical Society.
26. *Benjamin Franklin: Writings*, ed. J. A. Leo Lemay (New York: Library of America, 1987), 1140–41.
27. Benjamin Franklin, "The Pennsylvania Abolition Society to the United States Congress," February 3, 1790. Item among the unpublished papers of Benjamin Franklin included in database affiliated with the *Papers of Benjamin Franklin* project at this address: http://franklinpapers.org/franklin/framedVolumes.jsp.
28. *Benjamin Franklin: Writings*, 1157–60.

CHAPTER 2

WALT WHITMAN'S JOURNALISM

THE FOREGROUND OF *LEAVES OF GRASS*

DAVID S. REYNOLDS

WALT WHITMAN WROTE THAT HIS POETRY VOLUME *Leaves of Grass* (1855) grew from cultural ground that was "already ploughed and manured"; he declared that it was "useless to attempt reading the book without first carefully tallying that preparatory background."[1] Much of this preparation came in the form of the writings he contributed to newspapers during the two decades just before *Leaves of Grass* appeared. Exploring this journalistic apprentice work puts the lie to the standard view of Whitman as a solitary rebel against an American culture that was tame, prudish, or sentimental. To the contrary, many characteristics of Whitman's poetry—its defiance, its radical democracy, its sexual candor, its innovative imagery and rhythms—reflect his long-term participation in new forms of boisterous journalism that mirrored Jacksonian America's bumptious spirit in a time of urban growth, territorial expansion, and zestful reform movements. Whitman experimented with virtually every type of journalistic writing then popular, whose themes and images fed directly into his major poetry. If journalism helped generate his themes, it also led him to view poetry as the surest means of healing his nation, which was on the verge of unraveling due to the slavery controversy. In his newspaper pieces, Whitman, a free-soil Democrat, lambasted abolitionists and proslavery Southern fire-eaters, who were both calling for a separation of the North and the South. His journalistic denunciations of disunionists led him to fashion a new kind of poetic persona, a loving, democratic "I"

Figure 2.1 Walt Whitman, 1819–92, engraving by Samuel Hollyer. Courtesy of the Library of Congress.

who embraced not only Southerners and Northerners but people of all ethnicities and nationalities in verse of unparalleled expansiveness.

Whitman's introduction to journalism came in the summer of 1831 when, as a twelve-year-old Brooklynite trying to help out his struggling family after having dropped out of school the year before, he became a printer's apprentice for Samuel E. Clements's Democratic weekly *The Long Island Patriot*. Whitman soon switched newspapers, taking a job as a compositor for the Whig *Long Island Star*, edited by Alden Spooner. He stayed with the vibrant, influential Spooner for three years before taking on a similar job in Manhattan. These printing jobs, which involved working with an iron hand press, instilled in him a lifelong appreciation for the physical process of making books. He would help format and typeset the famous 1855 edition of *Leaves of Grass*, and he had a controlling hand in printing later editions of the volume. "I like to supervise the production of my books," he would say, adding that an author "might be the maker even of the body of his book (—set the type, print the book on a press, put a cover on it, all with his own hands)."[2]

In 1835, a tremendous fire destroyed much of Manhattan's newspaper district, and Whitman for a few years traversed Long Island, teaching in one-room schoolhouses while keeping his hand in journalism. In the spring of 1838, in between teaching jobs, he founded a weekly newspaper, the *Long Islander*, which he ran out of Huntington. Not only did he serve as the paper's editor, compositor, and pressman; each week he also did home delivery by riding his horse Nina on a thirty-mile circuit in the Huntington area.

He was no entrepreneur, however, and the exigencies of a daily schedule did not suit one who would famously write, "I lean and loafe at my ease."[3] After ten months he sold the *Long Islander*. He worked briefly as a compositor for a Manhattan newspaper and then as a typesetter for the *Long Island Democrat* in the town of Jamaica. For the latter paper he wrote "The Sun-Down Papers," a series of short prose pieces, including a didactic essay that denounced the use of tobacco, coffee, or tea and an allegory that questioned the idea of religious certainty.

Pursuing journalism, which at the time appeared to be his career choice, Whitman started writing in earnest for a variety of newspapers. After his arrival in New York City from Long Island in May 1841 he wrote for John L. O'Sullivan's *Democratic Review*, which would continue to publish works of his for years. In the fall he became a compositor for Park Benjamin's *New World*, a weekly magazine with a circulation of nearly 25,000. By January 1842 Whitman's writings were appearing in John Neal's magazine *Brother Jonathan*, which promised the "Cheapest Reading in the World." That spring Whitman edited the New York *Aurora*, a patriotic daily that leaned to nativism. After being discharged from the *Aurora*, apparently for laziness, he worked on an evening paper, the *Tattler*, for which he wrote a bulletin of murders.

Next he became a penny-a-liner for the *Daily Plebeian*, a Democratic Party paper run by the fiery, red-haired locofoco Levi D. Slamm. Whitman's most popular work, the temperance novel *Franklin Evans*, appeared in late 1842 as part of a weekly shilling-novel series. The next spring he edited the *Statesman*, a semiweekly Democratic paper, and that summer he covered the police station and coroner's office as one of eight reporters for Moses Beach's famous penny paper, the New York *Sun*. Early 1844 saw him writing for a time for the *New-York Mirror*, the popular weekly edited by N. P. Willis and George Pope Morris. In July he briefly edited the *Democrat*, a daily morning paper that was supporting James Polk for president and Silas Wright for governor of New York. The following spring he was writing tales for Thomas Dunn English's magazine, *The*

Aristidean. By August 1845, when his family returned to Brooklyn after five years in Dix Hills, Whitman left Manhattan for Brooklyn, where he would remain, with only brief periods away, for the next 17 years. In the fall of 1845 he wrote nearly a score of articles for Alden Spooner's *Star.* He had gained enough visibility to be hired as editor of the Democratic organ of Kings County, the *Brooklyn Daily Eagle,* which he edited from March 1846 to early 1848.

His antislavery views alienated his conservative employer, Isaac Van Anden, who fired him in January 1848. He was not long out of work. Within a few weeks he met a Southern newspaper owner, J. E. McClure, who hired him as a clipping and rewrite man for the *New Orleans Daily Crescent.* Along with his brother Jeff, Walt traveled south by train and boat, arriving in New Orleans in late February. He was there for three months, working for the *Crescent* and tasting the exotic delights of New Orleans life. His time in New Orleans gave him an attraction to Southern culture that, despite his antislavery position, never left him. As he later wrote, "O magnet-South! O glistening perfumed South! my South!"[4]

In late May, Walt returned to Brooklyn, where in the fall he founded and edited another Brooklyn newspaper, the *Daily Freeman,* designed to advance the cause of the antislavery Free-Soil Party. Like the party it supported, however, the paper was short lived; by the following fall it was taken over by conservative Hunker Democrats. He then entered a long period when he worked as a freelancer and sometime editor for a variety of newspapers and magazines—journalistic work that continued even beyond 1855, when his main creative energies were directed toward the successive editions of the ever-expanding *Leaves of Grass.*

Whitman as journalist and Whitman as poet were thus closely intertwined. By looking at his journalistic career, we see where many of his major themes came from.

This period saw a revolution in American journalism. Improvements in technology and distribution made possible the rapid printing and circulation of a new brand of popular journalism. With the publication of Benjamin Day's New York *Sun* in 1833 and James Gordon Bennett's New York *Herald* two years later, American papers suddenly became mass oriented. Papers that cost just one or two pennies largely supplanted the stodgy six-cent papers of the past. Lively, democratic, and informative, the penny papers attracted the attention of nearly all observers of American culture, including Whitman, who wrote of them in the *Aurora* in 1842, "Everywhere their influence is felt. No man can measure it, for it is immeasurable."[5] Whitman saw the penny papers as a democratizing influence that brought knowledge to the masses. "Among newspapers," he wrote, "the penny press is the same as common schools among seminaries of education."[6] This positive attitude toward the penny papers was reflected in "A Song for Occupations," where Whitman mentions among things to be sung "the column of wants in the one-cent papers" and "Cheap literature, maps, charts, lithographs, daily and weekly newspapers."[7]

Though Whitman saw the penny press as a force for egalitarianism, he knew well the brutal, sensational side of American journalism. He noted "the superiority of tone of the London and Paris press over our cheaper and more diffused papers," and concluded, "Scurrility—the truth may as well be told—is a sin of the American newspaper press."[8] The newspaper world he inhabited was an explosive one of colorful personalities and crude behavior. Newspapers editors often resorted to the bare-fisted tactics used also by the street gangs of the day. The controversial penny-press editor James Gordon Bennett was attacked on the street no fewer than three times; he played up the incidents in his *Herald*, regaling readers with details of each assault. Whitman leaped into the rough competition. As editor of the *Aurora* in 1842, he branded Bennett as "a reptile marking his path with slime wherever he goes, . . . a midnight ghoul, preying on rottenness and repulsive filth, . . . [a] despicable soul . . . whom no one blesses."[9] He would later use such slashing rhetoric in his political tract *The Eighteenth Presidency!*, where he compared corrupt politicians to lice, corpses, maggots, and venereal sores. Similarly demonic imagery governs his darkly ironic political poems "Respondez!," "Wounded in the House of Friends," and "Blood Money."

America's penny newspapers were known for their sensational content. Anything juicy or diverting—a "Mysterious Disappearance," a "Horrible Accident," a "Double Suicide," or "Incest by a Clergyman on His Three Daughters"—was considered fit news to print. Emerson noted in his journal that his countrymen spent their time "reading all day murders & railroad accidents" in newspapers.[10] Thoreau knew the popular press well enough to speak of the "startling and monstrous events as fill the daily papers."[11] In 1842 the London *Foreign Quarterly Review* generalized, "[T]he more respectable the city in America, the more infamous, the more disgusting and degrading we have found to be its Newspaper Press."[12]

Allied with the penny papers was a racy genre of urban fiction, on the "mysteries and miseries" of American cities, that was produced by best-selling writers such as George Lippard and George Thompson, who doubled as novelists and journalists. City-mysteries fiction ran with blood and reeked of murder and madness. It was voyeuristically erotic, featuring women whose "snowy globes" and sexual adventures were regularly described. Thompson's city-mysteries novels treated various kinds of sex: adultery, incest, child sex, orgies, miscegenation. In a newspaper article Whitman described the popularity of "blood and thunder romances with alliterative titles and plots of startling interest." "The public for whom these tales are written," he noted, "require strong contrasts, broad effects and the fiercest kind of 'intense' writing generally."[13]

Whitman had a vexed relationship to the culture of sensationalism. On the one hand, as a journalist he catered to sensation-hungry readers. He identified the love of sensationalism as America's leading characteristic: "If there be one characteristic of ourselves, as a people, more prominent than the others, it is our intense love of excitement. We must have our sensation, and we can no more do without it than the staggering inebriate can dispense with his daily dram."[14] The fact that he reported murders for the *Tattler*, wrote police and coroner's stories for the *Sun*, and used hyperbolic headlines about horrors in the *Daily Eagle* (e.g., "Horrible—A Son Killed by his Father" or "Scalded to Death")[15] suggests his willing participation in this sensational culture. As editor of the *Brooklyn Daily Times* he printed reports of rapes, murder, incest, and one case of homosexual rape. Nearly two-thirds of the poetry and short fiction he wrote before 1855 were dark or adventurous. A typical early poem, "The Inca's Daughter," portrays a native woman who is tortured on the rack and then commits suicide by stabbing herself with a poisoned arrow. Another, "The Spanish Lady," pictures a woman who is knifed by "one whose trade is blood and crime."[16] Whitman wrote several tales—including "Death in the School Room," "Richard Parker's Widow," and "The Half-Breed"—that likewise appealed to the popular appetite for the violent or grisly. He used dark images throughout his temperance novel *Franklin Evans*, and he began writing a city-mysteries novel, *Proud Antoinette: A New York Romance of To-Day*, involving a young man lured away from his virtuous girlfriend by a passionate prostitute who causes his moral ruin.

Still, Whitman increasingly tried to distance himself from sensational culture. In his major poetry, he included sensational imagery but made a willed effort to cleanse it of what he saw as its exploitative, purely diverting associations. Many moments in his poetry fall under the rubric of sensationalism. His most famous poem, "Song of Myself," contains an array of sensational images, including the suicide sprawled on the floor, the bedraggled prostitute, the opium addict, people afflicted with disfiguring illnesses, and the bloody battle of Goliad, where hundreds of soldiers were slaughtered. As a writer dedicated to absorbing his nation, Whitman knew he had to register such sensational phenomena in order to attain his goal of being a representative poet. But he adopted sensational themes with the specific intent of cleansing or uplifting them. In his best-known poems, sensational passages are framed by affirmative ones. Horrid occurrences, he showed, are a part of the rhythm of life, which also brings to the fore the beautiful and inspiring.

He was also aware of the public's fascination with sexual themes. In the mid-1850s, when he once spotted a teenager selling pornographic books, he snarled, "That's a New York reptile. There's poison about his fangs, I think."[17] Surveying the popular literature of the period, he lamented, "[A]ll the novels, all the poems, really dish up only . . . various forms and preparations of one plot, namely, a sickly, scrofulous, crude amorousness."[18] Whitman sharply distinguished *Leaves of Grass* from this material: "No one would more rigidly keep in mind the difference between the simply erotic, the merely lascivious, and what is frank, free, and modern, in sexual behavior, than I would: no one."[19] William Douglas O'Connor, Whitman's friend and strongest defender, asserted that *Leaves of Grass* must not be lumped with "the anonymous lascivious trash spawned in holes and sold in corners, too witless and disgusting for any notice but that of the police."[20]

Whitman tried to remove sex from the lurid, furtive realm of popular sensationalism and direct it toward what he described as the wholesome realms of "physiology" and "sanity." He treated sex with a candor that accentuated its naturalness and normality. Throughout his poetry, largely because of the influence of the physiologists Orson Fowler and Samuel R. Wells, who distributed the first edition of *Leaves of Grass* and published the second one, he treated sex and the body in what he considered to be a physiological, artistic way as a contrast to what he saw as the cheapened, often perverse forms of sexual expression in popular culture. "Who will underrate the influence of a loose popular literature in debauching the popular mind?" he asked in a magazine article.[21] Directly opposing the often grotesque versions of eroticism appearing in sensational romances, he wrote in the 1855 preface: "Exaggerations will be sternly revenged in human physiology. . . . As soon as histories are properly told, there is no more need for romances."[22] Priding himself on candid acceptance of the body, he announced in his first poem: "Welcome is every organ and attribute of me, and of any man hearty and clean."[23] He sang the naturalness of copulation and the sanctity of the sexual organs: "Perfect and clean the genitals previously jetting, and perfect and clean the womb cohering."[24] In poems such as "I Sing the Body Electric" and "Spontaneous Me" he listed the parts of the human body, including the sex organs, with the openness of a physiologist.

The same improving strategy Whitman applied to sensationalism and sex in his major poetry characterized his treatment of city life. The American city then was in many respects disagreeable. In a day before asphalt, the ill-lit streets of Manhattan were mostly unpaved. As Whitman often noted, they became mud sinks in the winter and dust bowls in the summer. Since sewage was primitive, garbage and slops were tossed into the streets, providing a feast for roaming hogs, then the most effective means of waste disposal. In addition to the pigs, there were cows that were regularly herded up public avenues to graze in outlying farm areas. Since police forces were not yet well organized, crime was a problem in Manhattan, which Whitman called "one of the most crime-haunted and dangerous cities in all of Christendom."

Whitman complained in newspaper articles that even his relatively clean home city, Brooklyn, had problems similar to Manhattan's. Since the city's drinking water still came from public pumps, Whitman feared Brooklynites were being slowly poisoned. He wrote in the *Brooklyn Daily Advertiser*, "Imagine all the accumulations of filth in a great city—not merely the slops and rottenness thrown in the streets and byways (and never thoroughly carried away)—but the numberless privies, cess-pools, sinks and gulches of abomination—the perpetual replenishing of all this mass of effete matter—the unnameable and unmeasurable dirt that is ever, ever filtered into the earth through its myriad pores, and which as surely finds its way into the neighborhood pump-water, as that a drop of poison put in one part of the vascular system, gets into the whole system."[25]

As for street animals, Brooklyn featured an even greater variety than Manhattan, since it was a thoroughfare to the farms on nearby Long Island. The problem provoked this outburst by Whitman in the *Star*: "Our city is literally overrun with *swine*, outraging all decency, and foraging upon every species of eatables within their reach. . . . Hogs, Dogs and Cows should be banished from our streets. There is not a city in the United States as large as Brooklyn, where the *cleanliness* and *decency* of its streets is so neglected as here."[26]

The city that appears in Whitman's poetry is not the squalid, perilous place he lamented in his journalism. In his most famous urban poem, "Crossing Brooklyn Ferry," he views both Brooklyn and Manhattan from the improving distance of a ferryboat that runs between them. The poem cleanses the city through distancing and through refreshing nature imagery. Manhattan is not the filthy, chaotic "Gomorrah" of Whitman's journalism but rather "stately and admirable . . . mast-hemm'd Manhattan."[27] Brooklyn is not the hog-infested, crowded city of his editorials but rather the city of "beautiful hills" viewed from the sparkling river on a sunlit afternoon.

If in his journalism he often lamented the city's filth and crime, in "Song of Myself" he turned to its dazzle and show: "The blab of the pave, tires of carts, sluff of boot-soles, talk of the promenaders."[28] In his poetry he calls New York City "Mannahatta," an ennobling Native American word that he called a "choice aboriginal name, with marvellous beauty."[29] Whitman used it as a synonym for "city of hurried and sparkling waters."[30] The water connotation became increasingly important to Whitman as urban squalor and political corruption grew in the late fifties. His poem "Mannahatta" delectates in the name while it minimizes less admirable features of the city:

> I see that word nested in nests of water-bays, superb,
> Rich, hemm'd thick all around with sailships and steamships, an island sixteen miles long, solid-founded,
> Numberless crowded streets, high growth of iron, slender, strong, light, splendidly uprising toward clear skies.

Just as he poeticized the city, so he improved on the denizens of the city streets. Because prostitution was by far the best-paying work women could then get, it was ubiquitous on the streets of Manhattan. If Whitman tried to uplift the city as a whole in his poetry, he also attempted to dignify the prostitute. In "Song of Myself" he mentions the "tipsy and pimpled" prostitute whom the world derides. He writes, "Miserable! I do not laugh at your oaths nor jeer at you."[31] He devoted a poem, "To a Common Prostitute," to investing a sex worker with dignity. "Be composed—be at ease with me," the persona announces. "My girl I appoint with you an appointment, and I charge you that you make preparation to be worthy to meet me."

He also presented flattering portraits of two types of males common on urban streets: the "b'hoy" (or "Bowery Boy") and the "rough." When Whitman describes himself as "Turbulent, fleshy, sensual, eating, drinking and breeding," he is not giving an accurate account of himself.[32] If the hard-hitting machismo of his persona says little about Whitman, it says a lot about the roistering street types he wrote about in newspapers. The b'hoy was typically a butcher or other worker who spent after-hours running to fires with engines, going on target excursions, or promenading on the Bowery with his g'hal. The b'hoy clipped his hair short in back, kept his long side locks heavily greased with soap, and perched a stovepipe hat jauntily on his head. He always had a cigar or chaw of tobacco in his mouth. As a New Yorker who fraternized with common people, Whitman mingled with the workers who made up the b'hoy population. One of his goals as a poet was to capture the vitality and defiance of the b'hoy:

> The boy I love, the same becomes a man not through derived power, but
>   in his own right,
> Wicked rather than virtuous out of conformity or fear,
> Fond of his sweetheart, relishing well his steak,
> Unrequited love or a slight cutting him worse than sharp steel cuts,
> First-rate to ride, to fight, to hit the bull's eye, to sail a skiff, to sing a
>   song or play on the banjo,
> Preferring scars and the beard and faces pitted with smallpox over all
>   latherers,
> And those well-tann'd to those that keep out of the sun.[33]

His whole persona in *Leaves of Grass*—wicked rather than conventionally virtuous, free, smart, prone to slang and vigorous outbursts—reflects the b'hoy culture. One early reviewer opined that his poems reflected "the extravagance, coarseness, and general 'loudness' of Bowery boys," with also their candor and acceptance of the body.[34] Others referred to him simply as "Walt Whitman the b'hoy poet" and "the 'Bowery Bhoy' in literature."[35]

Another street group Whitman wrote about in newspapers was variously called the "roughs," "rowdies," or "loafers": a class of gang members and street loungers who roved through Manhattan's poorer districts and often instigated riots. Rival companies of roughs formed gangs with names such as the Plug Uglies, the Roach Guards, the Shirt Tails, or the Dead Rabbits. In a time of rapid urbanization and economic dislocation, gangs provided certain of the urban poor a sense of identity and an outlet for violent impulses.

Whitman's poems presented an improved version of street types whose tendencies to violence and vulgarity he lambasted in newspaper articles. One of the constant themes of his journalism was that rowdiness and bad habits were all too common among the street toughs of New York and Brooklyn. He thought urban loafing was often mingled with viciousness. In an 1845 article he asked, "How much of your leisure time do you give to *loafing*? What vulgar habits of smoking cigars, chewing tobacco, or making frequent use of blasphemous or obscene language?"[36] In "Rowdyism in Brooklyn," a piece he wrote for the *Eagle*, he lamented the anarchic violence and loud obscenities of roving youths. A decade later, he feared the situation had worsened. "Mobs and murderers appear to rule the hour," he wrote in 1857 in the *Brooklyn Daily Times*. "The revolver rules, the revolver is triumphant."[37] "Rowdyism Rampant" was the title of an alarmed piece in which he denounced the "law-defying loafers who make the fights, and disturb the public peace"; he prophesied that "someday decent folks will take the matter into their own hands and put down, with a strong will, this rum-swilling, rampant set of rowdies and roughs."[38]

If he chastised the rowdies and loafers in his journalism, he presented an improved version of them in his poetry. "Already a nonchalant breed, silently emerging, appears on the streets," he wrote in one poem, describing the type in another poem as "Arrogant, masculine, naive, rowdyish[. . .]Attitudes lithe and erect, costume free, neck open, of slow movement on foot."[39] Early reviewers of *Leaves of Grass* saw the link between the poet and New York street culture. The very first reviewer placed Whitman in the "class of society sometimes irreverently styled 'loafers.'"[40] Another wrote, "Walt Whitman is evidently the 'representative man' of the 'roughs.'"[41]

Some, however, realized that Whitman was a rough with a difference. Charles Eliot Norton in *Putnam's* called him "a compound of New England transcendentalist and New York rowdy."[42] Those who saw Whitman's infusion of a philosophical, contemplative element into street types accurately gauged his poetic purpose. Appalled by squalid forms of urban loafing, he outlined new forms of loafing in his poems. "Walt Whitman, an American, one of the roughs, a kosmos": this famous self-description in "Song of Myself" uplifts the rough by placing him between words that radiate patriotism ("an American") and mysticism ("a kosmos").[43] Purposely in his poems Whitman shuttled back and forth between the grimy and the spiritual with the aim of cleansing the quotidian types that sometimes disturbed him.

The same recuperative process that governed his poetic treatment of popular literature and city life characterized his depiction of politics. He deployed his poetic persona to heal a nation he thought was on the verge of coming apart. Although Whitman associated with reformers of all stripes and absorbed their subversive spirit, he adopted none of their programs for social change. He feared was what then was called "ultraism," or any form of extreme social activism that threatened to rip apart the social fabric.

His ambivalence toward abolitionism was especially revelatory. On the one hand, he hated slavery and wished to see it abolished. As an antislavery, Barnburner Democrat, he came out against slavery in the *Brooklyn Daily Eagle* and the *Daily Freeman*. He editorialized on behalf of the Wilmot Proviso, a congressional proposal that would have banned slavery in any new territories conquered during the Mexican War.

At the same time, he could not tolerate abolitionism as it was advocated by the era's leading antislavery reformer, William Lloyd Garrison, who condemned the Constitution as "a covenant with death" and "an agreement with Hell" because of its implicit support of slavery. Garrison's battle cry, "No union with slaveholders!," reflected his conviction that the North should immediately separate from the slaveholding South.[44]

In the *Eagle*, Whitman, who prized the Constitution and the Union, called the Abolitionists "a few and foolish red-hot fanatics" and an "angry-voiced and silly set."[45] He wrote, "The abominable fanaticism of the Abolitionists has aroused the other side of the feeling—and thus retarded the very consummation desired by the Abolitionist faction."[46] He hated the nullification doctrines of Southern fire-eaters as much as he did the disunionism of the Garrisonians. He explained, "Despising and condemning the dangerous and fanatical insanity of 'Abolitionism'—as impracticable as it is wild—the Brooklyn *Eagle* just as much condemns the other extreme from that."[47]

His views were similar to those of Lincoln, who also opposed slavery yet hated abolitionism because he prized the Union above all. Despite their similarity of views, Lincoln and Whitman chose different methods of dealing with slavery. Lincoln chose the accepted method of politics. Whitman, in contrast, thought that politics, which he considered corrupt and impotent, could not resolve the slavery crisis. Only poetry could. His earliest jottings in his characteristic prose-like verse showed him attempting to balance antislavery and proslavery views in poetry. Fearing above all a separation of the Union, he penned lines in his notebook in which an imagined "I" identified lovingly with both sides of the slavery divide: "I am the poet of slaves and of the masters of slaves / I enter into both."[48] The message of these lines was clear: balance and equipoise by poetic fiat. The kind of balance he asserted in his notebook entry became far more crucial with the disturbing occurrences of the fifties, especially intensifying sectional debate over slavery. The poet was to be the balancer or equalizer of his land. "He is the arbiter of the diverse and he is the key," Whitman emphasizes in the 1855 preface to *Leaves of Grass*. "He is the equalizer of his age and land . . . he supplies what wants supplying and checks what wants checking."[49] Seeing that the national Union was imperiled by Northern Abolitionists and Southern fire-eaters, in the 1855 preface he affirmed "the union always surrounded by blatherers and always calm and impregnable."

He knew that Southerners and Northerners were virtually at each other's throats, so he made a point in his poems constantly to link the opposing groups. In the 1855 preface he assures his readers that the American poet shall "not be for the eastern states more than the western or the northern states more than the southern."[50] In his opening poem he proclaimed himself "A southerner soon as a northerner, a planter nonchalant and hospitable down by the Oconee I live, / [. . .]At home on the hills of Vermont or in the woods of Maine, or the Texan ranch." Whitman creates a loving "I" who assumes simultaneously a Northern and a Southern perspective.

In his search for healing agents to repair social divisions, Whitman didn't turn solely to an imagined first-person singular. He also drew off of several cultural phenomena—particularly art and music—he had come to know as a journalist.

Nearly half of his newspaper articles in the late 1840s and early 1850s were related to art. He wrote pieces on all the major New York–area art galleries. He became so closely associated with the art scene that he was chosen to give the keynote address at the Brooklyn Art Union's prize ceremony on March 31, 1851. He was nominated to be president of the Union and probably would have been elected to the position had the organization not disbanded later that year.

The galleries Whitman wrote about were filled with life-affirming, nature-affirming works: the Hudson River paintings of Thomas Cole, Asher B. Durand, and Thomas Doughty; the Greek revival sculpture of Horatio Greenough and Hiram Powers; the peaceful landscapes of Fitz Hugh Lane, Sanford Gifford, and John F. Kensett; the epic luminist canvases of Frederic Edwin Church. Whitman was committed to the union of matter and spirit, the real and the ideal that informed antebellum painting. He responded especially favorably to Doughty, whom he called "the prince of landscapists" and "the best of American painters," and Durand, about whom he wrote, "all he does is good."[51] These painters used a near-photographic style in the faith that nature in its unembellished details always pointed toward God's harmonious universe. They tried to allow the viewer to experience creation afresh, particularly in the form of still landscapes tinged with iridescence. Whitman, following the democratic trend to get directly back to the creation in art, gave the Adamic promise of unadulterated, sun-washed nature and a return to origins:

> Stop this day and night with me and you shall possess the origin of all poems,
> You shall possess the good of the earth and sun, (there are millions of suns left,)
> You shall no longer take things at second or third hand.[52]

Whitman regarded art as a powerful force for social unity and healing. In a newspaper article titled "Polishing the Common People," he called for the widespread distribution of artworks: "We could wish the spreading of a sort of democratical artistic atmosphere among the inhabitants of our republic."[53] He felt this democratic spirit especially strongly in the genre paintings of the day. Genre painters like George Caleb Bingham, William Sidney Mount, George Catlin, and Alfred Jacob Miller depicted hearty outdoor types (farmers, hunters, trappers, riverboat men) good-humoredly engaged in some form of leisurely, often prankish activity—ample fodder for similar images in Whitman's exuberant poetic catalogs. Genre painting also offered the promise of interracial bonding, since it treated blacks and Indians with little of the overt racism that permeated then American society. Whitman, in his concern over his nation's sectional and ethnic divisions, appreciated the sympathetic portraits of blacks by his fellow Long Islander William Sidney Mount. In an article on American art, Whitman mentioned having seen "Mount's last work—I think his best—of a Long Island negro, the winner of a goose at raffle."[54] Whitman's scenes of racial harmony, like the passage in "Song of Myself" about the African American team driver, whom the poem's speaker praises as a "picturesque giant," had precedent in Mount paintings.[55] Whitman also had high regard for genre paintings of Indians. In the *Daily Eagle* he wrote that George Catlin's paintings of Indians were a national treasure, and his moving description in "Song of Myself" of the marriage between the white trapper and the native woman is based on Alfred Jacob Miller's interracial painting *The Trapper's Bride.*[56]

Just as important to Whitman as painting was music, which he often wrote about in newspaper columns. Surveying all the entertainment experiences of his young manhood, he wrote, "Perhaps my dearest amusement reminiscences are those musical ones."[57] Music was such a strong force on him that he saw himself less as a poet than as a singer or bard.

Among the titles of his poems 72 different musical terms appear. In the poems themselves 25 musical instruments are mentioned. The dominant musical image group in his poetry derives from vocal music. Of the 206 musical words in his poems, more than half relate specifically to vocal music, and some are used many times. *Song* appears 154 times, *sing* 117, and *singing* and *singers* more than 30 times each.[58]

Whitman regarded music, like painting, as a prime agent for unity and uplift in a nation whose tendencies to fragmentation he sought to counteract. He had confidence in Americans' shared love of music. In the 1855 preface to *Leaves of Grass* he mentioned specifically "their delight in music, the sure symptom of manly tenderness and native elegance of soul."[59] As he explained in an 1855 magazine article, "A taste for music, when widely distributed among a people, is one of the surest indications of their moral purity, amiability, and refinement. It promotes sociality, represses the grosser manifestations of the passions, and substitutes in their place all that is beautiful and artistic."[60] By becoming himself a "bard" singing poetic "songs," he hoped to tap the potential for aesthetic appreciation he saw in Americans' positive responses to their shared musical culture.

America witnessed a musical explosion in the antebellum period. Whitman wrote newspaper articles about the succession of foreign musical masters—singers, instrumentalists, and orchestras—that toured America in the 1840s and 1850s. In his early journalism, Whitman reserved his highest praise for music that sprang from indigenous soil and embodied the idioms and concerns of average Americans. He discovered such music in the family singers that attained immense popularity in the mid-1840s. In a series of newspaper articles written from 1845 to 1847 he rejoiced over what he saw as the distinctly American qualities of the new family singers. The Cheneys, a quartet of three brothers and a sister from New Hampshire, thrilled him when he first heard them in November 1845 at Niblo's Theatre. In an article for the *Brooklyn Star* titled "American Music, New and True!," he raved, "For the first time we, on Monday night, heard something in the way of American music, which overpowered us with delightful amazement."[61] He declared that they "excel all the much vaunted foreign artists." He revised and expanded this article four times in the next year to include other singing families, particularly the Hutchinsons. In all its versions, the message was the same: what he termed the "art music" of the foreign musicians was overly elaborate and fundamentally aristocratic, while the "heart music" of the American families was natural and democratic.

The sudden popularity of the family singers fueled his dream that a thoroughly American musical style would overthrow the European: "Simple, fresh, and beautiful, we hope no spirit of imitation will ever induce them to engraft any 'foreign airs' upon their 'native graces.' We want this sort of starting point from which to mould something new and true in American music; if we are not greatly mistaken the spirit of the Hutchinson's and Cheney's singing will be followed by a spreading and imitation that will entirely supplant, as far as this country is concerned, the affected, super-sentimental kid-gloved . . . style of music which comes to us from Italy and France."[62]

Whitman in his poetry would strive for naturalness and what he called "a perfectly transparent, plate-glassy style, artless," characterized by "clearness, simplicity, no twistified or foggy sentences."[63] It was this kind of artlessness he saw in the Hutchinsons. "Elegant simplicity in manner," he wrote of them, "is more judicious than the dancing school bows and curtsies, and inane smiles, and kissing of the tips of a kid glove a la [Rosina] Pico."[64] Whitman valued the fact that the Hutchinsons sang about common American experience and the ordinary lives of average individuals. In the *Eagle* he noted that they "are true sons of the Old Granite State; they are democrats."[65]

The Hutchinsons also developed the stylistic device of solo and group singing. In their performances, male and female solos by each of the four singers were interspersed with tight choral harmonies. Whitman was fascinated by the technique. He was powerfully stirred by the rich vocal mixtures the singing families introduced, a mixture best captured in his poem "That Music Always Round Me," which describes a singing group that includes a tenor ("strong, ascending with power and health, with glad notes of daybreak"), a soprano ("at intervals sailing buoyantly over the tops of immense waves"), and a bass ("shuddering lusciously under and through the universe").[66] The family singers' extraordinary power, which he had often described journalistically, yielded the memorable line: "I listen to the different voices winding in and out, striving, contending with fiery vehemence to excel each other in emotion."

Responsive to the emotional music of the singing families, Whitman was also increasingly inspired by a more sophisticated form: the opera. He admired the great opera singers who came to America in the early fifties. The opera rage began in April 1847 when a famous Italian company opened at the Park Theatre. Whitman declared in the *Eagle* that "the *Italian opera* deserves a good degree of encouragement from us."[67] He heard at least 16 of the major singers who made their New York debuts in the next eight years.

Among the opera stars, the one that shone brightest for him was Marietta Alboni, the great contralto who also sang soprano roles. Having been coached in Italy by Rossini, Alboni, after several European tours, arrived in New York in the summer of 1852 and gave more than twenty performances over the next year. Whitman reported that he attended all her concerts. He paid tribute to Alboni in "Song of Myself," where he writes, "I hear the train'd soprano (what work with hers is this?), . . . It wrenches such ardors from me I did not know I possess'd them."[68] In another poem he writes, "The lustrious [sic] orb, Venus contralto, the blooming mother, / Sister of the loftiest gods, Alboni's self I hear."

Whitman had long sought a music that was at once sophisticated and populist, and he found it at last in Alboni. "All persons appreciated Alboni," he noted, "the common crowd as well as the connoisseurs."[69] He was thrilled to see the upper tier of theaters "packed full of New York young men, mechanics, 'roughs,' etc., entirely oblivious of all except Alboni." In an article titled "The Opera" he wrote, "A new world—a liquid world—rushes like a torrent through you."[70] He ended the piece by calling for an American music that might rival Europe's: "This is art! You envy Italy, and almost become an enthusiast; you wish an equal art here, and an equal science and style, underlain by a perfect understanding of American realities, and the appropriateness of our national spirit and body also."

In his poems Whitman tried to forge a new kind of singing, one that highlighted American themes but also integrated operatic techniques. "Walt Whitman's method in the construction of his songs is strictly the method of the Italian Opera," he would write in 1860, and to a friend he confided, "But for the opera I could not have written *Leaves of Grass*."[71] Many of the emotionally expressive, melodic passages, such as the bird's song in "Out of the Cradle Endlessly Rocking" or the death hymn in "When Lilacs Last in the Dooryard Bloom'd," follow the slow pattern of the aria. The more expansive, conversational passages in his poetry follow the looser rhythm of the operatic recitative.

Whitman's long and varied experience in journalism, then, exposed him to many cultural materials that provided fodder for his magnificent poetry. The poet fails, he says in the 1855 preface, if "he does not flood himself with the immediate age as with vast oceanic tides." For Whitman, this cultural immersion came when he was a journalist with an eye trained on his surroundings. "Remember," he would say, "the book [*Leaves of*

Grass] arose out of my life in Brooklyn and New York from 1838 to 1853, absorbing a million people, for fifteen years, with an intimacy, an eagerness, an abandon, probably never equalled."[72] The poet who boasted "I am large, I contain multitudes" had learned lasting lessons about democracy and art as a writer for American periodicals.[73] He had also developed a deep devotion to communicating with readers through the written word. In the *Daily Eagle*, he wrote, "There is a curious kind of sympathy (haven't you ever thought of it before?) that arises in the mind of a newspaper conductor with the public he serves. . . . Daily communion creates a sort of brotherhood and sisterhood between the two parties."[74] This statement anticipates the famous line in his 1860 poem "So Long": "Who touches this touches a man."[75] Journalism forged deep connections between Whitman and his readers, connections that produced poetry of both unprecedented intimacy and a democratic openness to the teeming nation around him.

NOTES

1. Walt Whitman, Preface to 1855 *Leaves of Grass* ("already ploughed") and "A Backward Glance O'er Travel'd Roads" ("useless to attempt"), *Complete Poetry and Collected Prose* (New York: Library of America, 1982), 11, 660, respectively. *Complete Poetry and Collected Prose* is hereafter cited as *CP*.
2. Horace Traubel, *With Walt Whitman in Camden* I (New York: Rowman and Littlefield, 1961[1905]): 194; and Traubel, *With Walt Whitman in Camden*, II (New York: Rowman and Littlefield, 1961[1907]): II: 480.
3. "Song of Myself," *CP*, 27.
4. "O Magnet-South," *CP*, 584.
5. *Walt Whitman of the New York Aurora*, ed. Joseph J. Rubin and Charles H. Brown (State College, PA: Bald Eagle Press, 1950), 112.
6. *Walt Whitman of the New York Aurora*, 12.
7. "A Song for Occupations" (original version), *Leaves of Grass: A Textual Variorum of the Printed Poems, 1855–1856*, ed. Sculley Bradley, Harold W. Blodgett, Arthur Golden, and William White, I (New York: New York University Press, 1980): 96.
8. *Brooklyn Daily Eagle*, February 8, 1847, and February 26, 1847.
9. *Walt Whitman of the New York Aurora*, 115.
10. Ralph Waldo Emerson, journal entry for May 1852 *Emerson in His Journals*, ed. Joel Porte (Cambridge, MA: Harvard University Press, 1982), 433.

11. Henry David Thoreau, *The Journal of Henry David Thoreau*, ed. Bradford Torrey and Francis H. Allen (New York: Dover, 1962), 267.
12. *Foreign Quarterly Review* (London), October 1842.
13. *Brooklyn Daily Times*, December 13, 1858; and *The Uncollected Poetry and Prose of Walt Whitman*, ed. Emory Holloway (Garden City, NY: Doubleday, Page, 1921), II: 20–21.
14. *Brooklyn Daily Times*, August 17, 1857.
15. *Brooklyn Daily Eagle*, October 5, 1846 ("Horrible") and *Brooklyn Daily Eagle*, December 23, 1847 ("Scalded").
16. *The Early Poems and Fiction*, ed. Thomas L. Brasher (New York: New York University Press, 1963), 10.
17. *New York Dissected*, ed. Emory Holloway and Ralph Adimari (New York: Rufus Rockwell Wilson, 1936), 127.
18. *Notebooks and Unpublished Prose Manuscripts*, ed. Edward F. Grier (New York: New York University Press, 1984), IV: 1604.
19. Horace Traubel, *With Walt Whitman in Camden*, IV (Carbondale: Southern Illinois University Press, 1959[1953]): 388.
20. William Douglas O'Connor, *The Good Gray Poet* (1866; rpt., Richard Maurice Bucke, *Walt Whitman* [New York: Johnson Reprint Corp., 1970]), 108.
21. *I Sit and Look Out: Editorials from the Brooklyn Daily Times*, ed. Emory Holloway and Vernolian Schwarz (New York: Columbia University Press, 1932), 119.
22. *CP*, 19.
23. *CP*, 190.
24. "The Sleepers," *CP*, 549.
25. *Brooklyn Daily Advertiser*, June 28, 1851.
26. *Brooklyn Evening Star*, May 21, 1846.
27. *CP*, 312. The quotation in the next sentence is also on this page.
28. *CP*, 195.
29. *CP*, 613.
30. *CP*, 586. The block quotation at the end of this paragraph is also on this page.
31. *CP*, 41. The quotation at the end of this paragraph is on *CP*, 512.
32. *CP*, 210.
33. *CP*, 243.
34. *Walt Whitman: The Contemporary Reviews*, ed. Kenneth M. Price (New York: Cambridge University Press, 1996), 131.
35. *New York Daily News*, February 27, 1856, and *New York Examiner*, January 19, 1882.

36. *Brooklyn Star*, October 10, 1845.
37. *Brooklyn Daily Times*, November 7, 1857.
38. *Brooklyn Daily Times*, February 20, 1858.
39. "By Blue Ontario's Shore," *CP*, 479; and "Song of the Broad-Axe" (1856 version), *Leaves of Grass: A Textual Variorum of the Printed Poems*, I: 204.
40. *New York Daily Tribune*, July 23, 1855.
41. *Washington Daily National Intelligencer*, February 18, 1856.
42. *Putnam's Monthly: A Magazine of Literature, Science, and Art* 6 (September 1855): 322.
43. *CP*, 50.
44. *The Letters of William Lloyd Garrison: To Rouse the Slumbering Land* (Cambridge, MA: Harvard University Press, 1981), 509. The quotation in the next sentence is on page vi.
45. *Brooklyn Daily Eagle*, February 25, 1847.
46. *Brooklyn Daily Eagle*, November 7, 1846.
47. *Brooklyn Daily Eagle*, December 5, 1846.
48. Whitman, *Notebooks and Unpublished Prose Manuscripts*, 1: 67.
49. *CP*, 9. The quotation at the end of this paragraph is on page 8.
50. *CP* 15. The next quotation in this paragraph is on pages 203–4.
51. *Brooklyn Daily Eagle*, November 18, 1847 (Doughty) and *Brooklyn Daily Eagle*, April 14, 1847 (Durand).
52. *CP*, 189.
53. *Brooklyn Daily Eagle*, March 12, 1846.
54. *The Uncollected Poetry and Prose of Walt Whitman*, I: 238.
55. *CP*, 199.
56. See *Brooklyn Daily Eagle*, July 9, 1846 (Catlin) and *CP*, 196 (trapper passage).
57. "November Boughs," *CP*, 1187.
58. Robert D. Faner, *Walt Whitman and the Opera* (Carbondale: Southern Illinois University Press, 1951), 122.
59. *CP*, 6.
60. *I Sit and Look Out: Editorials from the Brooklyn Daily Times*, 173.
61. *Brooklyn Star*, November 5, 1845. The quotation in the next sentence is also in this article.
62. *Brooklyn Star*, November 5, 1845.
63. *Notes and Fragments*, ed. Richard Maurice Bucke (Ontario: A. Talbot, n.d.[1899]), 70.
64. *The Gathering of the Forces*, ed. Cleveland Rodgers and John Black (New York: Putnam's, 1920), 346.
65. *Brooklyn Daily Eagle*, March 13, 1847.

66. "That Music Always Round Me," *CP*, 564. The quotation in the next sentence is also on this page.
67. *Brooklyn Daily Eagle*, February 13, 1847.
68. *CP*, 215. The quotation in the next sentence is on page 528.
69. *Faint Clews and Indirections: Manuscripts of Walt Whitman and His Family*, ed. Clarence Gohdes and Rollo G. Silver (Durham, NC: Duke University Press, 1949), 19. The quotation in the next sentence is on the same page.
70. *The Uncollected Poetry and Prose of Walt Whitman*, I: 98. The quotation in the next sentence is on the same page.
71. *Saturday Press*, January 7, 1860; and John Townsend Trowbridge, "Reminiscences of Walt Whitman," *Atlantic Monthly* 166 (February 1902): 166.
72. *Whitman in His Own Time*, ed. Joel Myerson (Detroit: Omnigraphics, 1991), 43.
73. "Song of Myself," *CP*, 246.
74. *The Early Poems and Fiction*, 6.
75. *CP*, 611.

Chapter 3

"Not Feeling Very Well . . . We Turned Our Attention to Poetry"

Poetry; Washington, DC's Hospital Newspapers; and the Civil War

Elizabeth Lorang

Over the course of the Civil War, Washington, DC, emerged as the medical center of the Union war effort. More than 150 hospitals treated patients in the district and the surrounding area, including Alexandria, Virginia.[1] These medical facilities ranged in size and type from large, formal general hospitals that treated thousands of patients for the duration of the war to small, impromptu hospitals established in response to momentary need, such as the four-bed Washburne Hospital set up in a former blacksmith shop for two months in the summer of 1862. Reading and writing were intimately connected with the hospital. An enormous textual record developed out of the hospitals, including medical reports, diaries and letters, memoirs, short stories, and verse. Recognizing the value of and the need for reading material, as well as for an outlet for the writing of hospital patients and staff, military and civilian leaders at several institutions established hospital newspapers. From the beginning, poetry was a crucial component of these newspapers. Often written by

I am grateful to Susan Belasco, Mark Canada, Kathryn Kruger, Kenneth M. Price, and Vanessa Steinroetter for help with this essay.

and for the sick and wounded and their caretakers, the poems published in hospital newspapers such as the *Armory Square Hospital Gazette*, the *Cripple*, and the *Soldiers' Journal* responded to and shaped the hospital experience; within the pages of the newspapers, the poems attempted to make sense of the war for readers at the hospital and at home.

The poems published and circulated in the hospital newspapers were part of a larger culture of poetry that played a central role in the experience of the Civil War. Americans responded to the Civil War in poetry, and poems helped readers and writers in the processes of commemoration and grief. They provided a space for contemplation, and they could distract and entertain. A range of examples highlights the powerful function of poetry during the war and provides a useful context for interpreting the poems published in the hospital newspapers. Julia S. Wheelock, for example, kept a diary during her time as a nurse in Alexandria, Virginia, and Washington, DC, hospitals. Published as *The Boys in White* in 1870, the diary includes nearly forty pieces of poetry, among which are poems and snippets of verse written by Wheelock herself and by others. Lemuel Donnell, a soldier in the Missouri State Guard, also wrote several poems in his Civil War diary: "A Camp scene described as I sit alone," "On Presenting a Ring," "Thoughts on the Moon," "Dedicated to the girls who have been so kind," and "The following is dedicated to my army comrades."[2] Donnell may have shared these poems—some on the war, others about domestic scenes surrounded by the war—with family and friends, but they do not appear to have been published in his lifetime or in later collections of Civil War verse. Another soldier, George McKnight, wrote poetry as well, but he sought a public audience for his work. A member of the Army of the Mississippi, McKnight was captured by Union soldiers at Hazlehurst, Mississippi, in mid-July 1863 and was sent to the military prison at Johnson's Island, Ohio. While at Johnson's Island, McKnight wrote poems under the pseudonym "Asa Hartz." The poems he wrote as a prisoner were published and circulated in the Southern press, including in the *Vicksburg Daily Whig* and the *Memphis Daily Appeal*.[3] Battles, camp life, and hospitals, however, were not the only experiences of the war, and John Willis Menard, possibly the first African American federal clerk, responded to other aspects of the war in verse.[4] No comprehensive bibliography of Menard's poetry exists, but during the war he published in both the *Christian Recorder* and in *Douglass' Monthly*.[5] On April 17, 1863, one of Menard's poems appeared in the *Washington Evening Star* in a larger article on the previous night's emancipation jubilee, held on the first anniversary of the emancipation of slaves in the District of

Columbia. After delivering opening remarks met with much enthusiasm by the audience—"One year ago to-day . . . the sun of slavery sunk down into its native hell"—Menard concluded with the poem he had written for the event: "One Year Ago Today."[6]

Even Abraham Lincoln wrote at least one poem during the war, "Gen. Lees invasion of the North, written by himself [sic]." As penned by Lincoln two weeks after the battle at Gettysburg, the poem reads,

> Gen. Lees invasion of the North, written by himself—
> "In eighteen sixty three, with pomp, and mighty swell,
> Me and Jeff's Confederacy, went forth to sack Phil-del,
> The Yankees they got arter us, and give us particlar hell,
> And we skedaddled back again, and didn't sack Phil-del.[7]

One term, *doggerel*, has become the ubiquitous descriptor of Lincoln's poem. Certainly the poem is not a literary masterpiece, and neither Lincoln nor secretary and poet John Hay, to whom Lincoln gave the poem, likely had any delusions about its so-called literariness. Until recently, the classification of Lincoln's poem as doggerel forestalled asking important questions about the poem. Why at this moment in the war—and, as far as we know, at no other during the conflict—did Lincoln turn to expressing himself in verse? What does the episode suggest about the role of poetry in Lincoln's life and more broadly? In *Lincoln: A Biography of a Writer*, Fred Kaplan begins to touch on these issues. Kaplan identifies poetry as "the métier natural to [Lincoln's] expression of emotion." Of the morning Lincoln drafted "Gen. Lees invasion of the North," Kaplan writes, "his notion of Sunday morning prayer [that day] was celebratory poetic frivolity for private amusement."[8] Kaplan's equation of Lincoln's poetry writing with prayer indicates the powerful role poetry—even doggerel—played during the war.

These examples are not anomalous, nor are they comprehensive. The poems produced during the war tackled all manner of themes, were recorded in diaries and letters, were published in a range of formats, and were written by the famous, infamous, everyday, and anonymous alike. They are perhaps countless, and they demonstrate the importance of poetry in the personal and communal experience of the conflict and in American culture. Even so, literary critics for decades bemoaned the dearth of major poems about the Civil War.[9] In recent years, however, a number of scholars have thrown the narrow-mindedness of this assessment into relief.[10] Cultural response to the war and attempts to make sense of and to chronicle it did not happen only, or perhaps even best, in the art of the exceptional, the experimental, and the epic; it occurred also in the art of daily life, including in the poetry that emerged out of the hospitals and was published in their newspapers.

Indeed, for much of the nineteenth century, poems of one form or another were ubiquitous in American newspapers, and they performed a variety of functions. They were published in daily, semiweekly, and weekly commercial, mass-market, and literary papers that might reach a few hundred or more than a hundred thousand subscribers per issue by the century's end. Poetic content took the form of full-length poems written expressly for the newspaper or reprinted from elsewhere, and it was a popular feature of obituaries and advertisements. In the first half of the century in particular, daily newspapers even cultivated resident poets, regular contributors to newspapers who editorialized the news and provided entertainment in verse. The presence of poems in the hospital newspapers was part of this larger cultural phenomenon. Readers encountered poetry in their daily lives, and such newspaper poetry had the potential to shape their experience and interpretation of major events, local happenings, and social and personal beliefs.

The hospitals in and around Washington, DC, were home to at least 5 of the 19 hospital newspapers published in the North and South during and just after the Civil War.[11] The first of the DC-area hospital papers, the *Finley Hospital Weekly*, appeared in late 1863. Two others were established shortly thereafter in January and February 1864: the *Armory Square Hospital Gazette* on January 6 and the *Soldiers' Journal* of Augur General Hospital at Rendezvous of Distribution near Alexandria, Virginia, on February 17. *Reveille*, the publication of Carver General Hospital in Washington, was probably published for the first time in early 1864 as well.[12] In February or March 1864, Henrietta C. Ingersoll, nurse and first editor of the *Armory Square Hospital Gazette*, edited *Roll Call*, a Washington-based triweekly, which may or may not have been associated with a hospital. Later that same year, on October 8, the *Cripple*, of the US General Hospitals in Alexandria, Virginia, appeared. Issues of all these newspapers are rare. In some cases, only a few issues are extant, and no complete run of any of the papers is known to exist. Fortunately, significant numbers of issues of the *Armory Square Hospital Gazette*, the *Cripple*, and the *Soldiers' Journal* are available; therefore, these three newspapers provide the basis of the current study.[13]

Little is known about the history or founding of these three papers aside from what can be deduced from the papers themselves. Ingersoll, a Maine woman and former nurse at Armory Square Hospital, may have founded the *Armory Square Hospital Gazette*, which she edited through the end of April 1864. Later editors of the newspaper included E. W. Jackson, chaplain of Armory Square Hospital, and H. E. Woodbury, acting assistant surgeon at the hospital.[14] Produced on a press owned by the surgeon in charge of the hospital and printed by soldier patients, the *Armory Square Hospital Gazette* pledged itself to the "support of Government, and to the destruction of copperheads and traitors," and the newspaper sought to chronicle the hospital as "an episode in a soldiers life [sic]—sometimes a painful termination of it."[15] Less is known about the *Cripple*, which featured only a short "Salutatory" in its first issue. "Published by and for sick and wounded soldiers," the *Cripple* was to be a "medium of Friendship and Information" between the hospitals under the charge of Edwin Bentley.[16] Only in its twelfth issue did the *Cripple* identify its editor, Leopold Cohen, who may have been a member of the US Army Hospital Stewards.[17] The inaugural issue of the *Soldiers' Journal*, on the other hand, described in some detail the process by which Amy Morris Bradley of the US Sanitary Commission established the newspaper. As special agent of the Sanitary Commission at Convalescent Camp (later Rendezvous of Distribution and Augur General Hospital), Bradley proposed the newspaper to the military leaders of the camp and then to the Sanitary Commission in Washington. All agreed on the utility of the newspaper, the proceeds of which were to be saved for the children of soldiers killed in the war, and the Commission provided Bradley with the necessary funding to start the paper. The *Soldiers' Journal* was to be "a pleasant and instructive companion to those who have left home and fireside to exchange them for the vicissitudes and dangers of military life."[18] The *Armory Square Hospital Gazette* and the *Cripple* were published primarily for patients at their hospitals, and the *Soldiers' Journal* was published both for patients at Augur General Hospital and for the larger military camp of which it was part, Rendezvous of Distribution. The newspapers' editors also solicited subscriptions from government officials nearby and from readers in the North. The *Soldiers' Journal* even had a number of volunteer subscription agents in the district and throughout the northeast.[19] At present, circulation figures for the newspapers are unknown. Circulations likely ranged from several hundred to a few thousand copies per issue per paper.

The papers were a blend of news, editorial, moral instruction, entertainment, practical information, record, and literature. They featured reports on the latest battles, the endeavors of the generals, and the political climate, as well as coverage of events at the hospitals, whether the arrival of a new publication, the donation of a quilt, or the celebration of holidays. Editorials commented on sanitary conditions at the hospitals, the presidential election of 1864, and the commissioning of African American soldiers, among other topics. The moral didacticism of the papers is most evident in articles, sketches, and poems that advocate temperance and giving oneself to God. Of the three newspapers, the *Cripple* was the least didactic, whereas the *Soldiers' Journal* had from the beginning a strong temperance agenda, which the *Armory Square Hospital Gazette* fervidly adopted in early 1865 when it set aside an entire page to the "Temperance Department." Likewise, the *Armory Square Hospital Gazette* and *Soldiers' Journal* were more religious in tone and sentiment than the *Cripple*. The newspapers were not entirely serious, however; jokes, selections from Artemus Ward, and other humorous items, including enigmas, or puzzles, and seemingly endless puns, provided entertainment and distraction from the reality of life in the hospital. All the newspapers sought to help the soldiers in more practical ways as well. They printed information on how to apply for artificial limbs and directories of officials and offices in Washington and Alexandria. The directories, for instance, included information for discharged soldiers seeking pay, local lodging, or transportation. In the *Soldiers' Journal*, a "Special Relief Department" identified the locations of relief offices and of DC's Home for Wives, Mothers, and Children of Soldiers.

The hospital newspapers also served as a source of record. Like many daily newspapers, the *Soldiers' Journal* regularly printed lists of addressees of unclaimed letters held at the Rendezvous of Distribution post office before the letters were returned to their sender or forwarded to the dead letter office. During the war and today, these lists provide useful information about who was at, or believed to be at, the camp.[20] To varying degrees, the *Cripple*, *Journal*, and *Gazette* all published information about the patients treated in their local hospitals. In the *Cripple*, this information appeared in weekly tabular reports, which included statistics on the number of patients in each of the five hospitals under the command of Edwin Bentley and the US General Hospitals of Alexandria, the number of deaths at each, the number of patients discharged, and so on.[21] In addition to tabular reports similar to those in the *Cripple*, the *Soldiers' Journal* also published the names of the dead at Augur General Hospital and causes of death in nearly every issue.[22] The *Armory Square Hospital Gazette*, on the other hand, rarely reported deaths as statistical information. Instead, in its first issues, the *Gazette* listed by name all patients admitted to the hospital, those returned from furlough, those returned to duty, those transferred, those discharged, and those who had died. In later issues, the *Gazette*'s practice of identifying hospital patients became irregular. Sometimes the paper featured a complete report like those of the first issues; other issues listed the names of the dead only; and at other times, the paper included very little information about hospital patients, aside from that conveyed in other articles.

Early issues of the *Gazette* also included short obituaries. The third issue, for instance, published obituaries for the two soldiers who died in the hospital that week: Caleb L. Depung and Chester Sheldon (both of whom were also included in the list of that week's arrivals). According to the newspaper, Depung "seemed religious, patient and uncomplaining. He had a great desire to see his family once more before he died. 'Only once more' he often repeated." Sheldon, the *Gazette* recorded, "came here from the Invalid Corps, was with us only one day, and was so sick when he was brought in, that it was with difficulty that his address could be obtained."[23] The obituaries, as personal as possible for being written by relative strangers, transform the soldiers from a statistic or just a name on a list to an individual, one with a life outside of the war and the hospital. Like the lists of names in the *Gazette*, the obituaries resist abstracting the deaths to statistics, even as they forgo individuality for literary conventions and types. This tension between the individual and the abstract continues in the poem that immediately follows the obituaries, "When the Boys Come Home," which situates "a one" among the "thousands on their way" to earthly and heavenly homes.

The contributions of soldiers to the newspapers indicate the important job the newspapers performed in the hospitals. A poem published in an early issue of the *Armory Square Hospital Gazette*, for instance, testifies to the newspaper's role in the hospital. While at Armory Square, soldier Isaac C. Dowling wrote "Acrostic," the first lines of which spell out "Armory Square Hospital Gazette." The narrator of the poem is the newspaper, which describes itself as a "spirit . . . on a mission true, / Resolved to enliven and comfort you." At the hospital, the newspaper's job is "soothing the minds of our soldiers true." Away from the hospital, "Parents shall bless me—lov'd ones find, / I bring them news of the brave ones gone." The ambiguity of these two lines leaves open to interpretation whether parents bless the newspaper because they find their loved ones in its pages, or whether it is the loved ones who find news of their deceased family and friends—in reality, probably both. The *Armory Square Hospital Gazette* and newspapers like it served as a vital connection between the battlefront and the home front. For both soldiers in the hospital and loved ones elsewhere, the newspaper spoke "to hearts in their lonely home," "encouraging hope where hope was dead." The purpose of the *Gazette*, as represented by Dowling, himself a reader of the newspaper, was to convey news and to offer hope and encouragement. One of the ways the *Gazette*, the *Soldiers' Journal*, and the *Cripple* accomplished this work was the publication of the stories and poems in their pages, described in "Acrostic" as "story and song" on the paper's "wings."

As "Acrostic" and "When the Boys Come Home" begin to suggest, poems, or songs, were an important feature of the three newspapers. In each newspaper, the first item in the first column of the first page was, with rare exception, a poem. Both the *Soldiers' Journal* and the *Cripple* published between two and three poems per issue, on average, and the *Armory Square Hospital Gazette* averaged one to two poems per issue. The majority of the poems in the newspapers deal with the war in a self-evident way, and poems not explicitly about the war typically have a figurative connection to it. There are poems on major events, such as the attempted siege of Washington, the battle of the Wilderness, and the assassination of Lincoln, and on major life events. The poems take place on battlefields and in domestic settings, and there are patriotic hymns and somber dirges as well as humorous verse. The prominence of poems in the hospital newspapers is similar to that of poems in other weekly and daily papers of the period with smaller circulations and geographic reach. During the Civil War, major metropolitan dailies and national weeklies also published poetry, but the presence and importance of poetry in their pages varied dramatically, based in part on the diversity of readership and the newspapers' geographic reach. In smaller-scale newspapers, such as those published at the hospitals, poetry played a significant role in building and reinforcing community. The poems published in the newspapers were local, and they interpreted the wartime experiences of the local community.

The newspapers reprinted verse by popular writers, including John Greenleaf Whittier, John G. Saxe, George H. Boker, and Oliver Wendell Holmes, but the majority of the verse was written by soldiers or nurses in hospital and camp or was sent to the papers from subscribers. Indeed, nearly every poem published in the *Cripple* was written for the newspaper. The poems were identified as "For the Cripple"—suggesting both the originality of the work and its intended audience—and the editor regularly acknowledged receipt of poems and decisions for publication on page two. In the "To Correspondents" column on January 28, 1865, for example, Cohen wrote, "L. H. S.—'The Dying Soldier' is very good for a little girl of nine years. 'Practice makes perfect.' Let us hear from you again." "The Dying Soldier" appeared in the next issue, on February 4, 1865. Two regular contributors to the *Cripple* were F. J. W., or Frederick J. Willoughby, and Sarah J. C. Whittlesey. By the time the first issue of the *Cripple* appeared in late 1864, Willoughby was a member of the 2nd US Veteran Reserve Corps Battalion (having been transferred from the 1st New Hampshire Cavalry), from which he was mustered out at Washington, DC, on July 31, 1865.[24] From October 1864 through April 1865, Willoughby contributed nearly 15 poems to the *Cripple*, which also featured his prose. Sarah J. C. Whittlesey, a native of North Carolina, had moved to Alexandria, Virginia, in 1848, and she wrote from Alexandria during the war.[25] Whether she was connected to the US General Hospitals in Alexandria in any official or unofficial capacity or she was only a subscriber to the paper is not clear. And the publication of her 1872 novel, *Bertha the Beauty: A Story of the Southern Revolution*, complicates Whittlesey's connection to the *Cripple*. In the romantic novel set during the Civil War, Whittlesey depicts Yankee men as villains and argues that reconciliation of the North and South is impossible.[26] In December 1864 and January 1865, however, four of her poems appeared in the Union hospital newspaper.

The *Soldiers' Journal* and *Armory Square Hospital Gazette* also published poems by local writers. More frequent contributors to the newspapers included Amy Morris Bradley, under the pseudonym May Morris, in the *Soldiers' Journal*, and H. E. Woodbury in the *Armory Square Hospital Gazette*. Other soldiers, nurses, and subscribers are marked by single contributions to the paper, such as N. Butler with "Banner of Fort Sumter," written for the *Soldiers' Journal* and published in the July 5, 1865, issue of the paper. Not all poems published in the papers were signed, however, and in some cases determining authorship may be impossible. Of the three papers, the *Armory Square Hospital Gazette* published the greatest number of unsigned poems. (The *Gazette* also featured the most verse by famous American authors.) Some of the unsigned pieces were poems identified as written for the *Gazette*, and others were poems reprinted from various newspapers and magazines. It is surprising that the hospital newspapers, which exchanged issues, only rarely reprinted poems from one another, especially in light of how common the practice was in the nineteenth century.[27] The rarity of this practice in the hospital papers suggests the amount of locally generated poetry on which the editors could draw.

The poems, as did the entirety of the newspapers, walked a poetic line between abstraction and individuality, generalization and specificity. Features of the poems, including datelines bearing the place and date of writing, served to mark the majority of the poems as unique, as could authorial attribution and identification of poems as "Original," "For the *Cripple*," or "Written for the *Soldiers' Journal*." Even as so many features rooted the poems in their specific geographic, situational, and textual environments, thereby identifying them as singular to some degree, the same poems could be markedly generic as well, particularly in their use and perpetuation of a common cultural vocabulary of the war. As propagated in the hospital newspapers and their poems—and elsewhere in the literary and visual culture of the war—the dying soldier, the reading and writing of letters, the appearance of phantom mothers (but no fathers), the role of angelic sisters and wives, and the uttering of last words emerged as evocative points of reference. One way of reading these repeated motifs is to see them as evidence of a lack of originality or artistry and to regard them as clichés, written to exhaustion. A more productive way to read them is as memes, or as "unit[s] of cultural transmission."[28] The recurring images of letters written and read and of dying words uttered were, on the most basic level, artistic renderings of literal scenes played out hundreds of thousands of times during the course of the war. The war was repetitive (620,000 deaths), and the representation and repetition of these images had resonance. The messages of these memes extend beyond the purely literal, as well. For instance, they carry information about how the culture regarded the written and spoken word, perceived gender, and understood death. Therefore, we should read the repetition and derivative motifs not as signs of aesthetic or intellectual failing but as a record of the experience of the war realized in poetry.

The sheer numbers of poems published in the newspapers is a rough measure of the poems' importance to their communities of readers; if readers did not value the poems, it is unlikely that poetry would have had such a prominent and prolific presence in the newspapers, with no shortage of news coverage or other material with which to fill their pages. Discussion of poetry in the newspapers further demonstrates the central role poems played in the *Armory Square Hospital Gazette*, the *Soldiers' Journal*, the *Cripple*, and the lives of their readers. An early editorial in the *Gazette* commented on the number of poems received by the newspaper: "[W]e seriously affirm that we have received from the soldiers *three* pieces of poetry to *one* of prose, ever since our paper began to live, and hereafter we shall ever declare that in the American Army, the Sword and the

Lyre go hand in hand, or side by side."[29] And a reprinted poem in the August 20, 1864, "Odds and Ends" column of the paper presents poetry as antidote or elixir for the physically and mentally downtrodden. In a note introducing a poem, the *Armory Square Hospital Gazette* describes the circumstances under which the piece was written: as a response to "[n]ot feeling very well the other day," the writers "turned [their] attention to poetry and Petersburg."[30] The resulting poem brought levity to a dire situation and to the news emerging out of the Richmond-Petersburg Campaign:

> Says U. S. Grant to R. E. Lee—
> 'Surrender Petersburg to me.'
> Says R. E. Lee to U. S. Grant . . .
> 'Have Petersburg? Oh, no you shan't.'
> 'I shan't!' said Grant, 'Oh very well . . .
> You say I shan't, I say I *shell*.'

Indeed, some of the readers of the poem as it appeared in the *Armory Square Hospital Gazette* may have been wounded in the Petersburg battles. Grim though the events were, the author of "[Says U. S. Grant to R. E. Lee]" turned to both poetry and humor, and the poem is reminiscent of Lincoln's poem on General Lee. The poems share an antagonist, Lee, and a plot, the fate of a city. Like Lincoln's poem, "[Says U. S. Grant to R. E. Lee]" might be dismissed as doggerel. The poem is not complex or especially insightful, but it did not require complexity or insight to achieve its work in the paper. Instead, it treated the dispiriting events of Petersburg with an easy rhyme scheme, meter, and a pun—a pervasive form of wordplay in the hospital newspapers. In other words, the poem served the role of the newspaper as characterized in Dowling's "Acrostic": "encouraging hope where hope was dead."

Likewise, an article on poetry in the *Soldiers' Journal*, apparently written for that newspaper, describes the value of poetry. Poetry, according to the author, "lifts the mind above ordinary life, gives it a respite from depressing cares, and awakens the consciousness of its affinity with what is pure and noble."[31] Reading this justification of poetry alongside the poems published in the paper points to the work that Bradley and others believed the poetry of the *Soldiers' Journal* performed. The language of healing that permeates both "Acrostic" and the "[Says U.S. Grant to R. E. Lee]" episode continues in this description from the *Soldiers' Journal*, as does the conquering of literal and figurative death. Here, poetry offers respite—certainly welcome from the "ordinary life" of the hospital. As the editors and contributors of the newspapers knew, a poem need not be a major literary accomplishment to achieve this work. Rather, the newspapers promoted accessible verse of shared experience.

The onus to lift spirits and to heal did not mean that all the poems published in the papers were light and humorous. In fact, if readers and writers turned to poetry because they were not "feeling very well," or they wanted "respite from depressing cares," some of the topics and treatments of themes in the newspapers' poems may seem surprising. In the weekly reports of death statistics and names of the dead, in news of battles, in descriptions of camp life, and in poems, death is a pervasive presence. A glance at titles alone illustrates the prominence of death in the newspapers' poems. In the *Armory Square Hospital Gazette*, poems included "The Soldier's Grave," "A Hero's Dirge," "The Soldier's Death," and "The Dying Soldier." The *Cripple* printed two different poems titled "The Dying Soldier";[32] other poems were "Remember the Brave," "I'll Be Thy Angel Wife," and "The Glory of Our Dead." In the *Soldiers' Journal*, poems with titles such as "The Memory of the Buried Brave," "How Glorious Thus to Die," "Life and Immortality," "The Dying Sister," "The Army of the Dead," and "Man Is Immortal till His Work is Done" were common. In addition to these poems, many others with more subtle titles, such as H. E. Woodbury's "The Coming Year," tackled the theme of death. New Year poems like Woodbury's—published in the December 31, 1864, *Armory Square Hospital Gazette*—were a common feature of newspapers in the nineteenth century. More than simply heralding the new year, however, Woodbury's poem imagines the end of the war. The end of the year and the end of the war are part of a larger cycle of life and death, seen most manifestly in the deaths of the soldiers.

How does this omnipresent theme of death, as presented in the newspapers' poems, fit with the rhetoric of healing and uplift elsewhere espoused in the papers? One explanation may be that they do not fit together; the emphasis on death and the rhetoric of healing, as juxtaposed in the pages of the papers, are simply one more contradiction of the war, explainable in part by the fact that the hospitals, their staffs, and their patients were surrounded by death, even as they held out hope for recovery. This reality certainly affected the portrayal and presence of death in the newspapers, but such an emphasis on death is not necessarily at odds with the goals of the newspapers and their poems to soothe, inform, and provide hope. In her influential study of death and the Civil War, historian Drew Gilpin Faust describes death as a "cultural preoccupation" at mid-century and during the war. In Faust's view, death became the subject of an "active and concerted work of reconceptualization," whereby it was "redefined as eternal life."[33] Given that the notion of death as eternal life is a fundamental tenet of Christian theology, it was not so much the redefinition of death as eternal life that took place during this period but more likely an increased cultural rhetoric about death as eternal life. Certainly there is a pragmatism to this perspective of death as eternal life in a culture facing loss on such a scale. The depiction of heroic and Christian deaths in the newspapers' poems participate in the creation of a narrative surrounding death and provide an opportunity to reflect on the faith of the dead and dying. A poem about the grave of an unknown soldier, written at Freedman's Village, Virginia, and published in the *Soldiers' Journal*, for example, offers solace: "If Jesus has known thee / Then all shall be well" and "if in Jesus he trusted, / 'Twere blessed to die."[34]

Even the nine-year-old author of "The Dying Soldier" had absorbed this lesson. The poem depicts a soldier dying alone in a field, "sadly thinking" "Of his dear young wife at home, / And his little children fair." Despondent, the soldier looks up in the sky, toward heaven, when he is bathed in the light of the sun. God sees the soldier on his deathbed and sends angels to comfort him. At this point, the soldier's sad and solitary death scene transforms; no longer alone, the soldier feels the angels' whispers as wind in his hair. Comforted, he prays, smiles, and dies.

Interpretation of "The Dying Soldier" is shaded by the item that immediately precedes it in the *Cripple*: "To Hospital." "To Hospital" gives the account of a soldier boy sent, with his regiment, to the Rappahannock, where he develops red fever. He survives in the woods as his regiment retreats and is taken by ambulance—"only a Government wagon"—and then by train to Alexandria. Along the way, he is treated with kindness by some, such as the minister who offers him a cup of hot tea; he is ignored by others, such as the women on the train, "sight-seers only." The boy eventually makes it to the hospital, where he recovers as a result of the "kind words, kind acts, kind friends, and kind Providence." "To Hospital" begins on the first page of the issue and it concludes on page four, just above "The Dying Soldier." The placement of the two pieces is distinctive, when compared to similar items in other issues of the *Cripple*. In all but two issues of the newspaper, a poem begins the final page of every issue. In the case of "The Dying Soldier," however, the poem is preceded by the conclusion of "To Hospital," which ends with a reminder to readers that not all soldiers are as lucky as the boy. His story "is but the story of many. He lived. Others suffered and *died*. May they rest in peace; may their country never forget them; may they rise in the first resurrection." A representation of one of those who suffered and died immediately follows these lines: "The Dying Soldier." The hope for resurrection and eternal life that ends "To Hospital" thus carries through to "The Dying Soldier," suggesting what kinds of messages the angels whispered in his ear and the reason for his final smile. The newspapers and their poems could not ignore death, because it was an inescapable reality of the war and of the hospital, so they shaped the narrative of death to soothe the dying and those left behind. One thread of the narrative was religious. Another thread situated death within a moral battle for freedom and ending slavery.

The newspapers used the conquering of slavery as justification for the deaths of soldiers, but as a whole they were not forward looking in regard to issues of race. Lines from "Report of the Medical Officer of the Day," published in the *Armory Square Hospital Gazette*, are telling:

> Through heaps of clothing foul I pass,
> Fatal to health as low morass,
> Midst sable daughters of old Ham,
> Now freed and fed by Uncle Sam,
> These, and some other nauseous stenches,
> The odor from a score of wenches.[35]

Not only are the African American women "wenches," but they also smell. And although it is technically the "heaps of clothing foul" that the narrator identifies as "fatal to health," the implications carry through to the women described in the following line. Similarly, despite the *Soldiers' Journal*'s emphasis on ending slavery—expressed in such poems as John Greenleaf Whittier's "The Mantle of St. John de Matha," for example—the newspaper regularly depicted African Americans in disparaging terms. In the same issue as Whittier's poem, for example, the newspaper printed what it called "an abstract" of a recent lecture by Ralph Waldo Emerson on American life. The piece describes Emerson's views on laughter: "How often is nature, hidden elsewhere, betrayed by a laugh! The Choctaw, or the negro element, sedulously concealed, except in this feature, will betray itself in the loud squeal of merriment which salutes a jest."[36] In addition, the issue included a piece from Artemus Ward that relies on the Sambo figure and Negro dialect for its humor. The paper also featured the latest installment in a several-issues-long editorial discussion about whether black soldiers should be commissioned, with the editor of the *Soldiers'*

Journal arguing that they should not. Doing so would "[tax] the generosity and credulity of our people too much to ask them to admit, at once, the equality of the negro in all respects."[37] The newspapers' and their poems' mediation of issues surrounding race and slavery is an important research area.

Even as they depicted African Americans as foul, primitive, and laughable, the newspapers used the freeing of the slaves to legitimize the soldiers' deaths. In fact, the depictions of African Americans elsewhere in the newspapers may have given greater rhetorical heft to the poems that sought to comfort soldiers with the righteousness of their cause: theirs was a great act of charity and compassion for "the least of these brothers and sisters." The *Soldiers' Journal* of August 3, 1864, for example, published "Lines," "suggested by the recent rebel invasion." (In mid-July, Confederate troops made a move toward Washington, DC, and nearby outposts, including Rendezvous of Distribution.) The poem proclaims, "We'll battle for freedom and freemen we'll die," in pursuit of a "'New Union' no slav'ry can mar." Similarly, an article later in the issue attempts to reassure soldiers about the precariousness of their lives, and it reinforces the message of the poem. Although a soldier may die alone in the hospital, he will die a "true American patriot." The piece asks, "Where are the soldiers who have shown more true courage than you? What cause more just than the one in which you are now engaged? Combining these true qualities, your bravery and the justice of the cause, when and where are the soldiers who have served with more glory than you? Do you despair? Why? Is not the cause most just?" In general, the questions are rhetorical, but the answer to *where* these other soldiers are is either that there are no braver soldiers, or, if there are, their bodies are literally in the ground, "mouldering," while their spirits live in memory with those of George Washington and other American patriots. The piece grants that "it is really sad that so many patriots have fallen," but they have "sealed their devotion to the country and the flag, the banner of freedom and liberty, and their love for the Union of the States by their hearts of blood."

The *Soldiers' Journal* reinforced this message in the next week's issue, which featured the poem "How Glorious Thus to Die" on the first page. The poem describes the death of a soldier:

Behold how gloriously he dies!
  The prize is gained for which he strove,
And the stained turf whereon he lies
  Is softer than the arms of love;

He lifts his weak head from the sod
  As the blithe bugle peals through the air;
And thanks for victory, to God,
  Commingles with his dying prayer!

Wherever the spirit of this soldier goes, "every slave shall rend his chain." The depiction of death as glorious in the pursuit of ending slavery offered some comfort, especially when the actual moment of death was likely to be, in the words of the *Soldiers' Journal*, "all alone, with no one to carry the last sentiments home, no mother to kiss the revered brow and whisper words of comfort and consolation; no sister to breathe a prayer to the All-Wise Creator for his Blessings to rest upon you, and to administer to your necessities."[38] Although the body may be injured, fractured, and ultimately mortal, poetry has the power to heal, reconcile, and conquer the harsh reality of war. As represented in the poems of the hospital newspapers, the soldiers' wounds and death are metonymic to the nation itself—fractured, injured, mortal—and the poems hold out hope of resurrection (to be known as Reconstruction) without the taint of slavery and bloodshed.

By the end of the nineteenth century, writers such as Ambrose Bierce and Stephen Crane criticized the glorification of the Civil War and its deaths in postbellum culture. Their darker, more realistic prose shapes our cultural memory of the war and has influenced the reception of Civil War–era verse in the twentieth and twenty-first centuries. In his influential assessment of Civil War literature, Edmund Wilson lamented that "a more authentic kind of poetry scarcely leaks through at all" in the body of Civil War verse. But in seeking authenticity—whatever that might mean—Wilson defined the value in opposition to the experience of writing and reading poetry in the Civil War, which was of the everyday, rather than the exceptional. Present-day readers may regard the poems' rationalizations of war deaths as simplistic, trite, or cliché. Within the midst of the Civil War and within Armory Square, Augur, and the US General Hospitals, however, the narratives that emerged surrounding death were functional, for both the dying and the survivors. The poems, written by soldiers, doctors, nurses, wives, and children, participated in the hospitals' and their newspapers' work of caring for patients. The poems attempted to make sense of death, to heal the souls of soldiers as well as their bodies, and to translate what were often horrific scenes into less terrifying, if not always comforting, ones. Together, the poems and the newspapers taught readers how to understand the war, the death of the soldier, how to die, and how to survive in the aftermath.

Notes

1. Susan C. Lawrence, Kenneth M. Price, and Kenneth J. Winkle, ed., *Civil War Washington*, Center for Digital Research in the Humanities at the University of Nebraska-Lincoln, http://civilwardc.org, 2012, have identified nearly two hundred places that served as hospitals in Washington, DC, and the surrounding area during the course of the war. See the project's database and mapping applications for information about hospitals, including locations.
2. Manuscript held at the Shiloh Museum of Ozark History, Shiloh, Arkansas. Donnell's diary has been digitized as part of the Missouri Digital Heritage project, available at http://www.sos.mo.gov/mdh.
3. Elizabeth Lorang, "From the Canonical to the Non-Canonical: Editing, the *Walt Whitman Archive*, and Nineteenth-Century Newspaper Poetry," *Documentary Editing* 32 (2011): 78–88, and "American Poetry and the Daily Newspaper from the Rise of the Penny Press to the New Journalism" (PhD diss., University of Nebraska-Lincoln, 2010).
4. Menard joined the Bureau of Emigration in the spring of 1862. See Joan R. Sherman, *Invisible Poets: Afro-Americans of the Nineteenth Century*, Second Edition (Urbana: University of Illinois Press, 1989), 99.
5. Philip W. Magness and Sebastian N. Page, *Colonization after Emancipation: Lincoln and the Movement for Black Resettlement* (Columbia, MO: University of Missouri Press, 2011), 138n30. Menard's contributions to *Douglass' Monthly* may be limited to a letter he wrote in response to Douglass's negative views of emigration and colonization.
6. *Washington Evening Star*, April 17, 1863, 3.
7. The manuscript of Lincoln's poem is held by the John Hay Library of Brown University and is featured in the digital exhibit "John Hay's Lincoln and Lincoln's John Hay," curated by the Center for Digital Scholarship, Brown University Library. The exhibit is available at http://dl.lib.brown.edu/lincoln/Lincoln_Hay/index.html. Lincoln's poem has previously been transcribed in several sources, including in Abraham Lincoln, *Speeches and Writings, 1859–1863*, ed. Ron E. Fehrenbacker and Roy P. Basler (New York: Literary Classics of the United States, 1989), 480; David Herbert Donald, *Lincoln* (New

York: Simon and Schuster, 1995), 447; Douglas L. Wilson, *Lincoln's Sword: The Presidency and the Power of Words* (New York: Alfred A. Knopf, 2006), 199; and Daniel Mark Epstein, *Lincoln's Men: The President and His Private Secretaries* (New York: Harper, 2009), 158. The opening quotation mark in the transcription presented here appears in the original manuscript; there is no concluding quotation mark in the manuscript.

8. Fred Kaplan, *Lincoln: The Biography of a Writer* (New York: Harper Perennial, 2008), 346.
9. Critical understanding of the poetry of the Civil War was, for decades, shaped by the negative assessments of Edmund Wilson, *Patriotic Gore: Studies in the Literature of the American Civil War* (New York: Oxford University Press, 1962); and Daniel Aaron, *The Unwritten War: American Writers and the Civil War* (New York: Alfred A. Knopf, 1973). Steven Conn's "Narrative Trauma and Civil War History Painting, or Why are these Pictures So Terrible?" *History and Theory* 41.4 (December 2002): 17–32, provides a useful context for thinking about Wilson's and Aaron's critiques as well as for considering the larger cultural output of the Civil War.
10. See, for example, Faith Barrett and Cristanne Miller, *Words for the Hour: A New Anthology of American Civil War Poetry* (Amherst: University of Massachusetts Press, 2005); Michael Cohen, "Contraband Singing: Poems and Songs in Circulation During the Civil War," *American Literature* 82.2 (June 2010): 271–304; Alice Fahs, *The Imagined Civil War* (Chapel Hill: University of North Carolina Press, 2001); Ellen Gruber Garvey, "Anonymity, Authorship, and Recirculation: A Civil War Episode," *Book History* 9 (2006): 159–75; Meredith McGill, *American Literature and the Culture of Reprinting, 1834–1853* (Philadelphia: University of Pennsylvania Press, 2003); Franny Nudelman, *John Brown's Body: Slavery, Violence, and the Culture of War* (Chapel Hill: University of North Carolina Press, 2004); Eliza Richards, "Correspondent Lines: Poetry, Journalism, and the U.S. Civil War," *ESQ: A Journal of the American Renaissance* 54.1–4 (2008): 145–69; Jessica Forbes Roberts, "A Poetic *E Pluribus Unum*," *ESQ: A Journal of the American Renaissance* 54.1–4 (2008): 170–97.
11. Earle Lutz, in "Soldier Newspapers of the Civil War," *Bibliographical Society of America* 46 (1952): 379, gives the total number of hospital newspapers as 19. Unfortunately, Lutz does not actually identify the 19 newspapers, naming only the *Reveille* (New Albany, Indiana) and the *Soldiers' Journal* (Alexandria, Virginia). The first

hospital newspaper of the war, the *Hammond Gazette* of Hammond Hospital in Point Lookout, Maryland, appeared on November 17, 1862. See H. E. P., Samuel Artus, and John T. Morton, "Lincolniana Notes," *Journal of the Illinois State Historical Society* 48.4 (Winter 1955): 456–65.

12. There is no extant copy of the first issue of the *Reveille*, and the newspaper may have been published less consistently than some of the other newspapers.
13. No single institution holds a significant run of the *Armory Square Hospital Gazette.* (The Library of Congress appears to have had a near complete run at one point.) Issues consulted for this project are held by the American Antiquarian Society; the Countway Library, Harvard University; the Thomas Biggs Harned Collection of the Papers of Walt Whitman at the Library of Congress; the Chicago History Museum; the National Library of Medicine; and the Raether Library of Trinity College in Connecticut. The *Cripple* is held by the National Library of Medicine in both print and microfilm formats. The Wisconsin Historical Society has a nearly complete run of the *Soldiers' Journal.* The Library of Congress makes available approximately one year's worth of the *Soldiers' Journal* via *Chronicling America* at http://chroniclingamerica.loc.gov. Issues of all three newspapers are available at http://civilwardc.org.
14. Jackson was the editor of the paper beginning with the issue of May 7, 1864. This issue also explained Ingersoll's departure: "The impossibility of giving to this paper the care and supervision which it needs, has induced the present Editor to resign her place to one who will, she trusts, be able much better to fill her place." Woodbury is identified as editor of the August 21, 1865, issue.
15. "Salutatory" and "Prospectus of the Hospital Gazette," *Armory Square Hospital Gazette,* January 6, 1864, [2].
16. "Salutatory," *The Cripple,* October 8, 1864, [2].
17. *The American Civil War Research Database,* Alexander Street Press, 2011, accessed October 5, 2011, http://www.civilwardata.com.
18. "Prospectus" and "The Soldiers' Journal—Salutatory," *Soldiers' Journal,* February 17, 1864, 4. In its first issue, the *Soldiers' Journal* identified Bradley as the newspaper's proprietor. Over the course of its run, R. A. Cassidy, Thomas V. Cooper, William P. Griffith, and R. J. Walradt served as editors of the *Soldiers' Journal.* Griffith and Walradt edited only the last few issues.
19. Subscriptions to the eight-page *Soldiers' Journal* were available for one dollar for six months or two dollars per year. Annual subscriptions to

the *Armory Square Hospital Gazette* and the *Cripple*, both four-page newspapers, cost one dollar. (Originally, a one-year subscription to the *Gazette* was fifty cents.) One-month, three-month, and six-month subscriptions were available for 10, 25, and 50 cents, respectively. The *Soldiers' Journal* was published on Wednesday mornings, and the *Cripple* and the *Gazette* were published on Saturdays.

20. On another occasion, the paper published a complete list of subscribers. The subscription list appears in the *Soldiers' Journal* of June 29, 1864. The printing and distribution of lists in newspapers, particularly of lists naming the dead, wounded, and missing, emerged as an evocative cultural touchstone in popular visual art and literature, as did the dead letter office. For more on the images of list reading and the dead letter office, see Vanessa Y. Steinroetter, "Representations of Readers and Scenes of Reading in American Literature of the Civil War" (PhD diss., University of Nebraska-Lincoln, 2011).
21. The quality of the microfilm reproduction of the newspaper makes it nearly impossible to determine an average number of deaths per week at the hospital.
22. Originally, this information appeared in the weekly "Chaplain's Report." After Chaplain William J. Potter was reassigned in May 1864, names of the dead appeared without a headline, just above or below the statistical report. Later, names were listed under the heading "Died," typically printed above the statistical data. As recorded in the pages of more than 70 available issues of the *Soldiers' Journal*, the number of deaths at Augur General Hospital averaged between three and four per week, with some weeks seeing no deaths and others as many as 18.
23. "[Caleb L. Depung]" and "[Chester Sheldon]," *Armory Square Hospital Gazette*, January 20, 1864, [3].
24. *The American Civil War Research Database*, Alexander Street Press, 2011, accessed October 5, 2011, http://www.civilwardata.com.
25. Ida Raymond, *Southland Writers: Biographical and Critical Sketches of the Living Female Writers of the South* (Philadelphia: Claxton, Remsen & Haffelfinger, 1870), 2:808.
26. See Sarah E. Gardner, *Blood and Irony: Southern White Women's Narratives of the Civil War, 1861–1937* (Chapel Hill: University of North Carolina Press, 2004), 62.
27. The November 5, 1864, issue of the *Armory Square Hospital Gazette*, for example, featured the poem "In the Hospital." Unsigned when it appeared in the *Gazette*, the poem, by Frederick J. Willoughby, had first appeared in the *Cripple* on October 22, 1864.

28. Biologist Richard Dawkins coined the term *meme* in *The Selfish Gene* (Oxford: Oxford University Press, 1987). In *The Selfish Gene* Dawkins writes, "The new soup is the soup of human culture. We need a name for the new replicator, a noun which conveys the idea of a unit of cultural transmission, or a unit of *imitation*" (206). Since the most common popular usage of the term today is to describe Internet fads, applying the term to nineteenth-century cultural phenomena may seem anachronistic. But Dawkins clearly imagined a much broader understanding of the word, one which encompasses "tunes . . . catch-phrases, clothes fashions," and even the idea of god (206–7).
29. "[We have received]," *Armory Square Hospital Gazette*, February 3, 1864, [2].
30. *Armory Square Hospital Gazette*, August 20, 1864, [3].
31. "[Poetry]," *Soldiers' Journal*, March 8, 1865, 22. (Pages of the *Soldiers' Journal* were numbered consecutively for all issues in a volume.)
32. For more on the dying soldier poems, see Fahs, *The Imagined Civil War*, 100–101.
33. Drew Gilpin Faust, *This Republic of Suffering: Death and the American Civil War* (New York: Alfred A. Knopf, 2008), 177.
34. *Soldiers' Journal*, April 5, 1865, [49].
35. *Armory Square Hospital Gazette*, April 9, 1864, [3].
36. "American Life," *Soldiers' Journal*, March 8, 1865, 19.
37. The exchange about the commissioning of African American soldiers begins in the issue of February 22, 1865. According to the editor of the *Soldiers' Journal*, the "race that has heretofore been admired for its unobtrusive patriotism" must first "win the respect of the nation, and prepare its people for a change that implies equality." Following the editor's remarks, the paper published a letter advocating for the commissioning of African American soldiers. A letter in the issue of March 1, 1865, rebutted the editor's comments, and one in the issue of March 8, 1865, argued against the commissioning of African American troops on the grounds of gradual change.
38. G. L. Mullock, "Federal Soldiers," *Soldiers' Journal*, August 3, 1864, 195.

CHAPTER 4

THE TRUE, THE FALSE, AND THE "NOT EXACTLY LYING"

MAKING FAKES AND TELLING STORIES IN THE AGE OF THE REAL THING

ANDIE TUCHER

IT WAS THE AGE OF THE REAL Thing. Americans in the late-nineteenth and early-twentieth centuries were famously smitten with science, enchanted by facts, hungry for authenticity, and preoccupied with realism, which, as one cultural mandarin wrote in 1887, had become "the state of mind of the nineteenth century. It affects the poet, fictionist, humorist, journalist, essayist, historian; the religionist; the philosopher; the natural scientist; the social scientist; the musician, the dramatist, the actor, the painter, the sculptor." This was the era, as many scholars have argued, when American culture took a decided turn away from idealism and romanticism and strove to see, represent, and embrace the world *as it truly was.*[1]

But it was also the age of the "fake." Americans in the late-nineteenth and early-twentieth centuries may have been reading Stephen Crane and mulling Herbert Spencer, gazing at Winslow Homer and scrutinizing Jacob Riis, and replacing their antimacassared armchairs with the stern seats of Stickley, but many were *also* preoccupied with the exact opposite of the real, and not *merely* to disapprove of it. It was at this high tide of America's romance with facts that the word *fake* itself emerged from the

---

I am grateful to the American Journalism Historians Association for the Joseph McKerns Research Grant that funded part of this research.

netherworlds that had previously been its main habitat to become a part of the public discourse.[2]

And it was the newspaper, the institution that had long ago established itself as the public's preeminent source for the truthful portrayal of the contemporary world, that was the instigator and main subject of the discourse about faking. As old journalistic customs confronted new modes of scientific observation and inquiry, new ideas about the relationships between citizens and politics, new competition from novelists who were claiming similar terrain, new technological possibilities, and new economic structures, many journalists found themselves rethinking the most basic assumptions about how facts worked, about how reporters established their credibility, about the relationship between language and reality, about the very role of journalism, all with the goal of building descriptions of the world that felt more true to life.[3]

In this complicated new world where all the rules for both fact and fiction were under reconsideration, some journalists briefly found their own potential for being what they saw as even *truer* to life in the practice one of them defined as "not exactly lying." But the debate over its propriety that was carried out both within and beyond the profession, the migration of the term into dozens of other arenas ranging from prize fighting to dairy farming, the precipitous decline into ignominy it endured, and the contrapuntal flourishing of the similarly problematic term *story* around the same time all offer intriguing insights into evolving understandings about exactly how to tell the truth in print about the world of the real.

FAKING DEFINED

The first journalists to talk about *faking* saw it as an insider's term. Its use was almost entirely confined to the nascent professional press, and it was usually sequestered inside quotation marks, emphasizing its strangeness as a bit of slang with a special meaning that ordinary folks could not be trusted to understand without expert guidance. The special meaning—faking "is not exactly lying."

Or so it was described in the monthly *Writer* magazine. Founded by William H. Hills in 1887, *The Writer*, the first significant periodical entirely devoted to the craft, claimed in its subtitle an expansive mission: "to interest and help all literary workers." But although the magazine welcomed everyone from preachers to novelists into that category, Hills, who was on the editorial staff of the *Boston Globe*, was clearly most interested in scrutinizing and guiding the yeasty world of journalism. There were tips on how to do an interview and how not to be sued for libel, advice about wearing eyeshades and preserving clippings, genteel battles over whether a reporter should use a typewriter and whether a female editor should be called an *editress*. In an article in the magazine's third number on varieties of journalistic style, Hills tossed off a casually appreciative reference to a kind of New York newspaper that requires a reporter to "be able to 'fake' brilliantly to do the work well. He must be a skilful romancer, and it will not hurt him any to be a poet. . . . He must have a brilliant imagination, a Niagara flow of language, and a vivid way of using words. . . . His style must have the quality of the French *feuilleton* writer and the snap of a Rocky Mountain stage-driver's long-lashed whip."[4] And five months later, in one of the very earliest published efforts to define and explicate the phenomenon of faking as it applied to journalism, Hills seemed delighted to explain to "the uninitiated moralist" why the practice of "not exactly lying" was no mere garden-variety hackery—in fact, no hackery at all. It applied to a very specific practice: "the supplying, by the exercise of common sense and a healthy imagination, of unimportant details, which may serve an excellent purpose in the embellishment of a dispatch. It differs from lying in this delicate way: the main outline of the skillfully 'faked' story is strictly truthful; the unimportant details, which serve only the purpose of making the story picturesque, and more interesting to the reader, may not be borne out by the facts, although they are in accordance with what the correspondent believes is most likely to be true."[5] Hills's breezy approach doubtless beguiled many readers into believing that faking was a harmless, even admirable practice ill served by its disreputable name. The point was to fill in any gaps that might have opened either in the dramatic appeal of the story or in a careless reporter's notes; to give a story color, interest, and charm; and to render newspapers more interesting and readable. Besides, everyone did it; it was "an almost universal practice, and . . . hardly a news despatch is written which is not 'faked' in a greater or less degree." It all seemed jolly fun. As an "experienced correspondent" was quoted as saying, "I hate to lie, but I love to 'fake.'"[6]

The "picturesque little details" that Hills offered as examples looked innocuous enough. A reporter following a story about the sober university professor who was fascinated into eloping with a young girl, for instance, might reasonably feel that "it doesn't do any serious harm to describe her as 'a bright and charming brunette of sixteen,' etc., etc.—we all know the 'faker's' phrases,—although, in reality, she might be a washed-out blonde of twenty-three." Readers would like it, and since they would never know the difference anyway, nobody would be hurt. It would simply be giving them the story they wanted and expected.[7]

Yet after painting this appealing picture of creative reporters and entranced readers, Hills did get down to wagging his finger, or at least wiggling it a little, navigating carefully between the duty of *The Writer* to set professional standards and his evident sympathy for any writer struggling to turn in a good story. Faking, he cautioned, was dangerous. For one thing, it was hard to do well; "the ordinary newspaper writer cannot 'fake' successfully," he said, and "the skilful 'faker' . . . is in danger of going beyond the bounds of probability, and of making it evident that he is not keeping to the facts." Since, he warned, the "experienced telegraph editor is quick to see when a correspondent is 'faking' immoderately" (the qualifying adverb is telling) and was unlikely to keep using material from any reporter suspected of faking, then "purely as a matter of business, it does not pay to 'fake' habitually or extensively. The man who has an itching desire to do that sort of thing, and an in-born consciousness that he can do it well, can make more money and a better reputation as a writer of legitimate fiction." It's best not to fake at all, Hills advised his readers, but "if you must 'fake' sometimes, use all the good sense and self-restraint that nature has given you."[8]

So by the end of the piece Hills's message was clear: faking, while fun, wasn't quite *comme il faut*. But the potential victim was also clear: not the reader, or the public trust, or society, or democracy; it was the *reporter*. A working editor who had taken on himself the task of defining an emerging profession was telling his readers that the real danger of shading the truth wasn't that it was unethical but that it might get them fired.

Other trade publications were equally indulgent about the practice. In 1886 *The American Bookmaker*, a journal "of technical art and information" about printing and typesetting, inducted its readers into the secrets of newspaper terminology and practice as if to a fraternity handshake. It defined faking in this way: "to cook up a story without materials, its excellence consisting in the interest and resemblance to truth which can be imparted to it. Very important journals sometimes do this. For instance, nearly all of the details in the accounts of the President's wedding trip to West Virginia [i.e., western Maryland] lately were 'faked.' Had they been true the different statements would have agreed with each other."[9] Here reporters seemed to have been not just embellishing the facts they had gathered but actually creating facts of their own, though even those had to bear a noticeable "resemblance to truth." Faking was even slipping into the first dawning of a journalistic curriculum. In 1894, more than a dozen years before the University of Missouri established America's first stand-alone school, Edwin L. Shuman, a reporter and editorial writer for the *Chicago Evening Journal*, was inspired by his experience teaching a Chautauqua journalism course to write a handbook for young journalists. Like Hills, he cautioned his readers that the fake was hazardous, "an edged tool" that could "wound fatally even the most skillful operator." Yet again like Hills he seemed tranquil in his acknowledgement that the practice was not only ubiquitous and inevitable but also beneficial—just what the public wanted. "This trick of drawing upon the imagination for the non-essential parts of an article is certainly one of the most valuable secrets of the profession. . . . Truth in essentials, imagination in non-essentials, is considered a legitimate rule of action in every office. The paramount object is to make an interesting story. If the number of copies sold is any criterion, the people prefer this sort of journalism to one that is rigidly accurate." No one wanted reporters to "fall into the dull and prosy error of being tiresomely exact about little things," Shuman concluded, "like the minutes and seconds or the state of the atmosphere or the precise words of the speaker. A newspaper is not a mathematical treatise."[10]

FAKING DEFENDED

For some fakers, the highest rewards of the practice were earthbound; it could fatten the pay envelope. Newspapers in this period commonly hired reporters "on space" rather than for a regular salary, which meant that what they were paid depended entirely on how many column inches of their copy made it into the paper. So a reporter might exhaust himself chasing a dozen leads all over town and still end up with empty pockets for the week if none of his stories passed muster with the editor. Canny reporters quickly learned to cram their copy full of the sort of piquant detail that would survive even the sharpest blue pencil, while equally canny press critics argued for the abolition of the space system as a giant first step toward improving journalism. "The space-writer finds it to his advantage to string out his subject by any possible artifice," grumbled the editor of a dignified literary magazine. "Every incident that can by any possibility be tortured in a sensational direction is distorted . . . [it] is not really to the advantage of the space-writer to adhere carefully to bare facts."[11]

But also clear in the late 1880s and early 1890s is the suggestion that faking could be an aesthetic pleasure and that, like the "experienced correspondent" quoted by Hills in 1887, some reporters just "love[d] to fake." It could be, simply, an escape from boredom, whether it was the journalists who were bored or their material that was boring. Many of the young men and women who had entered journalism looking for adventure or drama or novelty were dismayed to discover that what they actually had to do every day was crushingly humdrum. Local reporters on small-town papers faced the "overwhelming" challenge of filling five columns a week in places so dull, orderly, and newsless that, as Charles Edward Russell recalled of his apprenticeship on his father's paper in Davenport, Iowa, the arrival of a steamboat or the issuance of a new railroad timetable could be cause for rejoicing. Faking could repair the unbearable banality of reality.[12]

At the same time, some of the most eminent city papers had been moving decisively toward a kind of neutral, uninflected writing that young writers with literary ambitions—and there were many—often found irksome. In the 1890s Lincoln Steffens chafed at editor E. L. Godkin's mandate that *Evening Post* reporters "were to report the news as it happened, like machines, without prejudice, color, and without style; all alike." And long after Julius Chambers had gone on to lustrous careers as both a journalist and a novelist, he was still grumbling about the harm done to his talent by his first job in journalism, way back in 1870. The *New York Tribune* had employed a style "accurately described by John Hay, then a paragraph writer on the *Tribune,* as 'The Grocer's Bill,'" he complained in his posthumously published reminiscences. "Facts; facts; nothing but facts. So many peas at so much a peck; so much molasses at so much a quart. . . . It was a rigid system, rigidly enforced."[13]

For the ambitious, for the desperate, or for that aspiring novelist with the half-finished manuscript in the bottom drawer, the temptation to break loose with some personal or creative gesture must sometimes have been irresistible and, even better, the possible consequences mild. Even Russell, whose 1914 memoir included a sharp denunciation of faking, confessed that his old Davenport newspaper had occasionally resorted to using a story from an exchange paper with the names changed—something he *could* have chosen to call a fake rather than dismissing it, as he did, as a "sheer and perhaps clumsy invention."[14]

Pulling off a good fake offered other satisfactions to the reporter. It produced stories that readers noticed and liked. It reinforced reporters' sense of belonging to a select band with special skills and special privileges. It gave them a competitive arena with no holds barred where they could impress and (ideally) outdo rival papers or even their own colleagues. Grizzled old-timers who insisted that they had foresworn faking would nonetheless fondly recall the great fakes of their youth and pass on the stories to their successors as if they were founding myths. After a long day covering a mild and unproductive little anarchists' rally, as William Salisbury recorded in his memoir, the reporters sitting around the *Chicago Tribune* office plopped their feet on their desks and reminisced about "the hot times in the old days" of the Haymarket trials. They kept public excitement boiling even during lulls in the action, one veteran newsman recalled, with "all kinds of rumors" of plots and threats, but "the best faking in the anarchist days—" he went on, "the most artistic—was done by Dickson. . . . He got more scoops out of the cells of the condemned than anybody."[15]

It wasn't just reporters, either, who enjoyed a good fake. Faking could also drive up a paper's circulation, and while protocol required that editors officially frown on the practice, many let it be known, tacitly but unmistakably, that a story written with imagination and verve would not be taken amiss. During his brief stint on the *St. Louis Globe-Democrat* in 1892–93, the young Theodore Dreiser was assigned to write the regular "Heard in the Corridors" column that was supposed to have been based on interviews with guests at the various hotels in town. "One could write any sort of story one pleased,—romantic, realistic or wild," he later recalled, "and credit it to some imaginary guest at one of the hotels, and if it wasn't too improbable it went through without comment. It was not specifically stated by the management that the interviews could be imaginary," Dreiser went on, but the assistant city editor tipped him that the previous columnist "never tried to get actual interviews except once in a while," and Dreiser's own inventions soon won him a permanent assignment to the column. After being caught faking some theater reviews on a busy night, he fled the *Globe-Democrat* in a spasm of righteous remorse and moved over to the *St. Louis Republic*. There his fertile imagination again earned him acclaim and a steady assignment, this time covering baseball—and he eventually found that those faked reviews for the *Globe-Democrat* had been greeted with nothing more than hearty and sympathetic laughter by his colleagues.[16]

The journalistic fake was even recognizable enough to serve as a genially comic plot device in fiction. In a short story published in *Harper's Weekly*, the "Young Reporter" chivvied an older colleague for what he called a fake story involving a bear, a bicycle, and a handful of ball bearings, accusing him of "making journalism a byword and a reproach." But when the "Old Reporter" explained that his story had actually "tone[d] . . . down" an even more elaborate and incredible incident on the theory that "it is not so much the things which a man puts in as the things which he leaves out that makes a successful reporter," the callow youth looked at his colleague with new respect.[17]

SPEAKING OF FAKING

Journalistic embellishment, exaggeration, and fictionalization were, of course, nothing new for newspaper readers by the time Hills and his colleagues came along. Nor was the term *fake* unfamiliar to American ears. It *was* something new, however, that the practice was being named and discussed at all. And it was paradoxical that some journalists were launching their convivial discussion about the pleasures of faking at exactly the same time that others were opening a serious conversation about the duties, responsibilities, and standards of what was being seen for the first time as the *profession* of journalism.

For much of the nineteenth century, newspapers were only partly about "news," and nobody would have expected that everything appearing in one was factually accurate. Newspapers, especially local ones, which made heavy use of secondhand items copied from bigger papers and which had traditionally served as their readers' first or only regular encounters with print, had always had a dog's-breakfast feel about them, indiscriminately mingling intelligence about actual events near and far with poetry, fiction, homilies, travelers' letters, social notes, and jokes. And while those items were usually easy to categorize, others required careful evaluation.

Many papers indulged, knowingly or not, in hoaxes and tall tales. Dan De Quille, who once showed the ropes to the tenderfoot reporter Mark Twain, continued for decades to tickle gullible easterners with his accounts of seven-foot mountain alligators and eyeless hot-water fish. And one Joe Mulhatton, not a journalist at all but an ingratiating salesman with a fertile imagination, earned a certain notoriety as a "gorgeous and ornamental prevaricator" who planted so many tall tales about fallen meteors, treasure caves, and detached sunspots in papers across the country that when reports began circulating that he had died, canny newspapers covered themselves by hinting that the death notice itself might be another hoax. Practical jokes not infrequently wandered into print: as William Salisbury recalled, in his very first days on the job as a superabundantly energetic cub, his older and lazier rivals planted fake news notes for him, and "Patrolman Smith shot a mad dog in the West End while it was running eastward yesterday" actually slipped past his careless editor and into the *Kansas City Times*. And even the soberest paper was known to indulge in the occasional *jeu d'esprit*, as the *New York Tribune* did with its bizarre half-credible, half-frolicsome report of the burning of Barnum's Museum in 1865. Thus readers had become accustomed to papers that one week highlighted the president's message and the next a sentimental tale of the drunkard's redemption, and that claimed neither more nor less expertise in evaluating the latest weird natural phenomenon from the west than any of their own subscribers did. Readers understood that any encounter with a newspaper required them to continually monitor and readjust their assumptions about the authenticity and usefulness of what they were reading—that accurate news truthfully presented was just one category out of many that a newspaper might contain.[18]

Yet while the kind of *un*truthful embellishment Hills described was scarcely novel, what *was* unprecedented was that he was describing it in the first place. Reporters had never talked much before, or probably even thought much before, about exactly what they did, how they did it, and why. Reporters hadn't even been around very long; the figure known as the American reporter had been born only in the 1830s, a product of the ongoing transformation of journalism from a partisan argument among party-funded editors into a generally independent, enterprising, and commercially valuable information system. The new entrepreneurial journalism was unleashing new values, new competitive pressures, and new public expectations along with those new agents who were sallying forth, pencils in hand, into the streets, the courts, the ballrooms, and the battlefields to *find things out.*

A seedy lot they often were, too, those first generations of reporters. Just about the only thing that distinguished them from everyone else—other than that they were seen at best as busybodies, at worst as snoops, and that by most accounts they possessed a legendary capacity for beer—was that they claimed to *be* reporters. No special training was required to become one, and in fact the relatively independent and adventurous life of the journalist was a magnet for the scruffy, the footloose, and the anticonventional, while the work itself was not so much *un*conventional as nearly convention free. No recognized professional organizations or associations set standards or encouraged ethical norms. No generally accepted principles governed the publication of anonymous quotations or the limits of undercover reporting; no weight of tradition steered reporters toward the inverted pyramid or the anecdotal lead; no standardized credentials or press passes gave them leave to slip into crime scenes or committee meetings; and not many ordinary citizens, if stopped on the street and asked whether a public figure had any obligation at all to answer a question from a reporter, would have responded with an unequivocal "yes."

By the end of the nineteenth century, however, a sense of professional self-awareness was glimmering in the grime. Many journalists were joining members of other emerging professions and disciplines like law, medicine, social work, and librarianship in the widespread effort to identify, organize, and control the distinctive bodies of knowledge and codes of behavior that set them apart from ordinary people. Averse as they were to regulation both temperamentally and Constitutionally, journalists never quite kept pace with the lawyers and the doctors in some of the classic indicators of professionalism, such as establishing credentialing procedures, educational requirements, or enforceable codes of conduct. For some—but certainly not all—journalistic organizations, however, another aspect of the professionalization project was increasingly appealing: the use of special modes of inquiry that were different from what untrained people did, modes that were generally characterized as objective, empirical, informational, and rooted in the scientific method.[19]

Another way that evolving professions identified and defined themselves involved talking about themselves—that is, creating handbooks, textbooks, or journals written by professionals for fellow professionals. So when journalists did bring the topic of faking into the emerging conversation about who they were, the assurance that *The Writer* and other such publications were safe havens where insiders talked only to insiders may explain why they chose to deploy a word that at that point was associated almost entirely with louche company. In thieves' cant, *fake* embraced ingenious knavery of all sorts, from "faking a screw" (shaping a skeleton key) to "faking a pin" (injuring one's own leg for sinister purposes), and it was used around the kennel and the barn to describe illicit dye or clip jobs done on horses, show dogs, or even chickens to disguise their flaws. The term was also flourishing in the theater, where an actor who forgot his lines and "supplied the deficiency by words of his own immediate creation" was teased by his fellow troupers, not unsympathetically, as a faker. While it was the world of the stage, not the gamier purlieus of scheming invalids and doctored dogs, that was generally credited with inspiring the journalists to adopt the term as their own, even that world carried the sort of bohemian air that journalists would have found especially congenial.[20] Thus, like the swaggering drunk who insists *he* could be trusted to handle the hooch, journalists were telling each other in their safe journalists-only retreats that while the ordinary citizen and "uninitiated moralist" might not get it, they themselves understood perfectly well that "faking" was just another trick of the trade.

They knew better, however, than to make that point too vigorously in public. When they were addressing nonjournalists rather than yarning with their feet up, practitioners and advocates of faking tended to emphasize its utility, insisting that it actually made them better reporters, while quietly eliding its more freewheeling aspects. As a former news editor at the United Press wire service explained in 1894 in the widely read general-interest *Lippincott's* magazine, faking was a "legitimate and almost necessary" tactic, an ingenious way to cover a late-breaking story in detail and on deadline. Four years earlier, for instance, when the daughter of Secretary of State James G. Blaine inconsiderately scheduled her wedding to begin at two o'clock, just an hour before most afternoon newspapers had to close their final editions, reporters were sent the day before the great event to interview the family, the florist, and the dressmaker and had most of the story written 18 hours before the first guests arrived. Journalists simply had to take care, the UP editor cautioned, not to fall into the grievous error perpetrated by the New York news staff that had energetically and accurately collected all the details about a pending grand society wedding except for the most basic one and leapt into print with an elaborate account of "today's" nuptials a day before the ceremony actually took place.[21]

Sometimes journalists justified their fakery as a way to avoid the "unpardonable sin" of being scooped, which they presented as even more of a disaster for their news-hungry readers than for their own reputations. A 1901 column in another general-interest magazine quoted (or, possibly, faked an interview with) an ex-newspaper man who recalled the great tornado that, five years earlier in St. Louis, had knocked down all the telegraph wires and made it impossible for his distant paper to get any eyewitness accounts of the disaster. So his paper got hold of a man who "knew St. Louis and knew tornadoes by previous experience" to fake some details that felt true, and "the dear public read it with great gusto." Most reporters, the ex-newspaper man insisted, were as honest as anyone else and preferred not to write "fiction," but they also understood what their business required. "Better a thousand fakes to your discredit," he concluded, "than one beat."[22]

In both the professional press and the public mind, faking was closely associated with a journalistic tool that has now been accepted as one of the most basic and effective in the reporter's arsenal. In the nineteenth century, however, the interview was widely despised. A common complaint at the time, and one that has since received a great deal of attention from historians, was that the interview represented an unjustifiable intrusion into private life, a repellent expedient hatched by nasty busybodies and soulless snoops. But that wasn't the only objection. Interviews were also seen as, literally, incredible: there was no way, after all, of confirming that a given interview was authentic and no reason to trust what a reporter said anyway. It would be "ludicrous," grumbled a popular columnist for *Harper's Monthly*, to "quote a gentleman or lady as holding certain opinions because of a reported conversation printed in a newspaper."[23]

Ludicrous indeed, at least if you believed the many protests by such figures as the Rev. Charles Sheldon, whose madly popular novel *In His Steps: What Would Jesus Do?* catapulted him to the 1896 equivalent of rock-star status. "I have never," he wrote in *The Outlook*, "except once, to a reporter from my own home paper, been interviewed by a reporter for publication in a daily paper, and yet scores of supposed interviews have been published in daily papers." The same thing happened to other eminent men, too, he wrote; a politician friend of his was angry that he had been "reported as saying things he never said, and the 'interviews' were written, anyway, by 'enterprising' reporters, who must have so much matter daily for their papers."[24]

Reporters, however, contended that the fault lay not with the interviewer but the interviewee—with the amateurs, not the professionals. As a journalist named John Arthur argued in *The Writer* in 1889, "in nine cases out of ten" when a subject repudiates a published interview, "he lies. He doesn't like the look of what he has said, when he sees it in cold print." That was why, Arthur continued, if a man absolutely refused to be interviewed, then "no scruples of conscience keep me from obtaining my information through a third party, and 'faking' my interview accordingly." He even assured his nervous reader that such a response would not be "in any manner debasing his manhood."[25]

The Backlash

The heyday of the journalistic fake was brief.

Almost from the moment the word first emerged there had been murmurings in both the professional and the general press against the whole idea, and those murmurings only grew louder and more intense. *The Writer* itself embodied the changing climate of opinion. After running John Arthur's article, for instance, the magazine had quickly alerted potential interview-fakers that their manhoods might not be safe after all; the very next issue carried a rebuttal by a journalist who called Arthur's remarks "astounding." Faking, he spluttered, "is but an agreeable synonym for 'lying,' much as 'embezzlement' is a euphonism [sic] for 'stealing,'" and its prevalence was giving the press a bad name. Reporters must remember, he continued, that they have "no special ethical privileges or excuses. A reporter is a man (or woman) and has a soul, for which he is responsible."[26]

And seven years after editor Hills had chortled in print over the faked story of the charming brunette, he was publicly embracing the side of righteousness and denouncing Edwin Shuman's handbook for young journalists for its "bad advice" about faking. The practice may be legitimate in Shuman's notoriously freewheeling hometown of Chicago, wrote Hills (a Bostonian) in his 1894 review of the book, "but it is not so in the offices of the best newspapers throughout the country. . . . There are plenty of reporters everywhere who think that it is smart to 'fake,' but they are frowned upon by the best workers in the profession. . . . Nine times out of ten the reporter who 'fakes' details does so only because he is too lazy, or has not enough ability, to gather up the facts." Shuman got the message, too. His next book, *Practical Journalism*, which appeared in 1903, included a caution that could have been responding to Hills's very words: "The reporter who imagines it is smarter to 'fake' a story than to work hard and get the facts will fall by the wayside. Success follows the man whom a lie can not deceive and who scorns to resort to deception himself." (Shuman's most enduring legacy still embodies his mixed message: to this day his name is attached to a long string of prizes awarded by the English department at Northwestern, his alma mater, some of which honor essays or theses while others recognize fiction.)[27]

Now it was always someone *else* who faked. After the Western Associated Press broke its ties with the parent New York organization and established itself in Chicago as an independent corporation, its former partners in the original AP delighted in exposing it as an inveterate faker. The country press faked more often than the city press, said city papers; the British press faked more egregiously than the American press, said American papers; it was *other* papers that fell for the faked report, said *this* paper; it was in my youth that I myself faked, said the reformed veteran.[28]

The tipping point in the life of the fake, the moment when the word visibly crossed the border between excusable and dodgy, seems to have come with the eruption of the ruthless circulation war between Joseph Pulitzer's *New York World* and William Randolph Hearst's *New York Journal* in 1895–96. Critics saw plenty to complain about in what was becoming known as the "yellow press": the constant upward spiral of sensationalism; the fat Sunday editions crammed with gossip, fiction, comics, crusades, and crime; the shrieking banner headlines and gaudy illustrations; the pandering to proletarian taste; the brazen manipulation of public opinion. But in the eyes of many people, the yellow papers also seemed so cavalier about accuracy, so fond of embellishment and invention, and so unwilling to let the facts stand in the way of a good story that the label *faker* embodied a perfectly satisfactory summation of its worst evils and *fake* an acceptable synonym for *yellow.*

Throughout the lamentable episode of the Spanish American War, for instance—which the Hearst press did not, of course, actually ignite on its own, though it obviously had a wonderful time covering it—the mainstream press flung the accusation with abandon and fury both. And even during the first few days after the shooting of President McKinley, when he was responding to treatment and seemed likely to recover, the sensational press "contained columns, double-leaded and scare-headed, about the 'agony' and the 'torture' which the President was bravely bearing, all pure 'fake,'" complained the *Journal of the American Medical Association.* Apparently "the possibilities for the 'fake' in yellow journalism were too many to be ignored." In 1903 an encyclopedia entry on journalism gallantly tried to point out that while the yellow press was undeniably sensational, "it is not right . . . to describe as a 'fake' everything that is connected with so-called 'yellow' journalism." But in that four-letter word the nonyellow press had found what it needed—a pithy and evocative description of the distance between itself and its increasingly embarrassing cousins—and the gallant message was doomed.[29]

Thus, by the late 1890s, within a decade or so of the first appearance of the term in the professional press, hardly anyone was willing to publicly embrace faking as a harmless caprice or a nimble trick; hardly anyone was granting it the indulgent nudges and winks that had greeted its first years of life. In fact, as the word *fake* peregrinated out from the professional journals into the general discourse about journalism, everything about it was shifting and taking on a darker tone. No longer confined to describing cases of imaginative embellishment, innocent or otherwise, it now applied to a whole roster of outright trumpery, promiscuously serving as the word of choice for almost any journalistic ill. And because there were so many journalistic ills to describe—so much public dismay over what was widely seen as a sloppy, sensational, inaccurate press—the word got a workout.[30]

Journalistic practices condemned as "fake" were lambasted in the professional and general press alike, in publications ranging the full spectrum from the illustrated *Successful American* magazine to the

200-for-a-sawbuck socialist pamphlet. The term could refer to business practices from the tacky—the use of contests, coupons, giveaways, and premiums to boost circulation—to the crooked, as when drummers sold bogus newspaper subscriptions they never intended to honor. Or it meant the telegraph editors' habit of running long, prolix stories in the paper as if they had come verbatim (and at searing expense) over the wire. Or it was the sordid specialty of such supposedly artless provincial places as Sioux Falls, South Dakota, a favorite haunt of entrepreneurial hacks who would claim to be getting their intelligence by courier from Bad Axe Creek, the Black Hills, or other romantic locations safely beyond the reach of the telegraph, where anything *might* happen and no one was likely to point out that it hadn't. Or it was the instigator behind the brazenness of a sixteen-year-old schoolboy in Oakland, California, who had seen nothing wrong in planting dozens of sensation tales about western towns in eastern newspapers because, he said, after reading in a magazine that three New York papers published fake stories, "he could not see why he could not do the same thing."[31]

Or it was, according to the reform magazine *Arena*, a particular form of "gutter journalism" practiced by press bureaus that struck bargains with professional men who wanted publicity to lend their names as sources to invented stories of scandals or crime. *Arena*'s definition of "faking" marked a 180-degree turn from Hills's introduction of the term in 1887: "It is perhaps scarcely necessary to explain that 'faking,' in the newspaper sense, means the publication of articles absolutely false, which tend to mislead an ignorant and unsuspecting public." Around the beginning of World War I the socialist Max Sherover was using the term to describe news manufactured or distorted by publicity bureaus, press agents, or what he called the "kept press" to mislead the public and serve the money interests. By then, in fact, the term seemed to be shouldering out simpler, commoner words—*lies*, say, or *fraud*, or maybe even *propaganda*—and to a present-day ear, some of the uses of *fake* sound almost comically inadequate to the tasks it was called on to do—something akin to taunting a murderous thug as "you dirty rat!"[32]

Yet in an age when so many Americans were embracing the transformative power of the *fact*, the word describing its opposite was becoming too evocative, and too useful, not to share widely. By the very end of the nineteenth century the expressive term that the journalists had borrowed from the crooks, the touts, and the troupers had begun creeping for the first time into the general discourse. The particular deceptions, delusions, or frauds that characterized sports, agriculture, art, literature, medicine, politics, and a range of other fields were increasingly drawn in under the umbrella of "faking." Dairy farmers dismissed tinted margarine as "fake butter." City officials denounced saloons that carried out slapdash renovations to evade liquor laws as "fake hotels." Horticulturists were incensed at the hickory and pignut stock passed off as "fake pecans." Photographers who had routinely referred to conventional retouching techniques as "faking" switched to more innocuous locutions like "handwork" or "working up" after the former term acquired "a general not-to-be-mentioned-in-polite-society air." Works of art were described as fake, as were diagnoses of insanity, claims of streetcar injuries, books, antiquities, boxing matches, hypnotists, advertising, and weather forecasts. President Theodore Roosevelt himself popularized the term "nature fakers" as a gibe at the overly sentimental and unrealistic depictions of wild animals by such popular writers as Ernest Thompson Seton. And in 1896 the city council of St. Paul, Minnesota, passed an ordinance that lumped "faking" with grafting and swindling as practices it intended to "prevent and suppress" through the full majesty of the law.[33]

Although the meaning of the term had by now sprawled far beyond the jolly and relatively innocent sense first intended by Hills, Shuman, and the other journalistic enthusiasts, the roots remained the same. A fake was something whose essential nature had been changed or manipulated or tampered with in some consequential way; it betrayed the interested intervention of a human hand. The difference now in many eyes was that no matter how benign its intent, a manipulation could not possibly offer, as Hills and others had promised, a more appealing, more true-to-life, more *real* glimpse of the world. By definition, there was nothing benign or true or real about a fake.

Another Side of the "Story"

The rising tide of condemnation did not, of course, eradicate from the earth either the extreme or the less egregious forms of journalistic (or other) faking, but it did reflect the increasing urgency of the professionalization project and the drive among responsible journalists to distinguish their work from that of their yellower colleagues. The fissure that opened at the end of the century between the yellow press and the serious press has come to be routinely described as a split between the "information" model and the "story" model, with Adolph Ochs's *New York Times* emerging in 1896 as the premier example of an objective, authoritative, "professionally" produced publication geared to a respectable readership primarily interested in facts, while the Hearst and Pulitzer papers and their followers appealed to a mass audience by emphasizing entertainment even as they insisted that their entertaining stories were perfectly accurate.[34]

The labels *information* and *story*—a scholar's retrospective shorthand, it should be emphasized, not a contemporary description—do usefully evoke the difference in tone, spirit, and intent between visibly distinct journalistic enterprises. Part of what those emerging "information" papers were doing was learning to describe the world in ways that were different from what ordinary observers did, and part of what that press was doing was learning to *look like* it was describing the world in ways that were different from what ordinary observers did. Professionalization is at bottom a distancing project—an effort to set standards and draw boundaries not just between the trained practitioner who can carry out special tasks and the ordinary person who can't but also between the trained practitioner and the hobbyist, the journeyman, or the quack. Just as doctors differentiated themselves from homeopaths, and lawyers from notaries public, the new breed of professional journalists strove to present themselves as distinct not just from people who weren't writers but also from writers who didn't write *journalism*, at least as they conceived of it. For them, the fake was the necessary counterpoint against which the real could be defined.

Just as the novelists of the new Naturalism—current or former journalists many of them, including Frank Norris, Stephen Crane, and Theodore Dreiser, who later wrote that he had left the *New York World* in part over its propensity for faking despite its public reverence for "accuracy, accuracy, accuracy"—were driven by "a radical desire to suppress the 'literary'" in their effort to transmit rather than mediate real life, so too were the new journalists formulating their own new relationship between style and content.[35] Their intent was to convey to readers that they were receiving pure information—facts that had not been tampered with, facts that had been scientifically observed and dispassionately recorded—rather than an uncontrollable, unaccountable, unpredictable burst from someone's imagination or a fake manipulated by someone's interested intervening hand. The journalists of the "information" papers strove to embody authority, not chumminess; they exuded respectability and discipline, not rakish charm; they promised detached and value-free observation, not skylarking. More and more neutral, straightforward, and scientific was the literary style in these papers; less and less visible, or at least more closely corralled in special sections, were those traditional tall tales, bits of fiction, jokes, and other non-fact-based items that used to challenge their readers to continually monitor and readjust their assumptions about what was real and what was not. No longer faced with the anxiety (or pleasure?) of having to make those choices for themselves, readers could now, theoretically anyway, sail through one of these newspapers on a sort of authenticity autopilot in the serene confidence that everything in it was equally real. Contrary to Edwin Shuman's aperçu in his handbook for beginning reporters, a newspaper that sounded like a mathematical treatise in fact seemed exactly the right home for the Real Thing.

Yet while at the turn of the century the serious press was at the forefront of the widespread public turn against the "fake," it seemed much less interested in crusading against another bit of "newspaper parlance" that would seem to have posed an equally strong challenge to its accuracy, factuality, and ties to reality. To us present-day news consumers, the fundamental unit of journalistic work has been known for so long and so casually as the *story* that it's hard to step back and ponder how the same word could come to mean "[a]n account or report regarding the facts of an event" as well as "[a] lie," both of which senses appear within the first and primary definition of the word in the latest edition of the *American Heritage College Dictionary*. The label applies to the investigative report about prisoner abuse and the fluff piece about weight loss, to the pandect in *The New Yorker* and the photo spread in *People*. "Get that story!" probably ranks right there with "Stop the presses!" as the hoariest newsroom scene setter in Hollywood.[36]

It took some time, however, for journalists to settle on a term to describe the fundamental unit of the work they produced. The first generations of reporters referred variously to an "article" or an "item" or a "report" or a "despatch" or a "special" (a baggy term that could apply to everything from an important piece written by a "special correspondent" to a Sunday-edition human-interest softball) or even "stuff," which, as one handbook assured the neophyte reporter, was a "technical term" around the newspaper office for "reading matter." Around mid-century the first so-called story papers began to appear, but what the *New York Ledger*, *Frank Leslie's Chimney Corner*, *Fireside Companion*, and their readers meant by *story* was something with a semicolon and a thrill, something along the lines of "The Gun-Maker of Moscow; or, Vladimir the Monk"—it was, in other words, the accepted centuries-old usage referring to a fictional narrative.[37] The term did occasionally show up in the newsroom during those first decades of reportorial work, but rarely in a sense that could have been seen as "technical." A search through the memoirs of five Civil War correspondents written in 1865 and 1866, for instance, which numbered among the very first *reporters'* autobiographies ever written, turned up a liberal sprinkling of the words *story* or *stories*, but the writers were using them to mean general narratives—explanations, accounts, yarns. *Story* was not widely recognized (or debated) as "newspaper parlance" until around the same time that *fake* came into use; the same 1886 article on "newspaper expressions" that described the faking of Grover Cleveland's wedding trip also noted that "[t]he word 'article' is going out of use, although it is hard to see how it can be dispensed with altogether. The reporter applies 'story' to what he has written, although there may be nothing in it that the outside world esteems as such."[38]

Again like *fake*, the term *story* was bandied about inside the newspaper office with a nudge and a wink, and again journalists worried enough about the connotations it would carry for the uninitiated that they felt compelled to explain that it didn't mean what people thought it did. Professionals protected the term within quotation marks, helpfully included it in glossaries for lay readers, and stopped short in the middle of the page to explain, as Shuman did in his 1894 how-to manual, that "[a] 'story,' by the way, in newspaper parlance, is not simply a bit of romance, but anything written in narrative form, from the account of a royal wedding to a description of the state of the hog market." A writer who signed himself "Ex-City Editor" shared some of the secrets of his trade with the readers of the highbrow *Harper's Weekly*, describing how he would "despatch the reporters to various places, each one assigned to a definite piece of work, or, to use the technical expression of the newspaper world, each one given a definite 'story' to write," and a *World* reporter who published a collection of short stories about newspaper life proved her bona fides in a prefatory note defining some of the "colloquially technical expressions employed in a newspaper office" that she would be using, including both *story* ("almost any article in a newspaper except an editorial one") and *fake* (used if "the facts a story presents exist nowhere else"). And as late as 1914, the *Sun* newsman who took on the task of explaining to the clerical readers of the *Ecclesiastical Review* how to build a relationship with the press paused to clarify an important point:

> It must be stated here that the word "story" as applied in this article is used in its newspaper sense—there is no adequate synonym—as referring to a narrative published or publishable in a newspaper. Reporters, editors, newspaper men generally, refer to anything they write or handle as a "story." They speak of the "murder story in the Times," or the

> "political story." The word "story" carries no intimation of untruth or imagination. . . . When the account is entirely imaginary (what would be termed a short story), reporters refer to it as a "fiction story."[39]

The emphasis on the "technical" nature of so everyday a term, and on its special meaning in "newspaper parlance" (a favorite expression, complete with its almost visible hitch of the suspenders, that abounded in the professional literature), was doubtless a carefully calculated riposte to the wisecrackers and scolds who were, inevitably, inspired by the paradoxical range of meanings in the term. In 1907, for instance, a waggish Arkansas editor looked back on a youthful effort at "a very important and well-written special, or 'story,' as they now call them—and lots of them are *stories*, in truth." Even sharper was the anonymous 1906 screed in the highbrow *Scribner's* magazine that saw the acceptance of the "slang term of 'story'" to describe newspaper content as the perfect symbol of a disturbing trend. The "encroachment of the newspaper on the province of ordinary story-telling," the author of the piece grumbled, "modifies the reading habits" of the general public and encourages it to expect amusing trivialities in everything it sees in print.[40]

Other journalists went so far as to acknowledge a direct connection between the fake and the admittedly guilty pleasures of the "story," but they also hinted broadly that it was all the fault of the public, which *would* insist on liveliness in its reading matter. In fact the "whole secret" behind the ubiquity of the fake, Hills himself argued back in 1887, was "the constant demand for picturesque stories. . . . Descriptive details are expected from the correspondent, and he must do his best to supply the demand." And the columnist who in 1901 wrote with some sympathy about the St. Louis tornado fake remarked that "[t]he very word 'story,' used by newspaper men to describe a reporter's account of an occurrence, lends a certain color to [the] assertion that there is a demand for the art of the fictionist on the part of the papers. A bare recital of facts is not acceptable, except perhaps on a backwoods newspaper, if there are any such. The city daily must employ writers first of all who know how to tell stories."[41]

Despite these occasional sallies, however, the pejorative connotations simply didn't stick to the journalistic "story" with the same tenacity as they did to the journalistic "fake," and in neither the professional nor the popular literature of the time did the "story" inspire the kind of universal opprobrium that the "fake" had come to attract. The term was not widely applied in a dismissive sense, it was not pigeonholed as characteristic of the yellow press alone, and not even the papers that were staking their identity on their mathematical accuracy and impersonal authority seemed particularly troubled by the emerging convention of referring to realistic portrayals of news events with a term that bore a long, strong connection to the art of fiction. When even Ochs's *New York Times*, the archetype of the new "information" mode, could note casually that a business paper was about to "print a story" about an order of freight cars, or warn its readers that "[i]t is still too early to sift the news stories" about an "appalling fire," the *story* had clearly won general acceptance as a serious journalistic term.[42]

Language churns and changes, associations vary from user to user, and it's hard to know and easy to overanalyze exactly what connotations were drawn from so limber a term by its hearers and speakers a century gone. The word might have slid into the general discourse not because of any subtle cultural commentary it might have expressed but simply because it was handy and comprehensible. Yet it's striking that the term *story* was becoming the term of choice for just about anything published on newsprint at exactly the same time that the new "information" newspapers were staking their claim to greater respectability and authority by avoiding emotion, resisting literary flourishes, renouncing creativity, and exalting the discrete fact—in other words, by sounding as different as possible from the traditional story, that old-fashioned, comfortable, supple device for explaining the world that Charles Tilly has called "one of [humankind's] great social inventions."[43] In the emerging competition between the professional and the mass-entertainment press, the pros may have won on reputation, but their victory came, literally, on their rivals' terms.

In the complex literary world of the turn of the century, where a story paper could be a polar opposite to a newspaper story, where some journalists sounded like novelists *and* the other way around, and where all the old rules and cues governing the relationship between style and content were changing, the efforts of the "fakers" to invent and embellish their way to a more true-to-life portrayal of the real world went too far. What was, perhaps, not yet clear was whether the austere new style of factual and objective journalistic writing could go far enough.

NOTES

1. Richard Watson Gilder, "Certain Tendencies in Current Literature," *New Princeton Review* 4 (July 1887): 4. Useful secondary sources in the large literature on this topic are Miles Orvell, *The Real Thing: Imitation and Authenticity in American Culture, 1880–1940* (Chapel

Hill: University of North Carolina Press, 1989); Jackson Lears, *Rebirth of a Nation: The Making of Modern America, 1877–1920* (New York: Harper, 2009), esp. chap. 6; David E. Shi, *Facing Facts: Realism in American Thought and Culture, 1850–1920* (New York: Oxford University Press, 1995).

2. My research into the words *fake* and *story* would have been impossible without the use of a variety of digitization projects and full-text search engines, including Google Books, JSTOR, the Proquest and Readex databases of historic newspapers and periodicals, "Chronicling America" at the Library of Congress, the "Making of America" projects at Cornell and the University of Michigan, and the online archives of *Harper's Weekly*. Like many scholars, however, I have also developed a keen appreciation of how frustrating and perilous these invaluable tools can be. OCR systems often confused *fake* and its derivatives with forms of *sake* or *take*, and it was impossible to search so commonplace and versatile a term as *story* in a consistent way across an array of search engines whose capacity for precision varies so widely. Thus while I am confident that I am accurately describing *trends* in how the words were used, I do not attempt to quantify my findings or indulge in absolutes ("the first," "the most widespread"), which would imply an exactness I cannot defend.
3. Michael Schudson, *Discovering the News: A Social History of American Newspapers* (New York: Basic, 1978); James W. Carey, "American Journalism On, Before, and After September 11," in *Journalism After September 11*, ed. Barbie Zelizer and Stuart Allan, 71–90 (London: Routledge, 2002); Karen Roggenkamp, *Narrating the News: New Journalism and Literary Genre in Late Nineteenth-Century American Newspapers and Fiction* (Kent: Kent State University Press, 2005).
4. William H. Hills, "Advice to Newspaper Correspondents III: Some Hints on Style," *Writer* 1 (June 1887): 51.
5. Hills, "Advice to Newspaper Correspondents IV: 'Faking,'" *Writer* 1 (November 1887): 154.
6. Hills, "Faking," 154.
7. Hills, "Faking," 155.
8. Hills, "Faking," 155–56.
9. "Newspaper Expressions," *American Bookmaker* 3 (August 1886): 46. Determined to keep the press at arm's length, Grover Cleveland had announced his engagement to his twenty-one-year-old ward just days before the private White House ceremony was held, but undaunted reporters had stalked, besieged, and beset the

honeymooning couple with a vigor and a creativity that became legendary.

10. Edwin L. Shuman, *Steps into Journalism: Helps and Hints for Young Writers* (Evanston, IL: Evanston Press, 1894) 122, 123; on his life see s.v. *National Cyclopaedia of American Biography* 15: 275–76.
11. John Brisben Walker, "Some Difficulties of Modern Journalism," *Cosmopolitan* 24 (January 1898): 328. See also Ralph Pulitzer, *The Profession of Journalism: Accuracy in the News: An Address before the Pulitzer School of Journalism, Columbia University, New York, Delivered at Earl Hall December 16, 1912* (New York: The World, 1912), 14–15.
12. Charles Edward Russell, *These Shifting Scenes* (New York: Hodder & Stoughton, 1914), 19–21.
13. Lincoln Steffens, *Autobiography* (Santa Clara: Santa Clara University Press, 2005[1931]), 179; Julius Chambers, *News Hunting on Three Continents* (New York: Mitchell Kennerley, 1921), 7.
14. Russell, *Shifting Scenes*, 19.
15. William Salisbury, *The Career of a Journalist* (New York: Dodge, 1908), 108–9.
16. Theodore Dreiser, *Newspaper Days: An Autobiography*, ed. T. D. Nostwich (Santa Rosa: Black Sparrow Press, 2000), 166–67, 247–54, 263–65, 285–88.
17. Walker Aken, "A Lesson in Reporting," *Harper's Weekly*, July 4, 1896, 663.
18. On De Quille, see C. Grant Loomis, "The Tall Tales of Dan De Quille," *California Folklore Quarterly* 5 (January 1946): 26–71; see also E. D. Cope to De Quille, on American Naturalist letterhead, Philadelphia, September 18, 1880; and Thomas Donaldson to T. T. Orbiston, on US Centennial Commission letterhead, Philadelphia, March 7, 1876; both in the Dan De Quille Papers, BANC MSS P-G 246, Bancroft Library, University of California at Berkeley. On Mulhatton, see "Western Writer of Fakes," *New York Daily Tribune*, January 13, 1901, B4; and "Joe Mulhatton Dead—Or Joke?" *Chicago Tribune*, December 21, 1913, 6; Salisbury, *Career*, 5–6. On the *Tribune*'s story about the fire, see Andie Tucher, "In Search of Jenkins: Taste, Style, and Credibility in Gilded-Age Journalism," *Journalism History* 27.2 (Summer 2001): 51–52. On the cognitive processes for judging fact and fiction, see Lisa Zunshine, *Why We Read Fiction: Theory of Mind and the Novel* (Columbus: Ohio State University Press, 2006), esp. 47–54.

19. On journalism and professionalism in general, see Andie Tucher, "Reporting for Duty: The Bohemian Brigade, the Civil War, and the Social Construction of the Reporter," *Book History* 9 (2006): 131–57; Schudson, *Discovering the News*; Schudson and Chris Anderson, "Objectivity, Professionalism, and Truth Seeking in Journalism," in *The Handbook of Journalism Studies*, ed. Karin Wahl-Jorgensen and Thomas Hanitzsch, 88–101 (New York: Routledge, 2009); and Stephen A. Banning, "The Professionalization of Journalism: A Nineteenth-Century Beginning," *Journalism History* 24. 4 (Winter 1998/99): 157–63.
20. "Fake, v.2," *Oxford English Dictionary*, Second Edition, 1989, http://www.oed.com/view/Entry/67778; on the theatrical derivation, John S. Farmer, ed. and comp., *Americanisms Old and New: A Dictionary of Words, Phrases, and Colloqiualisms Peculiar to the United States, British America, the West Indies, &c., &c . . .* (London: Thomas Poulter & Sons, 1889), 232–33.
21. George Grantham Bain, "Newspaper 'Faking,'" *Lippincott's Monthly*, August 1894, 274–75.
22. "The Spectator," *Outlook* 67 (February 23, 1901): 438.
23. Tucher, "Jenkins," 51–52; George William Curtis, "Easy Chair," *Harper's New Monthly Magazine* 42 (April 1871): 774.
24. Charles M. Sheldon, "The Daily Papers and the Truth," *Outlook* 65 (May 12, 1900): 117.
25. John Arthur, "Reporting, Practical and Theoretical," *Writer* 3 (February 1889): 37.
26. H. R. Shattuck, "Reporters' Ethics," *Writer* 3 (March 1889): 57–58.
27. Hills, "Book Reviews: *Steps Into Journalism*," *Writer* 7 (August 1894): 120–21; for another review chastising Shuman for his comments on faking, see "Briefs on New Books," *Dial* 17.202 (November 16, 1894), 298–99; Edwin Shuman, *Practical Journalism: A Complete Manual of the Best Newspaper Methods* (New York: D. Appleton, 1903), 119.
28. On the Western AP, see for example "Unfounded Political Rumor," *New York Times* (copying the *Rochester Union and Advertiser*), August 30, 1894, 4; "A Fakir Assaulted," *Atlanta Constitution*, June 28, 1895, 3; "'Fake' Story of the Race," *New York Tribune*, September 9, 1895, 2. On the country press, see "Famous Newspaper Fakes," *Washington Post* (copying the *New Orleans Picayune*), August 11, 1907, MS3; on the British press, see "Fake Journalism," *Our Paper* 18 (July 12, 1902): 441; on the other papers that fell for it, see "Baron Mulhatton: The Latest Effort of the Modern

Rival of Munchausen—That Big Snake Fake from Kentucky," *Missouri Republican*, March 24, 1888, 3; on the veterans, see Salisbury, *Career*, 111–12.

29. On the yellow papers and the war, see for example "Cartoons and Comments: Yellow Papers Don't Make Yellow People," *Puck* 43 (March 9, 1898): 7; "The Week," *Nation* 66 (May 5, 1898): 334; Elizabeth L. Banks, "American 'Yellow Journalism,'" *Nineteenth Century* 44 (August 1898): 330–32; and "In the Lion's Den," *Land of Sunshine* 7 (November 1897): 251. On McKinley, see "The President's Case and the Newspapers," *JAMA* 37 (September 14, 1901): 705. (By the time this cheery but premature report on the president's recovery saw print, the yellow papers had become, accidentally, correct: he died in great pain that very day.) See also "Journalism," *Consolidated Encyclopedic Library*, ed. Orison Swett Marden (New York: Emerson, 1903), 11:3126.
30. A search with the Google Books Ngram viewer for the frequency of the terms *fake* and *faking* in the American English books in its database that were published between 1850 and 1950 offers a rough corroboration for their increasing popularity in general use at the turn of the century. For *faking*, the line is relatively flat between 1850 and 1890, beginning and ending that segment at about .0000030% with some wavering in between, but then it registers a steep and consistent rise, to about .0000110% in 1910, .0000200% in 1930, and .0000325% in 1950. The line for *fake* is slightly more erratic between 1850 and 1890: it starts at around .0000300%, crests just above .0000400% around 1865, and slumps to just above .0000200% in 1890. It then reverses itself, however, climbing steadily, hitting just above .0000800% in 1910 and holding around .0001800 in the mid-1930s to mid-1940s, before declining gently to just below .0001700% in 1950.
31. "Fake Journalism," *Journalist* 19 (March 17, 1894): 2 (copied from the *New Haven Register*); "Stolen Information: How it is Handled by 'Fake Newspaper Men,'" *Successful American* 4 (September–October 1901): 563–64; "Faked Cable News," *Independent* 61 (November 1, 1906): 1068; "Where Fakes are Made," *Journalist* 31 (December 14, 1901): 101; "High School Lad Stirs Up a Hornet's Nest by 'Fake' Tales," *San Francisco Chronicle*, November 15, 1905, 26.
32. J. B. Montgomery-M'Govern, "An Important Phase of Gutter Journalism: Faking," *Arena* 19 (February 1898): 240; Max Sherover, *Fakes in American Journalism* (Buffalo: Buffalo Publishing, 1914), 1.

33. These examples represent just a tiny sampling of usages found in the popular press between 1890 and 1910: on butter, see George Lang Jr., "Comments on Missouri Bulletins," *American Food Journal* 3 (April 15, 1908): 14; on hotels, see "Mr. Raines and His Law," *Nation* 63 (December 10, 1896): 433–34; on pecan stock, see Elizabeth Higgins, "The Lure of the Pecan," *Harper's Weekly* 55 (February 11, 1911): 19; on retouching in photography, see C. H. Claudy, "Working Up a Picture," *Photo Era* 13 (July 1904): 112; on art works, see "Forgeries in Collections," *New York Times*, August 16, 1896 (copying the *Contemporary Review*), 22; on insanity, see "Murderer Fales's Will: A Writing That Suggests Both Lunacy and 'Faking,'" *New York Times*, March 24, 1893, 2; on alleged injuries from streetcar accidents, see Edward Hungerford, "The Business of 'Beating' Street Railway Companies," *Harper's Weekly* 51 (September 14, 1907): 1340; on a faked book, see "Now Who is Mr. Vandam? And is 'The Englishman in Paris' Really a 'Faked' Book?" *New York Times*, October 15 1892, 4; on antiquities, see "Faking Antiquities: How Imitation Treasures of Former Ages Such as Furniture, China, and Pictures Are Made," *Chicago Tribune*, July 12, 1903, A4; on boxing matches, see "Was It A Fake? The Mitchell-La Blanche Fiasco," *San Francisco Chronicle*, February 21, 1891, 10; on hypnotists, see "Fake Hypnotists Reap a Harvest: Humbugs Make Easy Livings Out of Dupes," *San Francisco Chronicle*, November 21, 1897, 23; on advertising, see L. J. Vance, "Advertising Fakes," *Printers' Ink* 6 (March 30, 1892): 420–21; on forecasting, see F. J. Walz, "Fake Weather Forecasts," *Popular Science Monthly* 67 (October 1905): 503–13. On nature faking, see generally Ralph H. Lutts, *The Nature Fakers: Wildlife, Science and Sentiment* (Charlottesville: University Press of Virginia, 1990). On St. Paul's ordinance, see Hiram David Frankel, comp., *Compiled Ordinances of the City of St. Paul, Minnesota, Corrected and Revised to January 1, 1906* (St. Paul: Review Publishing, 1908), 127. The term *fake book* as applied to music came later, around the 1940s: see Barry Kernfeld, *The Story of Fake Books: Bootlegging Songs to Musicians* (Lanham, MD: Scarecrow, 2006).
34. Schudson, *Discovering the News*, 88–120; Roggenkamp, *Narrating the News*, 27–47. Other scholars have referred to "hard" vs. "soft," "important" vs. "interesting," or "news" vs. "human interest"; see S. Elizabeth Bird and Robert W. Dardenne, "Myth, Chronicle, and Story: Exploring the Narrative Qualities of News," in *Media, Myths, and Narratives: Television and the Press*, ed. James W. Carey (Newbury Park: Sage, 1988), 68–69.

35. Dreiser, *Newspaper Days*, 644–46; Michael Davitt Bell, *The Problem of American Realism: Studies in the Cultural History of a Literary Idea* (Chicago: University of Chicago, 1993), 113.
36. It is, however, striking that the term *story* does not seem to have found a comfortable place in the vocabulary of Internet journalism, where even the sites run by established news organizations are dominated by "clips," "links," "posts," "blogs," "updates," "tweets," and "feeds." Whether the brisk and participatory conventions of digital media are killing the traditional news story itself—the self-contained, single-authored narrative that unfolds at its own pace—is a hotly debated topic well beyond my scope here. (For an entry point into a recent and sprawling outbreak of that debate, see Jeff Jarvis, "The Article as Luxury or By-Product," *Buzzmachine.com*, posted May 28, 2011, http://www.buzzmachine.com/2011/05/28/the-article-as-luxury-or-byproduct.)
37. The first three headings in the *OED*, all of them labeled "obsolete," refer to historical writing; the sense of "a narrative of real or, more usually, fictitious events, designed for the entertainment of the hearer or reader" (heading 5a) dates to the sixteenth century. Under its sixth heading (6e) comes the definition "*orig. U.S.* A narrative or descriptive article in a newspaper; the subject or material for this," though the OED's earliest example, the Ex-City Editor's 1892 *Harper's Weekly* article cited in note 39, appeared a good six years after the term was used in "Newspaper Expressions" (see notes 9 and 38). "Story, n. 1," *Oxford English Dictionary*, Second Edition, 1989, http://www.oed.com/view/Entry/190981.
38. On *stuff*, see Charles H. Olin, *Journalism: Explains the Workings of a Modern Newspaper Office, and Gives Full Directions for Those Who Desire to Enter the Field of Journalism* (Philadelphia: Penn Publishing, 1910), 187; "Newspaper Expressions," 42. The Civil War memoirs were George Alfred Townsend, *Campaigns of a Non-Combatant, and His Romaunt Abroad During the War* (New York: Blelock, 1866); Albert D. Richardson, *The Secret Service, the Field, the Dungeon, and the Escape* (Hartford: American Publishing, 1865); Junius Henri Browne, *Four Years in Secessia: Adventures Within and Beyond the Union Lines: Embracing a Great Variety of Facts, Incidents, and Romance of the War . . .* (Hartford: O. D. Case, 1865); Thomas W. Knox, *Camp-Fire and Cotton-Field: Southern Adventure in Time of War; Life with the Union Armies, and Residence on a Louisiana Plantation* (New York: Blelock, 1865); and Charles Carleton Coffin, *Four Years of Fighting: A Volume of Personal Observation with the*

Army and Navy, from the First Battle of Bull Run to the Fall of Richmond (Boston: Ticknor and Fields, 1866).

39. Shuman, *Steps into Journalism*, 7; Ex-City Editor, "Gathering the Local News," *Harper's Weekly* 36 (January 9, 1892): 42; Elizabeth G. Jordan, *Tales of the City Room* (New York: Charles Scribner's Sons, 1898), viii; Horace Foster, "The Priest and the Newspaper," *Ecclesiastical Review* 51 (September 1914): 285–86.
40. Fred W. Allsopp, *Twenty Years in a Newspaper Office* (Little Rock: Central, 1907), 27; "Spectator," 437; "The Point of View: The Newspaper and Fiction," *Scribner's Magazine* 40 (July 1906): 122, 123.
41. Hills, "Faking," 155.
42. "15,000 Freight Cars Ordered," *New York Times*, October 28, 1899, 3; "The Theatre Fire," *New York Times*, January 2, 1904, 8. Equally unperturbed by the paradoxical meaning was Ralph Pulitzer, who on succeeding his father in 1911 continued the *New York World* as an entertaining mass-circulation paper while launching a crusade for journalistic standards. He established a sort of prototype ombuds office "to promote accuracy and fair play, to correct carelessness and to stamp out fakes and fakers," and warned the first class of students at the Columbia Journalism School that the newspaper that "prints a deliberate fake" becomes "a degenerate and perverted monstrosity." But in that same speech he routinely used the term *story* to refer to the contents of his strenuously fake-free paper. Merle Harrold Thorpe, ed., *The Coming Newspaper* (New York: Holt, 1915), 321; Pulitzer, *Profession of Journalism*, 16.
43. Charles Tilly, *Why?* (Princeton: Princeton University Press, 2006), 65.

Chapter 5

Elizabeth Jordan, "True Stories of the News," and Newspaper Fiction in Late-Nineteenth-Century Journalism

Karen Roggenkamp

On February 25, 1947, the *New York Times* ran a nine-paragraph obituary commemorating the life and accomplishments of journalist, editor, and author Elizabeth Garver Jordan. Noting Jordan's influence at the helm of *Harper's Bazaar* from 1900–1913 and her enduring friendships with Henry James and William Dean Howells, the obituary revealed that Jordan's career began 57 years earlier when she wrote for the *New York World* and its "True Stories of the News" daily articles that "chronicle[d]" the "humorous to the deeply tragic" everyday dramas of New York and "took their author into every phase of the city's life."[1]

The *Times* obituary underscores Jordan's importance in terms of late-nineteenth-century and early-twentieth-century literary production. More specifically, it invites consideration of Jordan's narrative roots in the *New York World* and "True Stories of the News," a series that featured Jordan as principal reporter and that consisted of more than ninety articles printed between November 1890 and May 1891.[2] While the series spanned only a brief period of time, it nevertheless magnifies the finely webbed intersections between journalism and literature at the turn of the twentieth century.[3] "True Stories of the News" introduces a new thread into that web when placed in the context of newspaper fiction.[4] As an emerging popular genre in the late nineteenth century, newspaper fiction dramatized news making by casting reporters as heroes of both the newsroom and the city's streets and by providing readers with an insider's view of the romance and rigor of reporting. A series like the *World*'s "True Stories of the News" built on the conventions of early newspaper fiction, just as newspaper fiction built on the conventions of articles like those that appeared in "True Stories of the News," and the work of Elizabeth Jordan, who authored newspaper articles and newspaper fiction alike, offers a particularly useful window into this generic interaction. In keeping with the stylistic project that characterized Joseph Pulitzer's "New Journalism" of the 1880s and 1890s, Jordan constructed her *World* articles so that they "read" the city as an unfolding book, a real-life "novel" that cast the reporter as an essential character in its plot. Jordan's newspaper fiction, in turn, drew (sometimes directly) on the stories she covered for "True Stories of the News." In fictionalizing these stories, Jordan examined the reporter as a character and the nature of reporting itself more critically, thereby disrupting the simplistic picture of heroic reporters and benevolent newspapers that was prevalent in the pages of the *World* and other mass-market periodicals.

This essay begins by situating "True Stories of the News" within the context of new journalism, as practiced in Pulitzer's *New York World*. I lay out the narrative framing of the stories in the series, with their self-conscious use of the reporter as a character in the writing. I then turn to the genre of newspaper fiction itself and explore its use by Elizabeth Jordan. In particular, I examine her 1902 story "In the Case of Hannah Risser," which uses as its springboard one of the articles Jordan wrote for "True Stories of the News" a decade earlier ("The Happiest Woman in New York"). Ultimately, I argue that Jordan's story line, appearing first in a newspaper article and then in a short story, reflects the shifting—and shifty—nature of how "true stories" could unfold in journalism and literature alike at the turn of the twentieth century.

New Journalism and "True Stories of the News"

Long before the age of Truman Capote and Tom Wolfe, late-nineteenth-century urban newspapers popularized a reportorial style called new journalism. Emerging at a critical junction in the development of the modern newspaper industry, papers like Pulitzer's *St. Louis Post-Dispatch* and *New York World* and, later, William Randolph Hearst's *San Francisco*

Examiner and *New York Journal* offered an exciting alternative to staid, information-oriented papers such as the *New York Evening Post* and the *New York Times*. By the early 1880s, Pulitzer popularized a fresh mixture of human-interest stories, dramatic prose, and detailed illustration in the pages of his mass-market newspapers. Based simultaneously on an aesthetic of "the real thing" and on sensationalism, Pulitzer's papers delivered the news in an entertaining, story-like fashion, even in much of its everyday reporting. In contrast, highbrow papers like the *Post* and the *Times* promoted what Michael Schudson calls an "information model" of reportage—drier, less dramatic writing centered around the ideals that would eventually emerge as the industry standard of "journalistic objectivity" in the early twentieth century.[5] Matthew Arnold, on viewing Pulitzer's work in 1887, coined the phrase "new journalism," remarking that the style "has much to recommend it. It is full of ability, novelty, variety, sensation, sympathy, generous instincts."[6] However, he added, its "one great fault is that it is feather-brained. It throws out assertions at a venture because it wishes them true; does not correct either them or itself, if they are false; and to get at the state of things as they truly are seems to feel no concern whatever."[7] Other critics were even more pointed, especially as the 1890s drew to a close and new journalism turned increasingly "yellow." Doggerel in an 1897 issue of *Life* magazine, for example, described new journalism with disgust:

> Sixty-nine pages of rubbish,
> Twenty-two pages of rot,
> Forty-six pages of scandal vile,
> Served to us piping hot. . . .
> Thirty-four sad comic pages,
> Printed in reds, greens and blues;
> Thousands of items we don't care to read,
> But only two columns of news.[8]

Serious and comic jabs notwithstanding, new journalism proved that sensation sold and that the pursuit of a popular audience translated into financial success within a crowded periodical marketplace. New journalism privileged stories that would titillate and sell, as even a glance at headlines makes evident: "They Died in Sin," "She Was Crazed by Terror," "She Fought Three Wildcats," "An Eight Year Old Wife," "Scenes in an Opium Joint," "Whose Hand Held the Ax?"[9] The list goes on.

In the news market of the 1880s and 1890s, sensationalistic papers were the locus of the greatest circulations and the highest profits.

However, sensationalistic papers also felt the force of competition with the fiction marketplace and with literary realism at the end of the century. Papers like the *World* positioned themselves in explicit competition with realism as they crafted stories that stood alongside and against their fictional counterparts. In addition to drawing liberally on basic literary techniques such as vivid imagery, strong characterization, and compelling dialogue, reporters also used narrative frames from detective tales and historical romances in composing their stories. Still, they manipulated the framing to suggest that their "true" stories were superior to the imaginary stories invented by authors of fiction. In story after story, reporters produced a narrative that looked and read like fiction in terms of its aesthetic and entertainment value. However, the news articles reminded readers at every turn that what lay in the morning or evening paper was a *true* story, a story "drawn from life," unlike the mere figments of imagination that novelists created. A subheadline might remark, then, that an article about a family reunited after years apart was a "Story of Actual Facts That Discount Fiction," or that a piece about an apprehended criminal was "LIKE AN ACT FROM A MELODRAMA," to provide just two examples.[10] Although the entertainment-model newspapers were based on dramatic reportage, these frequent references to truth suggest that journalists for sensationalistic papers respected the influence and marketability of the rising "objectivity" and crafted stories that would resonate with truthfulness—or at least with the illusion of truthfulness.

The *World*'s "True Stories of the News" feature (initially published under the headline "Stories of the News") drew attention to this interplay between journalism and literature by deliberately positioning itself as an alternative to literary realism and by extolling the virtues of its true stories, which transcended the fictions that they sometimes resembled. The first 25 articles were numbered, as if each were a chapter in the unfolding drama of city life—chapters of a serialized novel, a notion reinforced by one advertisement that referred to the articles as "clever news feuilletons" which "set forth" the "romance, the pathos and the humor of actual everyday life in this big town" (see Figures 5.1 and 5.2).[11]

Authored without a byline, as was typical of most late-nineteenth-century articles, "True Stories" took "from the daily happenings in New York—those bits of drama which are often covered by a few lines in a newspaper," such as "the finding of an unknown body in the river; the suicide of an unknown girl; some pregnant incident in the prisons or courtrooms or hospitals of the big city," as Jordan later explained in her memoir.[12] The reporters' job—"dig up all the facts back of the news

ONE OF MANY.

[Sketched from Life on the Third Avenue L.]

What is this young lady doing?

It's hardly necessary to explain, for, of course, you have seen her yourself.

She has cut out one of THE WORLD'S "True Stories of the News," and she is enjoying it all by itself. A lot of her friends are doing likewise.

Those clever news feuilletons are cet. a great hit when readers go to all this trouble to preserve them. Well, New York always appreciates anything new, and the "True Stories of the News" are new in several ways. They are new in matter and new in method. The romance, the pathos and the humor of actual every-day life in this big town were never set forth in such fascinating shape before.

If you are not already reading them, you should begin at once, or you will be altogether out of fashion.

Figure 5.1 Advertisement for "True Stories of the News," *New York World*, January 15, 1891. Image courtesy of Mullins Library, University of Arkansas.

leads and write each story as fiction, hung on its news hook."[13] Reporters became "daily frequenter[s] of the Tombs, of Bellevue Hospital and the Charity Hospital on Blackwells Island, of the Police Courts and the City Prisons."[14] Following tips gleaned from workers in these various institutions or inspired by random news stories, reporters ventured "into all

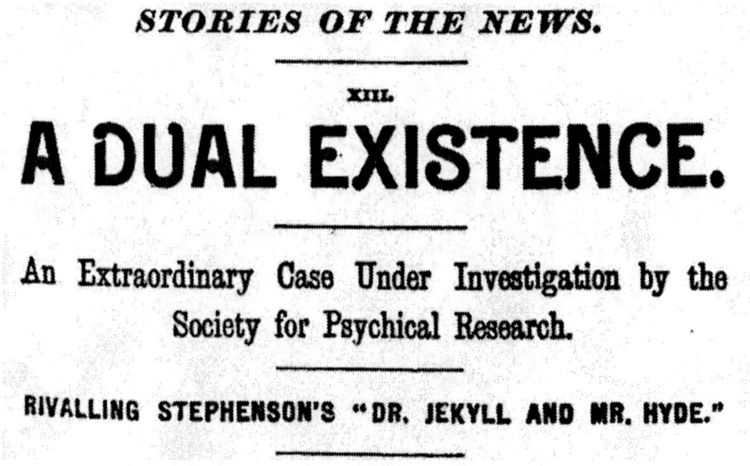

STORIES OF THE NEWS.

XIII.

A DUAL EXISTENCE.

An Extraordinary Case Under Investigation by the Society for Psychical Research.

RIVALLING STEPHENSON'S "DR. JEKYLL AND MR. HYDE."

Figure 5.2 Representative headline from "True Stories of the News," including Roman numeral "chapter number" and literary reference, *New York World*, December 10, 1890. Image courtesy of Mullins Library, University of Arkansas.

sorts of places and among all types of human beings" as they sought to uncover what newspaper admirer Jules Verne called "the real psychology of life," available, in his view, only through the news, which offered genuine "truth—truth with a big T" courtesy of "the police-court story, the railway accident, . . . the every-day doings of the crowd."[15]

While novelists may have taken umbrage at Verne's characterization of news as the locus of Truth, the writing in "True Stories of the News" asserted that the news easily surpassed the inventions of fiction and that the most intriguing drama unfolded every day on the streets of the teeming city—and thus on the pages of the city's biggest paper as well. The series covered a diverse range of topics, from humorous to mocking, from tragic to shocking. Read collectively, the subjects of the articles fall into five rough categories: poverty, immigration, love, crime, and humor. Articles about poverty described the depressing living conditions in New York's most downtrodden neighborhoods by spotlighting tragic tales, such as an eviction, a tenement fire, a suicide, a mutilation, or a kidnapped child. Often, articles about poverty involved immigrants, whose invariably sad stories constitute another central subject for the series. Such pieces, which frequently included ethnically suggestive dialogue, sketched the disappointing experiences of newcomers to America, people who had been lured across the Atlantic by tales of golden streets and unimagined wealth, like the Romanian mother of six who had been deserted by her cap-maker husband, or the German child accused of theft after fingering the toys in an abundant department store Christmas display—a pathetic tale whose moral for poor immigrant children was sadly ironic on Christmas Eve: "Never even look at the toys intended for happier children."[16]

The theme of love offered both comic and tragic endings. Readers could be amused, for instance, by the wealthy couple who divorced and remarried multiple times in a "curious drama of real life," or by the absurd picture of "an epidemic of love sweep[ing] over" the cast of a Bowery "freak show," in which "the earliest symptoms were undoubtedly noticed in the living skeleton" before the disease of infatuation struck the "conical-headed Australian with the boxing gloves," the "Hibernian sword-swallower," and the "Missing Link."[17] Still, love turned sour in many of the "true stories" through pieces that described jilted lovers, love-torn suicide cases, and even a young woman seemingly tricked into marriage because of hypnotism—an article heralded as an "intensely dramatic chapter from real life."[18]

As in most urban newspapers of the late nineteenth century, crime offered yet another theme that invariably satisfied readers. "True Stories of the News" placed its own imprint on crime reportage by exposing the unsavory activities of the "better" class of people, as when the column accused Mrs. A. M. Gardner, a "well-known woman of letters," of skipping out on an enormous bill at the Park Avenue Hotel. Despite "the intense desire of all parties to keep the particulars from the press," the *World* described the case in what must have been, to Mrs. Gardner and hotel management alike, embarrassing detail.[19] Other crime stories verbally convicted street thugs, drunkards, conmen, and opium smokers.[20]

Finally, a smaller number of "humorous stories" served the purpose of outright amusement and entertainment. Readers learned, for instance, of three-year-old Winnie Vance, with "big blue, inquiring eyes and . . . mane of fluffy brown ringlets," who followed a dog (frankly irresistible with his "sardonic grin" and beckoning tail) onto the track for an elevated train and held up traffic as "the youngest of flagmen—or flag-women—on record."[21] Some of the most humorous stories involved people who had been led astray by reading too much fiction. One story, for instance, described a young man who joined the navy under the misleading influence of *Three Years before the Mast* and "a pile of cheap paper-covered literature" that extolled the glories of a sea-faring life. "The salt of the brine which he had tasted in the pages of his favorite dime novels made him thirsty to be an actor in those same spirited adventures," the writer chortled, as if with a knowing wink to *World* readers. The young man spent only a few days before the mast before securing a discharge and "burn[ing] the books which he used to read."[22] The moral to such book-oriented articles seems clear. Reading is all well and good, but be mindful of the slippery line between truth and fiction—and keep buying the *World*, which will never lead you astray!

The various subjects of "True Stories of the News" reveal the scope of the series, and closer examination of the writing itself uncovers the manner in which reporters constructed the news—the "true" part of the title—around the scaffolding of literary elements—the "story" behind the headline. Each article liberally employs standard literary elements, including vivid description, simile, imagery, dialogue, and even cliffhangers. Stylistically, "True Stories of the News" reads as an unfolding, multi-plotted novel of the great city—a story that can only be narrated with the immediacy and skill of the journalist's craft. Indeed, the journalist himself (or, in the case of Jordan, herself) emerges as perhaps the most provocative feature of the articles, and the reporter character becomes a central link between news articles and the parallel genre of newspaper fiction. Nearly every article references "the reporter," "the WORLD man," the "woman from the WORLD," and so on. Readers watch the characters—whether they are poor immigrants, accused criminals, or wayward children—as they play out the drama of the day. More pointedly, readers watch those characters being watched, in turn, by the *World's* representatives. The articles remind the audience of the process and craft of news gathering by making the reporter an important part of the setting and the action, a feature that would be pivotal in newspaper fiction as well, as I discuss later. Hearst praised this reportorial involvement as a keystone of a "journalism that acts," reporting that proudly manufactured (sometimes quite literally) the news and ensured that readers could see the reporter's (often heroic) part in the process. Narratologically, the immersion of the reporter—the agent of print—in the journalistic scene also closes the gap between writer and subject and thus, theoretically, between reader and subject. Placed bodily within the room where a young girl has committed suicide, at the bedside of a dying woman, or alongside an insane immigrant girl as she wanders on the wharf, the reporter becomes the physical stand-in for the reader who is absorbed in this "true story."

The ostensible goal of verbal proximity between reader and subject in "True Stories of the News" is sympathetic identification, as illustrated in the inaugural story of the series: "Jessie Adamson's Suicide." Attempting to explain "Why a Girl of Nineteen Killed Herself Yesterday in This City," the article describes how "the reporter" uncovers, piece by piece,

Jessie's desperate history of immigration, ruined prospects, and emotional decline.[23] The writer imagines readers who might say, "If we had known, we might have stretched a hand to her, poor thing, in her distress." Such thoughts are useless now, the reporter remarks, and while people seem to forget the needy while they are alive, "[w]e take care of the dead always" (a stark sentence that refrains through the article). A subtly critical voice leaks into the article, then, as the writer wanders to the side of Jessie Adamson's corpse and endeavors to show what the body of an impoverished young woman looks like:

> She was dead.
>
> She was very fair to look upon yesterday morning when they had prepared her for the grave. She had blue eyes, but they were hidden underneath the lids. Her nose was small and delicate as if cut in a cameo. Her fair hair had been carefully brushed back against her pillow, and her hands were folded peacefully across her breast. The people in the house saw that everything that could be done was done, and then they came away and left her there.

The "people in the house" leave, but the reporter lingers, as do readers, to examine the sparse contents of the cold room, reading the "pitiable story" that it imparts and reminding the public, lest it venture too far into voyeuristic fancy, that "you must remember that she was very, very poor. That is why she killed herself yesterday morning." As a literary offering, the article draws on sentimental conventions, but it also draws attention to the power of the reporter. She is the one who controls the true story of why a 19 year old killed herself; she is the one who claims responsibility for guiding readers to the truth behind the suicide, rather than allowing them to revel in the dead girl as spectacle and thus consume the news in only the most superficial of fashions.[24]

"Jessie Adamson's Suicide" is merely one example of how journalists used the reporter figure in "True Stories of the News." Another piece in the series shows a reporter as he watches a pathetic, demented woman wander along the Battery seawall day after day, looking vainly into the horizon for her lover's ship to return. "This poor, unfortunate, stranded woman is not the young, beautiful girl that the romantic pathos of her story might suggest," the reporter muses. "That kind of woman you meet with in novels."[25] Still another describes a *World* reporter who is following up on a story about an abandoned woman, which had been reported in the general news columns the previous day—a story that was incomplete because it lacked the full "sad history of the household at No. 189 Division street" until "a WORLD reporter spent an hour . . . with the deserted woman and learned from her own lips the story of her misery."[26] Countless other illustrations of the active reporter emerge in the *World*, and these articles attempt to balance the inclusion of an active reporter with the ideal of actuality—that is, the stories are meant to be read as things that really happened, without extensive interference from or manipulation by the reporter. That person was present to chronicle an event and then to translate for readers the significance of what he or she had seen. Even though they are "artful" creations—that is, the stories are not intended to appear artificial in any way—they are the true stories of the city. Nevertheless, the actual instability between reporter as artificer and reporter as chronicler emerges when we place "True Stories of the News" beside the genre of newspaper fiction, which could look more directly at the story behind how "true stories of the news" are manipulated and constructed. In the hands of Elizabeth Jordan, in particular, newspaper fiction exposes the overpowering influences of profit and ambition in the news making process and ultimately asks readers to question where the boundaries between invention and actuality lie in journalism and literature.

Newspaper Fiction, Elizabeth Jordan, and "The Case of Hannah Risser"

If reportorial involvement in "True Stories of the News" contributes to a "journalism that acts" by casting the reporter as a character in the drama of the city, the genre of newspaper fiction takes the idea further. Newspaper fiction deliberately toys with the lines between fact and fiction by depicting the life and work of reporters—by turns arduous, glamorous, and heroic—and drawing plots from real-life experiences that the writer had encountered in covering the news. Inherently metatextual, newspaper fiction draws its plots from actual scenarios and stories that reporters had encountered on the job, affording an entertaining insider's view of life in the newsroom. Newspaper fiction, as such, differs from fiction that simply includes journalist characters but that does not feature news gathering as a central plot point, such as William Dean Howells's *A Modern Instance* or Henry James's *Portrait of a Lady*. Newspaper fiction, then, frequently includes such plot turns as the investigation of criminal activity or a romantic entanglement, but at its self-conscious core is an examination of the profession and practice of journalism itself.

Fueled by the rising celebrity of professional journalists, the genre emerged during the last two decades of the nineteenth century and continued into the twentieth century. While magazines in the 1870s and 1880s published nonfiction articles about the newspaper industry, that topic did not merge with fiction until the mid-1880s—arguably the first example of newspaper fiction is "Scoresby's Mistake: A 'Newspaper' Story," published in *Frank Leslie's Popular Monthly* in 1885.[27] The genre came to true prominence five years later when dapper reporter Richard Harding Davis published several newspaper fictions, beginning with his popular 1890 "Gallegher, A Newspaper Story."[28] Davis demonstrated a penchant for deliberately confusing his fictional and journalistic personae. Davis's fictional reporter Courtlandt Van Bibber, "an affable, handsome, debonair bachelor," served as a thinly disguised and "idealized portrait of Davis himself."[29] In fact, this reporter hero appears throughout Davis's work—as Van Bibber in the fiction and as Davis or "Reporter Davis" in the news stories he wrote for the *New York Evening Sun*. On his first day of work at the *Sun*, for instance, Davis, in an almost unbelievable turn of events, was approached by a famous con artist. Recognizing the man's swindle, Davis accosted him and handed the criminal over to the police. Then, rushing on to the *Sun* offices, he wrote the experience up as his first article, presenting himself as an actor in the story: "The prisoner slipped out of his overcoat but Reporter Davis seized him round the neck and held on until Policeman Lyna came along and took the bunco sharp to the Oak Street Station."[30] Ultimately, newspaper fictions rested (as did new journalism and, in some respects, literary realism itself) in the liminal space between news articles and purely imaginative writing, and they enjoyed brisk sales in the late-nineteenth-century and early-twentieth-century literary marketplace.[31] As a whole, these fictions epitomize how new journalism sought to blend "the real" and "the story," casting the professional reporter / hero into a dramatic participant role. As one critic noted, "The 'new journalism' of which we hear so much nowadays has developed a new breed of newspaper men and women," and it was that "new breed" that newspaper fiction strove to accent.[32]

Unsurprisingly, the stories soon grew repetitious and redundant, and while reviewers in the 1890s enthusiastically took note of fresh newspaper fictions, by the turn of the century they were easy targets for humor writers, as evidenced by this "advice" from a tongue-in-cheek 1912 *Life* article describing how to find success writing newspaper fiction: "First essential, gruff city editor. After that four 'star' reporters and one unappreciated 'cub.' The conversation must be replete with 'scoops' and 'clean copy' and 'throbbing presses.' Let the 'cub' get the big 'beat' and have the story printed on the first page just as it comes from his typewriter 'pulsing with human interest.' On the strength of the story raise the 'cub's' salary to seventy-five dollars a week. (Remember, we are speaking of fiction.)"[33] Initially, though, critics were more appreciative of the genre, as the positive reviews of Jordan's 1898 *Tales of the City Room*—the first of her many newspaper fictions—attest. Indeed, a notice in the periodical *Independent* speaks to the appeal of newspaper fiction at the turn of the century—the prize promised to the winner of its weekly puzzle contest was a copy of *Tales of the City Room*.[34]

Tales of the City Room offers a solid representation of the genre, though reviewers were also drawn to the novelty of its feminine author—Jordan was among the first female reporters to publish newspaper fiction, though similar women's stories were more commonplace a decade later. In addition to the pieces collected in *Tales of the City Room* (several of which were first published in magazines), Jordan revisited the icon of the female reporter in several other works published in popular magazines, as well as in the novel *May Iverson's Career* (1914). Jordan was well suited to write about what it meant to rise in the profession. She had come to big-city reporting in 1889 as an aspiring writer from Milwaukee. With incredible good fortune, she worked her way into the inner sanctum of the editorial offices at the *New York World* and secured a reporter's job. At first confined, to her utter dismay, to the social page, Jordan soon revealed her reportorial acumen and advanced to the city room. Women were still not a common presence in newsrooms at the time Jordan stormed the city, though their numbers swelled during the last two decades of the century. In 1880 only 288 women were reporters or editors, a number that shot up to 600 just ten years later and that continued to rise as the century closed.[35] Regardless of this phenomenal career growth, women occupied an uneasy position in the city room. In an era that still saw the mass-market newspaper—and certainly the rough world of the reporter—as a masculine venue, given its responsibility to bear witness to the darkest realities of life, women struggled to claim space for themselves against critics who argued the newsroom would destroy one's femininity. As a result, while most women were relegated to homemaking pages or society reporting, figures like Jordan proved more than capable of producing the kind of dramatic and sensational news that drove late-nineteenth-century new journalism. Recognizing the novelty of her position, Jordan, who harbored literary aspirations along with her journalistic ambitions, drew on her experience as a reporter to craft fictions about reporters, just as she drew on her experience as a fiction writer to craft stories for the newspaper. In much of her fiction, Jordan depicts the drama beneath the newsprint, the action behind the scenes that was, indeed, the "true story of the news" for reporters.

Though Jordan's newspaper fiction as a whole offers insight into the intersections between literature and fiction in the late nineteenth century and early twentieth century, one piece in particular situates the genre within the context of "True Stories of the News"—a 1902 story titled "In the Case of Hannah Risser," which builds on and directly responds to Jordan's 1890 article for the *World*, "The Happiest Woman in New York."[36] The shift from article to newspaper fiction opens a space for Jordan's critical commentary, not only on the existence of poverty and suffering in the great city—themes already manifest in practically every chapter of "True Stories of the News"—but, more strikingly, on the commodification of poverty and suffering for an ambitious reporter and her potentially voyeuristic reading audience.

Jordan's *New York World* "source document," "The Happiest Woman in New York," tells of Mrs. Dora Meyer, an impoverished and feeble old woman who has, at the time of the article's publication, gained enough health to leave her tenement room for the first time in 13 years (thanks in part to the *World*'s Charity Fund). In the article, Jordan describes how "the woman reporter of THE WORLD" had accidentally found Mrs. Meyer "during a mercy trip among the tenements" a month earlier. Mrs. Meyer's leg had deteriorated to such a degree that the doctor accompanying "the reporter" could not promise the old woman's recovery—indeed, "to the writer's untrained eye it seemed hopeless." Almost out of pity, "the woman reporter promised [Mrs. Meyer] a long drive through the city and the Park just as soon as she was able to be out." In the wonderful world of the *World*, however, dreams do come true. Though "it all seemed like a fairy tale to the old woman," Mrs. Meyer received "money from THE WORLD'S Charity Fund to buy nourishing food and supply her most urgent wants," and her health improved. Finally, accompanied "by the WORLD reporter," Mrs. Meyer drives around the city in grand style in a carriage hired by the reporter, taking special note of "the glittering gilt dome of THE WORLD'S home," as depicted in the illustration for the article (see Figure 5.3).

The bulk of the article recounts this journey through the city and describes how the teeming metropolis appears to someone who has been housebound for over a decade. The end of the carriage ride and the article finds a tired but exuberant Mrs. Meyer exclaiming still over the glories of her day—and of the *New York World*.

Figure 5.3 *World* reporter Elizabeth Jordan accompanies Mrs. Dora Meyer on a ride through New York City, with the dome of the new *World* building in the background, *New York World*, December 19, 1890.
Image courtesy of Mullins Library, University of Arkansas.

Twelve years later, Jordan fictionalized—to what degree we can only speculate—the story of "the happiest woman in New York" through her newspaper fiction, "In the Case of Hannah Risser." The 1902 story provides, as it were, the story behind the original "true story of the news." In Jordan's fiction, female reporter Miss Underhill pitches to her editor a story idea about one Hannah Risser, an elderly woman whose ill health has trapped her in a tenement room for 29 years, not the 13 of "The Happiest Woman in New York." The cynical city editor is not enthusiastic about the potential profit in such a story. "Don't see much in it," he tells Miss Underhill flatly. "Old woman, old attic, old story. We've done it too often."[37] In Jordan's framing, the old woman and her personal "true story of the news" are, from the start, simply commodities, objects that readers will literally buy—or not—and the editor sees Hannah Risser as an oversupplied commodity at that; the market, it would seem, has suffered a glut in feeble-old-woman stories. Miss Underhill, however, convinced that her lead "is unique, and has fine possibilities" of an extremely marketable "pathos," persuades her editor that it "might almost evolve into a 'teary tale,'" the kind of article that evokes sensational public response and thus more profit for the paper.[38] Her "slant" on the story? She, the journalistic heroine, will write herself as a character into the story by rescuing Miss Risser from the confines of her hovel, at least for a day, by providing a pleasant drive around the "better" neighborhoods of the city. She will play fairy godmother to an ironic Cinderella, and a thorough description of Hannah Risser's response, sure to be filled with tears of joy and gratitude, will provide the substance of the story.

From the start, however, actuality threatens to derail the news, even though Miss Underhill has taken care to secure Miss Risser's consent—a "small detail," the narrator dryly comments, "that Miss Underhill sometimes forgot" when writing her articles.[39] While Miss Underhill approaches the drive with Miss Risser with "a comfortable sense of satisfaction in her breast" and identifies the "unique privilege to open such a vista to a starved human soul and mind," she discovers, much to her annoyance, that the old woman does not exhibit a similar degree of satisfaction.[40] When Miss Underhill arrives at the tenement to pick up her subject, she finds the old woman weeping and fretting that she will not be able to return to her home of 29 years. With some effort, Miss Underhill coaxes Miss Risser into the carriage, and the women begin their drive around the city.

The reporter's spirits rise as the carriage passes into more pleasant neighborhoods, but her irritation grows when, at every turn, the old woman refuses to acknowledge the superiority of the modern city in comparison to her own humble home. Driving through the "silence and green restfulness" of Central Park, for instance, Miss Risser merely sniffs, "I got a geranium . . . in my winda."[41] When Miss Underhill points out the wide expanse of visible sky, Miss Risser protests, "In my little room, . . . by the winda where my chair iss. There I can see a big piece of sky, 'most as big as a little carpet."[42] And the sight of well-fed children playing on the park carousel simply brings forth the cry, "Little Josie Eckmeyer iss only four yearss old, but she comess to me efery night to kiss me when she goes to bedt."[43] With every turn of the carriage wheel, Miss Risser registers a new disappointment and begs to return to her tiny room.

Miss Underhill's panic rises as she realizes that the "special" she has promised her editor is "not developing quite in accordance with her wishes," and she sees "her story fading to a dim outline of what it should have been."[44] But Miss Underhill is the consummate professional journalist—at least by the standards of new journalism. As the two women travel back to the tenements, inspiration strikes the reporter and in her mind she eagerly begins to draft a story for the next day's paper: a pathetic, triumphant, heartfelt tale of a woman who has broken out of the bondage of three decades trapped in a suffocating room (courtesy of the reporter and her paper). "She [Miss Risser] looked out over the expanse of water," Miss Underhill mentally *writes*, and "tears filled her dim old eyes, those eyes which for thirty years had gazed upon nothing but the grimy walls of the opposite tenement and a tiny patch of blue sky which the great building could not quite shut off."[45] If the real Hannah Risser will not cooperate in crafting the "true" story of the news, the reporter will simply craft it herself. Miss Underhill smugly reflects that "her story could tell what Hannah Risser should have felt during that drive" and even decides to add flourish by casting Miss Risser as "an educated woman who has seen better days," a move sure to enhance the story's pathos.[46] By the end of the carriage ride, Miss Underhill finishes mentally drafting the article she will soon set down on paper by envisioning Hannah Risser in a melodramatic good-bye:

> This was her life: she must return to it, for He who put her there had some good purpose in it. She seized the reporter's hand and kissed it.
>
> "Good-by," she said: "Thank you, and God bless you. You have shown me to-day a glimpse of what I hope awaits me after I take my next—and last—long drive."

How wonderful of Miss Underhill to have given the poor woman a glimpse of heaven on earth, simply by driving her around the city! This emotional ending suits the reporter much more than the reality she witnesses as the carriage pulls in front of Miss Risser's building: "Her face was transfigured. The listless, sick little old woman had become an ecstatic creature, hysterical with joy. 'Ach Gott!' she shrieked, 'Ach Gott!—there's my little home. I'm back again, I'm back.'"[47] Clearly, though, Miss Underhill knows what her readers want, and she pens the perfect "teary tale"—so much so that "New York wept over it the following morning." Indeed, so many letters offering a new home to Miss Risser flood the newspaper's office "that Miss Underhill was forced to write a brief supplementary article explaining that Hannah Risser was 'permanently and happily provided for'" by the benevolent efforts of the newspaper. One lie has begotten another, and Miss Underhill's carefully constructed story about a suffering old woman has necessitated another news fabrication—another false article about the paper's continuing aid to Hannah Risser—to staunch the overwhelming flow of reader support for the "fictional" woman. Fortunately, as Miss Underwood realizes, print can easily smooth over any inconsistency between fact and fiction in the world of new journalism.[48]

Miss Underhill's story slathers on florid language and heart-rending images with an obviously heavy hand, and while Jordan does not directly quote herself in the 1902 story by repeating what she originally wrote for

"True Stories of the World," her fictional creation does simply amplify the tone of writing seen in "The Happiest Woman in New York," which includes such lines as "her story is an interesting and pathetic one" and "it was a pathetic sight to see the happiness of this woman, among other people and like other people." Furthermore, while Miss Underhill reveals the shameless self-promotion of the paper when she writes her follow-up notice, in the original article Jordan describes Dora Meyer proclaiming that reporters for the *World* "all are angels," as indicated both by their behavior toward her and by the towering golden top of the Pulitzer building. The original article even ends by reminding readers of the *World's* Charity Fund and reassuring them that a donation will help "complete the work which THE WORLD has begun in rendering this poor old woman the happiest woman in New York."[49] In both news article and fiction, then, the newspaper itself emerges as a heroic force, but only the fiction reveals the reporter's cynical machination in creating that heroism.

Jordan's self-conscious transfiguration of her original story from "True Stories of the News" points to the flexibility that late-nineteenth-century reporters saw in their definitions of "the news" and to Jordan's ability to reflect both on the sensational and the ethical implications of new journalism. A decade after the fact, Jordan as fiction writer returned with a humorously critical voice to a plot line that was already familiar to her—perhaps already familiar because she had played a part not only in narrating it but in manufacturing it to some degree as well. At its core, all newspaper fiction demonstrates the business end of reporting. In the hands of a reflective writer like Jordan, though, newspaper fiction also ponders and criticizes what that business end means in terms of journalism and literature alike.

CONCLUSION

Half fiction, half fact, the story that Miss Underhill mentally composes as she returns her rebellious charge to the tenement provides sly commentary on the process of news gathering and narration at the turn of the twentieth century. The reporter's central task is to chronicle the news, but only so far as it coincides with the story the audience expects to encounter. If news and story diverge, story takes precedence. By early May 1891, however, "True Stories of the News" had come to an end. Although "the macabre dance of daily news gathering went on," as Jordan put it, the feature had run its course and was replaced in the *World* by other running columns, including the "Drama of a Day" series, which covered in dramatic prose such topics as "A Bird's-Eye View of New York City Life: From the Police Records," and the "Yesterday" series, exemplified by headlines like "Yesterday with the Coroners: While Sunny June Smiled on the City, a Dark Record Was Making" and "Yesterday in the Tombs: Tales of Woe and Pictures of Misery, Crime and Depravity Under Review."[50] It's a small wonder that "True Stories of the News"—or any similar feature—would enjoy a relatively short life, given the amount of work it entailed. Jordan later reminisced that writing "True Stories of the News" "represented one of my most strenuous periods. It was no simple task to find from the news climax of some dramatic episode all the facts preceding it, to write two or three columns about them, and to do this six days a week."[51]

The strenuous work paid off for the paper, though, and for Jordan as well. Thanks to the ethos of new journalism and the *World*, Jordan was able to compose the news in a way that engaged her fundamental sense of storytelling, and that experience in writing the news served, in turn, to nourish her literary development. But even though she continued to work in journalism for many more years, Jordan turned a critical eye toward what it means to write news that reads like a story (or vice versa), and her newspaper fiction reveals some of the assumptions about how readers, reporters, and editors viewed news subjects as commodities. If news is merely a story and real people simply characters in a drama, then what is finally true?

"True Stories of the News" and similar features invite us to relish the provocative—and, for increasingly objective-minded news readers of the era, provoking—interplay between journalism and literature in late-nineteenth-century new journalism. Literary elements such as figurative language and dialogue helped to bring true stories to life, but the urge to tell a good story sometimes lured journalists away from the truth they were supposed to be reporting. Read in concert with newspaper fiction, the articles that Elizabeth Jordan and other reporters contributed to the *New York World* and other mass-market papers point toward the hybridity between genres and disciplines and help us to continue reconstructing the story of "the true" in news and literature.

Notes

1. "Elizabeth Jordan, Journalist, Dead," *New York Times*, February 25, 1947.
2. Because several articles in "True Stories of the News" reference male reporters, one can assume that Jordan was not the sole author of the

articles in the series (though one should be open to the thought that these male figures could be fabrications of a female reporter). However, obituaries for Jordan, as with the *Times* example that opens this essay, indicate that she was the principal author, and in her memoir *Three Rousing Cheers*, Jordan characterizes the series as her singular responsibility.

3. As I have argued in another context, the use of literary discourse was widespread in the most popular mass-market newspapers of the 1880s and 1890s. See *Narrating the News: New Journalism and Literary Genre in Late Nineteenth-Century American Newspapers and Fiction* (Kent, OH: Kent State University Press, 2005).
4. Newspaper fiction was also referred to by the labels *newspaper stories* and *newspaper novels*.
5. Michael Schudson, *Discovering the News: A Social History of American Newspapers* (New York: Basic Books, 1978), 89. See also Michael Robertson, *Stephen Crane, Journalism, and the Making of Modern American Literature* (New York: Columbia University Press, 1997); and David Mindich, *Just the Facts: How "Objectivity" Came to Define American Journalism* (New York: New York University Press, 1998) for rich accounts of these two journalistic styles and the emergence of "objectivity" as a primary news principle.
6. Mathew Arnold, "Up to Easter," *Nineteenth Century* 21 (1887): 638.
7. Arnold, "Up to Easter," 638.
8. Tollen Smith, "New Journalism," *Life* 30.775 (October 28, 1897): 345.
9. *World* headlines from January 4, 1898; January 7, 1889; January 9, 1889; January 16, 1889; February 10, 1889; and March 10, 1889.
10. "The Lost Is Found," *New York World*, January 17, 1891; "A Natural Criminal," *New York World*, November 28, 1890.
11. Advertisement, *New York World*, January 15, 1891. The articles appeared in most, but not all, weekday issues of the *World* during this time span and typically ran across the bottom third of page six or nine in weekday editions. As the series came to an end in May 1891, they appeared with less frequency. The idea of a news feuilleton was also used in a series called "Sporting Feuilletons," which ran roughly concurrent to "True Stories of the News" and also featured "chapter numbers."
12. Elizabeth Jordan, *Three Rousing Cheers: An Autobiography* (New York: D. Appleton-Century Company, 1938), 49.
13. Jordan, *Three Rousing Cheers*, 49.

14. Jordan, *Three Rousing Cheers*, 49.
15. Jordan, *Three Rousing Cheers*, 49. Jules Verne, qtd. in "Will the Novel Disappear?" *North American Review* 175.550 (September 1902): 289–98.
16. "Seven Mouths and One Loaf," *New York World*, April 6, 1891; "A Christmas Larceny," *New York World*, December 24, 1890.
17. "A Divorce Tangle," *New York World*, January 10, 1891; "A Bowery Museum Romance," *New York World*, January 1, 1891.
18. "Because He Was Jilted," *New York World*, December 3, 1890; "'Les Miserables,'" *New York World*, March 19, 1891; "Was it Hypnotism?" *New York World*, December 4, 1890.
19. "The Lady and—the Hotel Bill," *New York World*, April 1, 1891.
20. "A Life for an Apple," *New York World*, March 24, 1891; "A Night on 'Post Thirteen,'" *New York World*, March 7, 1891; "Here's a Very Clever Rogue," *New York World*, March 14, 1891; "In an Opium Trap," *New York World*, December 12, 1890.
21. "That Tiny Girl on the Track," *New York World*, March 12, 1891.
22. "Uncle Sam Was a Hard Master," *New York World*, March 30, 1891. "'Red, the Boy Burglar,'" *New York World*, April 8, 1891, was another story that exposed the "dangers" of too much fiction reading.
23. "Jessie Adamson's Suicide," *New York World*, November 25, 1890.
24. It is obvious that many readers did, in fact, sympathize deeply with the people they read about in the pages of the *World*—both in "True Stories of the News" and in more general articles as well. After the series details the eviction of a worthy, poor family in a powerfully vivid story ("'Put Yourself in His Place,'" *New York World*, March 18, 1891), readers responded with multiple offers of work for the unemployed father ("The Silver Lining of the Cloud," *New York World*, March 21, 1891). In a very concrete sense, readers helped "author" subsequent stories by their own actions and reactions to the news.
25. "The Ophelia of the Battery," *New York World*, November 29, 1890.
26. "Seven Mouths and One Loaf," *New York World*, April 6, 1891.
27. "Scoresby's Mistake: A 'Newspaper' Story," *Frank Leslie's Popular Monthly* 19.3 (March 1885): 286–90. For nonfiction accounts of how newspapers work, see, for instance, A. E. Watrous, "Some Experiences of a Reporter," *Lippincott's Monthly Magazine* (May 1887): 829–34.
28. Richard Harding Davis, "Gallegher: A Newspaper Story," *Scribner's Magazine* 8.2 (August 1890): 156–72.

29. Arthur Lubow, *The Reporter Who Would Be King* (New York: Scribner, 1992), 2.
30. Richard Harding Davis, "Our Green Reporter," *New York Evening Sun*, November 2, 1889.
31. A complete compilation of newspaper fictions is not available, but some titles (in addition to those by Davis and Jordan) include Francis C. Regal, "By Telephone," *Lippincott's Magazine* (January 1895): 126–35; Arthur McEwen, "The Vengeance of Pendleton," *Overland Monthly and Out West Magazine* 26.153 (September 1895): 283–91; H. Pearson, "A Newspaper Woman's Romance," *Peterson Magazine* 6.2 (February 1896): 218–21; Ernest Shriver, "A Frustrated 'Scoop,'" *Peterson Magazine* 6.5 (May 1896): 531–35; Eva Madden, "The Only Woman's Page," *Youth's Companion* 72.18 (May 5, 1898): 213–14; John A'Becket, "Miss Upton's First 'Assignment,'" *Youth's Companion* 72.34 (August 25, 1898): 390–91; Jesse Lynch Williams, *The Stolen Story and Other Newspaper Stories* (New York: Charles Scribner's Sons, 1899); Robert Barr, *Jennie Baxter, Journalist* (New York: Frederick A. Stokes, 1900); Kate Masterson, "The Love-Making of Loo," *Smart Set* 2.3 (September 1, 1900): 99–104; Ellen Olney Kirk, *Good-Bye, Proud World* (New York: Houghton Mifflin, 1904); Mrs. Fremont Older, *The Giants* (New York: D. Appleton, 1905); Miriam Michelson, *A Yellow Journalist* (New York: D. Appleton, 1905) and *Anthony Overman* (New York: Doubleday, Page, 1906); William Budd Trites, *John Cave* (London: A. Treherne, 1909); Josephine Simrall, "Her Best Stuff," *Lippincott's Monthly Magazine* 89.530 (February 1912): 298–307; Thomas T. Hoyne, "The Ego of the Metropolis," *Life* 66.1710 (August 5, 1915): 234–35; George Ethelbert Walsh, "Jane Eddington, Editor," *National Stockman and Farmer*, serialized December 25, 1915, through February 26, 1916; Hartford Powel Jr. and Russell Gordon Carter, "Broken Wings," *Youth's Companion*, serialized August 1928 through January 1929; Malcolm Ross, *Penny Dreadful* (New York: Coward-McCann, 1929); Mildred Gilman, *Sob Sister* (New York: Grosset & Dunlap, 1931).
32. "Collections of Short Stories," *Literary World* 29.9 (April 30, 1898): 141.
33. Hinton Gilmore, "Hints for Fiction Writers," *Life* 60.1573 (December 19, 1912): 2500.
34. "Puzzles," *Independent* 50.2579 (May 5, 1898): 41. Sample reviews include John Corbin, "Clever Short Stories," *Book Buyer* 16.3 (April 1, 1898): 254; "Cosmopolitan Literary Juggling," *Life* 31.800 (April

7, 1898): 298; Review of *Tales of the City Room*, *Critic* 29.843 (April 16, 1898): 265; "Collections of Short Stories," *Literary World* 29.9 (April 30, 1898): 141; "The Library," *Art Interchange* 40.5 (May 1, 1898): 121; "New Books," *Interior* 29.1459 (May 12, 1898): 598; Review of *Tales of the City Room*, *Bookman* 7.6 (August 1898): 524.

35. See Howard Good, *The Journalist as Autobiographer* (Metuchen, NJ: Scarecrow, 1993), 73; Maurine H. Beasley and Shelia J. Gibbons, *Taking their Place: A Documentary History of Women and Journalism* (Washington, DC: American University Press, 1993), 10; and Marion Marzolf, *Up from the Footnote: A History of Women Journalists* (New York: Hastings House, 1977), 26. The first women's press organization, the Ladies' Press Club of Washington, DC, was formed in 1881. See Elizabeth V. Burt, ed., *Women's Press Organizations, 1881–1999* (Westport, CT: Greenwood Press, 2000).
36. "The Happiest Woman in New York," *New York World*, December 19, 1890. Elizabeth Jordan, "In the Case of Hannah Risser," *Harper's Bazaar* 36.8 (August 1902): 710–17.
37. Jordan, "In the Case of Hannah Risser," 710.
38. Jordan, "In the Case of Hannah Risser," 710.
39. Jordan, "In the Case of Hannah Risser," 711.
40. Jordan, "In the Case of Hannah Risser," 711, 712.
41. Jordan, "In the Case of Hannah Risser," 712.
42. Jordan, "In the Case of Hannah Risser," 714.
43. Jordan, "In the Case of Hannah Risser," 714.
44. Jordan, "In the Case of Hannah Risser," 714.
45. Jordan, "In the Case of Hannah Risser," 716.
46. Jordan, "In the Case of Hannah Risser," 716.
47. Jordan, "In the Case of Hannah Risser," 717.
48. Today, we have no way of knowing which parts—if any—of "True Stories of the News" might be fabrications of the sort that Jordan describes in her short story. I have not located a "follow-up" article describing continuing care for Dora Meyer, though the *World* story does conclude by beseeching readers to contribute to the paper's Charity Fund. Readers did respond enthusiastically to the *World*'s calls for help in many other instances, and this case most likely drew a similar response. The notable difference in the short story, of course, is that the charity of readers is an unanticipated (and rather undesired) consequence of Miss Underhill's fabrication, while the *World* article about Dora Meyer solicits funds more directly.
49. "The Happiest Woman in New York," *New York World*, December 19, 1890. Construction on a new, 16-story *World* building—complete

with dazzling gilt dome—on New York's Park Row drew to completion in 1890, and the paper wasted no opportunity to extol the literal and symbolic superiority of the city's tallest structure.

50. "Yesterday with the Coroners," *New York World*, June 11, 1891; "Yesterday in the Tombs," *New York World*, June 13, 1891.
51. Jordan, *Three Rousing Cheers*, 51.

CHAPTER 6

WHERE THE MASSES MET THE CLASSES

NINETEENTH- AND EARLY-TWENTIETH-CENTURY AMERICAN NEWSPAPERS AND THEIR SIGNIFICANCE TO LITERARY SCHOLARS

CHARLES JOHANNINGSMEIER

UP UNTIL THE 1980S, THE THOUSANDS OF literary works—even those by popular and well-respected authors—that were first published in late-nineteenth- and early-twentieth-century American periodicals had received only minimal attention from scholars. Found only in musty bound volumes, decaying piles of newsprint, or hard-to-read microfilm, these publications were widely regarded either as low quality productions or as inferior, nonauthoritative versions of texts later published in book form; in both cases, it was believed, they well deserved to be consigned to the shadows of literary history. With the rise of New Historicism, however, this situation began to change dramatically. Because the chief goal of New Historicism is understanding how literary texts influenced readers and their cultures, scholars employing this approach highly value the versions of literary texts that reached the greatest number of readers. And since the texts with the largest audiences before 1920 were typically serialized, a steady stream of scholars in the 1980s started investigating American periodicals and the literary works they contained. Soon thereafter, in 1991, the field had its own organization—the Research Society for American Periodicals—as well as a journal: *American Periodicals*. As a result of all this interest, the past few decades have produced a substantial number of monographs, essay collections, and journal articles about American periodicals and literature that have greatly broadened the horizons of inquiry for students of this period. Those investigating the serialization of literary works between 1880 and 1920, however, have focused almost exclusively on the role played in American culture by the important magazines of the period, including *Atlantic Monthly*, *Harper's Monthly*, *Century*, *Scribner's*, *The Ladies' Home Journal*, and the *Saturday Evening Post*. In doing so, they have implicitly defined *periodical* quite narrowly, as synonymous with *magazine*. Consequently, the connections between American newspapers and fiction have been almost completely neglected, and very few people even today appreciate how incredibly important newspapers are to the study of American literature during these decades.

Such a scholarly lacuna is especially disappointing to me, for almost 15 years ago, I published *Fiction and the American Literary Marketplace: The Role of Newspaper Syndicates in America, 1860–1900* (1997), in which I documented the histories of the first newspaper syndicates in America, the major role they played in the literary marketplace, and the impact they had on fiction-reading audiences. This book also suggested numerous potential topics for future research in the field. Yet since that time, besides my own articles on serialized fictions in newspapers, to my knowledge only one monograph (Karen Roggenkamp's *Narrating the News: New Journalism and Literary Genre in Late Nineteenth-Century American Newspapers and Fiction*), one essay collection (*Transnationalism and American Serial Fiction*, edited by Patricia Okker), and a handful of articles have been chiefly devoted to the intersections of American newspapers and literary history.[1] While I am heartened by those scholars who have started to briefly mention that many authors of the period published their fictions first in newspapers, and by the efforts of others who have begun to more deeply delve into the small print of newspaper pages and analyze what was printed there, there is much more work that needs to be done. To better understand the careers of numerous authors and how their works impacted American culture between 1880 and 1920, it is simply imperative that scholars more fully investigate the role newspapers played in American literary history. Fortunately for such scholars, there has never been a better time to conduct such research—and the situation promises to continue to improve in the years ahead. This article will highlight just some of the most promising areas for research in this field.

POTENTIAL USES OF NEWSPAPERS

There are many ways newspapers can be valuable to literary scholars. One traditional use, yet one that is not employed often enough, is to help locate the sources for particular literary works. David S. Reynolds, in his magisterial *Beneath the American Renaissance: The Subversive Imagination in the Age of Emerson and Melville* (1988), convincingly argued that even many well-known literary authors from earlier in the nineteenth century, often thought of as having stood separate from their culture, in actuality incorporated in their works many of the issues evident in contemporaneous newspapers. Writers from later in the nineteenth century and early in the twentieth were similarly inspired by their newspaper reading to create great fictions. It is relatively well known, for instance, that Frank Norris based his novel *McTeague* on the real-life murder of a San Francisco cleaning woman by her alcoholic husband, that a 1904 article in the *Berkshire Evening Eagle* about a young girl's sledding accident served as Edith Wharton's inspiration for the climactic scene in *Ethan Frome*, and that Theodore Dreiser transformed newspaper reports about the murder of a pregnant woman from upstate New York into *An American Tragedy*.[2] More recently, scholars involved in the Willa Cather Project at the University of Nebraska-Lincoln have spent countless hours searching through the contents of newspapers from Cather's hometown of Red Cloud, as well as those from nearby Hastings and Lincoln, from the late 1880s through the 1920s to find a great deal of information about the real-life counterparts and events on which Cather based her fictions. Undoubtedly there is much more "source" information about other major fictions of the period still to be found.

Newspapers can also yield a good deal of previously unknown biographical information about authors, which in turn can prompt looking at their texts in new ways. Interviews with authors, often printed only in newspapers, can be especially revealing. For instance, few examine the works of Sir Arthur Conan Doyle for their racial import or imperialist registers; however, in an 1892 interview published in the *Boston Herald* he is quoted as saying, "America and England[,] joined in their common Anglo-Saxonhood, with their common blood, will rule the world. We shall be united. And the sooner that day comes the better." Such a comment, one might suppose, could prompt an examination of how Conan Doyle's advocacy of white imperialism might affect one's understanding of his fictions, including even those about Sherlock Holmes. In another article of interest, a reporter for the *Boston Globe* in 1899 asked American regionalist Mary Wilkins Freeman, as well as other women authors, about their childhood dolls. In response, Freeman provided numerous interesting details about her own favorite, named "Topsy." Besides hinting that Freeman possibly admired the character of "Topsy" from *Uncle Tom's Cabin*, this article affords insight into why Freeman included numerous dolls in her fictions and why she sometimes signed letters to her close women friends with the nickname "Dolly." In addition, this article represents further evidence of the widespread attempt at the end of the nineteenth century to infantilize women—especially high-achieving women—to maintain the patriarchal status quo. In another article related to the turn-of-the-century gender wars, fellow regionalist Sarah Orne Jewett—an author commonly regarded today as having advocated resistance to patriarchal forces in her fictions—revealed to an inquiring reporter a quite ambivalent attitude about women exercising power in the public sphere. In an 1894 article published in the *Los Angeles Times* under the title "Woman in Politics," Jewett opined, "Personally I have no wish to hasten the day when women suffrage will be allowed, but I believe that day to be inevitable, and I should certainly consider it my duty to vote."[3] Such a comment should certainly be taken into account when determining to what degree Jewett's texts should be interpreted as promoting women's rights.

Newspapers have also been quite valuable in filling in details about the life and career of naturalist author Frank Norris. Just a few years ago I found a short piece from the *Lincoln [Nebraska] Star* titled, "A Lincoln Man Tells of Norris," which includes an interview with his maternal uncle shortly after Norris's death. The uncle, who had had little contact with Norris during his adult life, recounted his memories of Norris as a young child: "'The boy was inclined to be melancholy,' said Mr. Doggett. 'At times he was full of activity and animal spirits, but ordinarily he was slow and thoughtful. Instead of playing with the other boys he would hang back by himself, interested perhaps, but in a passive degree." This information helped Norris biographers Joseph R. McElrath Jr. and Jesse S. Crisler establish that Norris's disposition was probably not as different from his father's as had been previously supposed.[4] One also sees here the youthful beginnings of an introspective writer who was fascinated by, yet distanced himself from, the masculine world around him.

More recently, I discovered three printings of a story written by Norris and syndicated to the *Boston Globe*, *Omaha Bee*, and *Portland Oregonian* in April 1898, which have helped answer two questions long discussed among scholars: what, exactly, were Norris's duties at the McClure enterprise's New York City offices in 1898–99, and what role did this position play in his career? This story, "Easter Bonnets (Marked Down)," is a greatly revised version of a piece Norris had earlier published in *The Wave* magazine of San Francisco. A comparison of this earlier version with the syndicated newspaper versions reveals that Norris was applying to his own work the editing skills he was learning at his new job, such as how to make his dialogue more realistic. As I conclude, "this discovery suggests that the non-novel-writing work that Norris did during his time working at McClure's should not be slighted as having completely bogged down Norris's career; in fact, some of this work appears to have helped improve his fiction writing."[5]

In addition, newspapers often contain information that is invaluable in establishing the publication history of particular fictional works. Biographers of Henry James, for instance, have never understood how and why his story "The Real Thing" ended up in various American newspapers in 1892. Scrutiny of one Galesburg, Illinois, newspaper, though, turned up a speech delivered by S. S. McClure, the famous newspaper syndicator who bought "The Real Thing" from James and subsequently sold it to various papers. Speaking in Galesburg at his alma mater, Knox College, McClure recounted how in the late spring of 1888 during one of his many "recruiting" trips to England, he used a letter of introduction from Robert Louis Stevenson to obtain a meeting with James. McClure explained, "When I went to see Mr. James I found him engaged with some other man, but as soon as he heard that I had but recently been with Stevenson, he dismissed the gentleman with the plea of a most important engagement. In a few minutes he came to me and begged me to tell him of Stevenson. So for two hours I talked to him of nothing but Stevenson." Because Stevenson had made a great deal of money selling his own work to McClure prior to 1888, the letter he provided McClure probably told James something such as, "If you ever need money, sell something to this man—he's a gold mine." The information gleaned from this small-town newspaper thus helps explain why, when James needed a great deal of money a few years later to finance his ventures in the theater, he sold the first serial rights of "The Real Thing" to McClure for newspaper syndication, rather than to a magazine that would have yielded more prestige—but less cash.[6]

In addition, literary scholars would be well advised to locate and read some of the thousands of book reviews that were printed in newspapers of this time period. These allow scholars to go beyond how the more elite reviewers for magazines such as *Harper's Monthly*, *Century*, *Scribner's*, and *Atlantic Monthly* understood literary texts and get closer to what more typical readers, outside of the urban Northeast, probably thought of particular works. In recent years, a growing number of contemporary newspaper reviews have started to be read as a result of their having been reprinted in the pages of Norton Critical Editions, as well as on authors' websites. Nevertheless, for the patient researcher, there are still hundreds if not thousands of undocumented reviews of books by authors of interest that are waiting to be unearthed. The rewards of patient research searching for reviews can be great. For instance, an independent scholar from North Carolina, John Freiermuth, has in the past few years located a great number of reviews of Charles Chesnutt's works in papers from large and small cities, in the South as well as the North and West, and in African American newspapers as well as white-controlled ones.[7] Reading the reviews of Chesnutt's short story collection *The Conjure Woman* that were published in white-controlled newspapers reveals that, contrary to current scholarly opinion, the stories' ex-slave narrator Uncle Julius did not succeed in educating white readers about the injustices of slavery and prejudice; instead, judging from these reviewers, they regarded him chiefly as a self-interested, humorous black storyteller.

Other reviews that would be of great interest to scholars—and which could be useful in starting a classroom discussion—are ones I have found of Frank Norris's *McTeague* and Kate Chopin's *The Awakening*. Jeannette Gilder excoriated *McTeague* in a review published in the *Chicago Tribune* in 1899. Strongly contributing to the popular consensus that sought to connect Norris with the demonized French author Emile Zola, Gilder asserted "he has out-Zolaed Zola," and as a result "the reader . . . will be inclined to throw the book aside as hopelessly vulgar and plebeian." Gilder concluded by expressing her desire that *McTeague* "will not be tolerated by American readers of fiction." Unfortunately, despite the insights such a review can provide for modern readers, neither this review nor any other newspaper reviews are reproduced in the most recent Norton Critical Edition of the novel. And although editor Margo Culley does include a number of excerpts from newspaper reviews of *The Awakening* in the widely distributed Norton Critical Edition of this novel, she does not reprint a lengthy one written by Gilder and printed in the *Chicago Tribune*, titled "NOVEL LEAVES A BAD TASTE | 'The Awakening' Treats of a Woman's More Than Weaknesses. | LOVE CAME TOO LATE | Title of the Book Seems to Apply to the Husband with Force. | TYPE IS NOT COMMON." To my knowledge, this review has never been documented or reprinted, but it deserves to be better known. Gilder's review strongly reminds present-day readers that there were many women at the turn of the century who did not view the novel's protagonist, Edna Pontellier, in starkly black-and-white terms. Somewhat surprisingly, Gilder—probably reflecting the views of many of her readers—could grudgingly approve of Edna's inclination to have an affair in order to find happiness outside a loveless marriage, but when she could not even be faithful to her lover, she had apparently crossed a different kind of moral line. Gilder writes, "I do not know whether Mrs. Chopin intends that we shall have any sympathy for Mrs. Pontellier or not. To my mind she deserves none. I could have forgiven her being married to a cold, practical sort of man, had she loved the rather insipid Robert Lebrun even to her undoing. But while she was supposed to be eating her heart for Robert she was behaving in the most shameless manner with another man. Her conduct seems to have been that of a wanton."[8]

BIBLIOGRAPHY

One of the most important reasons literary scholars should more closely examine newspapers of this period is that they can be invaluable to the project of completing authors' bibliographies. There is no late-nineteenth- or early-twentieth-century fiction author of interest today who did not publish at least one short story or novel first in the pages of a newspaper. Search the pages of any big-city newspaper after 1880 and you will find works by Mark Twain, Charles Chesnutt, Rudyard Kipling, Robert Louis Stevenson, William Dean Howells, Sarah Orne Jewett, Sir Arthur Conan Doyle, Hamlin Garland, Thomas Hardy, Bret Harte, Kate Chopin, Henry James, Stephen Crane, Frank Norris, Albion Tourgée, Theodore Dreiser, Joseph Conrad, H. Rider Haggard, Ouida, Frank Stockton, and countless others. Although some of these printings were "corrupted" by the interventions of editors, typesetters, and/or printers, and thus do not represent the final artistic intentions of their authors, they are nonetheless important to document and take into consideration, for they allow us to make more informed, authoritative arguments about authors' career trajectories, their actual audiences, and the cultural impact of their works.

There are four main ways that perusing newspapers can rectify various authors' incomplete publication records. First, there are many cases where it is known from an author's letters, diary, or even publicity materials that he or she wrote a particular fiction, but no one has ever been able to find its actual publication. For example, Mary Wilkins Freeman once referred to a story called "The White Frost Snake" in a letter, but until recently this story had not been located, possibly because, as it turns out, it was printed in numerous newspapers under the title "The White Witch: Her Christmas Dealings With the Children of Polaria." Similarly, Joseph Conrad wrote to his friend Edward Garrett in 1897 that "The *Nigger* is bought in the states by the Batchelor [sic] syndicate for serial," referring to Conrad's short novel *The Nigger of the 'Narcissus': A Tale of the Forecastle* and Irving Bacheller's newspaper syndication service. Thanks to the efforts of assiduous Conrad scholars, the serialized installments of this short novel (from August to September 1897) have now been located in eight different American newspapers, including the *Rocky Mountain News* to the *Utica [NY] Daily Journal.* In addition, William Dean Howells was known to have written a children's story for publication in late December 1895, but no one knew whether the work had been published or not until "The Flight of Pony Baker. A New Story of Boy Life" was discovered in the *Atlanta Constitution.* For many years, too, bibliographers had been aware of an 1899 publicity broadside that listed Frank Norris's short story entitled "A Salvation Boom in Matabeleland" as available to McClure syndicate subscribers for purchase. However, an extensive search of 14 different newspapers by Joseph Katz and six graduate research assistants in the early 1970s turned up no printings. Since their search, eight printings of this story have been located, in the New York *Sun*, *Atlanta Constitution*, *Boston Globe*, *Syracuse Evening Herald*, *Rocky Mountain Weekly News*, *Omaha Daily Bee*, and *Raleigh News and Observer* (twice)—and there are probably more to be discovered. Facing similar situations over the years, I have found two early Jack London stories ("The Unmasking of the Cad" and "The Grilling of Loren Ellery") in the *Utica Daily Observer*, as well as Robert Louis Stevenson's final work, the "Weir of Hermiston," in the *Nebraska State Journal.*[9]

Second, newspaper research can often correct the mistakes made by bibliographers and biographers who have incorrectly asserted that a particular work's magazine appearance was its only serial printing. Newspaper sleuthing has revealed numerous such errors. Henry James's "The Real Thing" was, for instance, long believed to have been serialized in 1892 only in the British magazine *Black and White* until David J. Nordloh revealed that it was first serialized in a number of American newspapers. Similarly, Mary Wilkins Freeman's "The Long Arm" was assumed to have been published only in the American *Pocket Magazine* rather than in multiple newspapers affiliated with the Bacheller Syndicate.[10]

Third, there are a number of instances where bibliographers and/or biographers have, to their credit, listed a newspaper appearance of a certain work—but have not noticed that in fact more than one newspaper printed the same work, either through the operations of a syndicate or through piracy. The former was the case with the Henry James stories "Pandora" and "Georgina's Reasons." In their generally authoritative bibliography of James's works, Leon Edel and Dan Laurence correctly list these two stories' publication in the New York *Sun* in the summer of 1884; however, they overlooked their syndication by *Sun* editor Charles A. Dana to, and subsequent simultaneous publication in, the *San Francisco Chronicle, St. Louis Globe-Democrat, Chicago Tribune,* New Orleans *Times-Democrat, Savannah Morning News, Syracuse Daily Standard, Cincinnati Enquirer,* Philadelphia *Times,* and *Springfield (MA) Republican.* One sees a similar situation in the case of many of the individual Sherlock Holmes. To their credit, Richard Lancelyn Green and John Michael Gibson, in *A Bibliography of A. Conan Doyle* (1983), list for each Holmes story its publication in approximately seven to ten American papers; however, I have found numerous other printings of these stories in other newspapers. This type of mistake has been repeated by the bibliographers of many authors from this period, among them Charles Chesnutt, Hamlin Garland, Mary Wilkins Freeman, and Sarah Orne Jewett.[11] Consequently, scholars have drastically underestimated and misunderstood the audiences that these authors reached with their fictions.

It should also be mentioned that closer attention to newspapers can often uncover textual versions of certain works, approved by their authors, that prompt interpretations very different from the ones typically reprinted and/or anthologized. Stephen Crane's 1894 story "An Experiment in Misery" is a case in point. In its original newspaper appearance in the New York *Press,* this story was prefaced by a dialogue between two presumably middle-class men "regarding a tramp." On the subject of how the tramp feels, the older of the two says to the younger man, "You can tell nothing of it unless you are in that condition yourself. It is idle to speculate about it from this distance," and the narrator writes, "from those words begins this veracious narrative of an experiment in misery." These words establish an important frame to the core story of a young man who poses as a homeless man and comes to see—at least briefly—how it might feel to be poor and with little hope. Without these words from the newspaper version, which make it appear as a work of reportage rather than of fiction, the reader loses the original text's sense of immediacy and realism. Unfortunately, despite the preface being somewhat common knowledge among scholars, it is not included in the authoritative University Press of Virginia edition of Crane's short works and is rarely included in the versions used in the classroom.[12]

The most valuable and exciting type of bibliographic "find," of course, is the previously unknown work by a famous author. Almost forty years ago, Joseph Katz stated, "[A]nyone with the patience to turn over the pages of old periodicals is bound to turn up unknown writings of the realists as well as significantly variant texts of their known writings." This is certainly true in the case of newspapers. The potential finds, however, are probably not limited to works by realists alone; the diligent scholar is likely to locate unknown texts by romance writers such as E. P. Roe, Elizabeth Stuart Phelps, Rudyard Kipling, Mary E. Braddon, and Robert Louis Stevenson, too. Because my own areas of interest involve realist authors, here I will briefly describe just a few of the discoveries recently made of realist texts. During the past few years I have had the good fortune to discover three undocumented short stories by Sarah Orne Jewett: "A Business Man" (1885), "Mrs. Blackford's Only Rose" (1895), and "Dolly Franklin's Decision" (1899). Thus far, only the latter has been critically analyzed. In the case of Mary Wilkins Freeman, a search of multiple newspapers turned up "Emma Jane's Checkerberry Lozenges," "My Lady Primrose," "Lost in the Snow," and "Lauretta." The discovery of these stories is evidence of possibly greater productivity and popularity than is commonly assigned to Freeman. In addition, the fact that so many of her previously unknown works are children's fictions raises the question of whether she was better known at the time as a writer for young people than as one for adults. Charles Chesnutt is another author from this time period whose bibliography, thanks to various scholars, is gradually being filled in by the discovery of fictions published in newspapers. Charles Gilmore, for instance, in the late 1990s discovered a Chesnutt sketch entitled "Frisk's First Rat" in the Fayetteville, North Carolina, *Educator* of March 20, 1875.[13] Overall, one would imagine that the prospect of discovering new versions of known works or previously unknown works by particular authors should be more than enough incentive to tempt literary scholars into more assiduously searching the pages of late-nineteenth- and early-twentieth-century newspapers.

Information about Readers and Reading

Newspapers can do much more than reveal important information about authors and the works they created or help complete the bibliographies of their works. The publication information gleaned from assiduous searching in newspapers can also tell a great deal about the actual audiences for various authors and genres, as well as about the cultural work performed by fictions among millions of previously overlooked readers.

According to a commonly accepted paradigm, the agents of print culture most responsible for purveying fictions to mass audiences in the United States between 1880 and 1920 were magazines such as *Harper's Monthly, Century, Munsey's, McClure's, Ladies' Home Journal,* and the *Saturday Evening Post.* Unlike previous magazines that had measured their audiences in tens of thousands, these publications reached hundreds of thousands of readers; around the turn of the century, some were read by millions. Nonetheless, such large readerships pale in comparison to those of many newspapers during this period, most of which contained some type of fiction. Especially when a fiction was distributed to multiple newspapers by one of the early syndicates such as S. S. McClure's Associated Literary Press or Irving Bacheller's variously named enterprises, it had the potential to reach millions of readers nationwide.

The implications of these larger circulations for our understanding of how many people were reading works by particular authors are far reaching. Sarah Orne Jewett, for instance, an author commonly associated almost exclusively with the genteel *Atlantic Monthly* and its select audience, reached many more people with her newspaper fictions than she ever did with her works published either in this periodical or in books. A single story of hers appearing in the *Boston Globe* of the 1890s, such as "A Financial Failure: The Story of a New England Wooing," when this newspaper's circulation was approximately 150,000, would have reached ten times as many readers as one of hers that appeared in the *Atlantic Monthly.* If a story were syndicated, it would have appeared in at least a dozen other newspapers nationwide, further increasing its circulation. Even *Harper's Monthly* could boast a circulation of only about 200,000 in the mid-1880s, less than that of some of the leading New York dailies. Mary Wilkins Freeman was one author who frequently published in *Harper's Monthly,* but one 1895 report stated about her story "The Long Arm," syndicated in a number of different newspapers, "Her latest effort has been more widely commented on than any previous production and will be as thoroughly appreciated as if it had appeared through the usual channels for this author's stories."[14]

In addition, newspaper publication prompts reconsideration of the geographical scope of various authors' audiences. While the distribution areas of most mass-market magazines until the end of the nineteenth century were quite circumscribed, newspapers containing imaginative literature saturated the entire country. After the Civil War, the major literary magazines, almost all of which were printed in the Northeast, were able to reach across the country by rail, but they usually were read only by people living in cities along the major rail lines that distributed them. Not until the late 1890s and early 1900s, with the introduction of Rural Free Delivery, were these magazines able to reach readers west of the Mississippi River and in rural areas more frequently.

In striking contrast, poems, short stories, and novels published in newspapers enjoyed widespread circulation in rural and urban areas alike during the late nineteenth and early twentieth centuries. Newspapers were widely dispersed outside their local areas via the US mail because of the special low rate privileges they were accorded. Later in the century, large urban dailies—almost all of which printed fiction—were distributed far and wide throughout their regions by railroad trunk lines. Both magazines and newspapers were unloaded at stations along the main lines, but only newspapers were subsequently picked up at all these smaller rail stations and carried by horse-drawn wagons into rural areas. A 1907 report by J. Lincoln Steffens undoubtedly had held true for some time previous to that date: "At every station on the way bundles of papers are left, at a moment's pause, or are flung off upon the platforms . . . as the train slows up for an instant, in the darkness. . . . They are [then] carried in all directions by wagons which are in waiting, and it must be a very remote and scantily populated hamlet that wholly escapes their visitation." An editorial in the *Atlanta Constitution* in 1884 noted that it "reaches almost every point in Georgia, and penetrates into every adjoining state on the day of publication"; also in the 1880s, the *St. Paul Pioneer Press*'s circulation area extended "east into Wisconsin, south into Iowa, north into the British possessions [Canada], and west to the Dakotas," where the Laura Ingalls Wilder family is known to have read copies of this paper, far from its original site of publication. In 1891, editor Edgar Watson Howe observed, "Even in the west the big St. Louis dailies are delivered three hundred miles away by ten o'clock on the morning of publication," and he noted that the "Chicago dailies are delivered on the Mississippi River by breakfast time."[15]

It is important to remember, too, that public library reading rooms across the country regularly made newspapers from distant towns and cities available to patrons. In large metropolitan libraries, the number of newspapers carried far outmatched the number carried today by these libraries. To give just one example, the Denver Public Library in 1895 had in its reading room 101 different daily and weekly papers, ranging geographically from the *Boston Herald* to the *San Francisco Examiner*, *Seattle*

Post-Intelligencer, and *Laramie [Wyoming] Boomerang*; it also carried dozens of small Colorado newspapers such as the *Ouray Herald* and *Silver Cliff Rustler*. Even a relatively small city library such as the one in Council Bluffs, Iowa, in 1894 carried five local and regional dailies, as well as the weekly editions of four New York City newspapers, the *Philadelphia Times*, *Chicago Inter-Ocean*, *Atlanta Constitution*, *Salt Lake City Tribune*, and *San Francisco Bulletin*.[16]

All this information about the geographic reach of newspapers can have a significant effect on our understanding of the cultural work performed by the fictions printed on their pages. For instance, the fact that papers containing works by a wide spectrum of regionalist authors such as Garland, Freeman, Jewett, Chesnutt, Harte, and many others penetrated into rural areas refutes the contention, first voiced by Richard Brodhead and now widely accepted, that the main audience for regionalist fiction consisted of voyeuristic, condescending Northeastern readers of elite magazines and that thus "the literature of regionalism is a product more particularly of the high-cultural literary establishment."[17] Based on this understanding of the audience for regionalist fiction, Brodhead and a number of others have concluded that works of this genre trained these magazine readers to view rural and small town inhabitants and locations as exotic, yet relatively unimportant, components of the new, urban-centered, industrial American nation, thereby bolstering their own cultural hegemony. While magazines may indeed have performed this type of cultural work among more urbanized readers, newspapers were likely performing a different kind of work with small-town and rural readers, many of which probably interpreted regionalist fictions set in their locales as more celebratory than patronizing.

In addition to having broader geographic distribution coverage than magazines, newspapers also reached a broader socioeconomic spectrum of readers. Through studying these newspapers, modern scholars are afforded a better view of which fictions were actually available to such readers, in what contexts they were read, and how readers responded to them. Not until the 1890s did monthly magazines lower their prices from the relatively expensive 35 cents to 15 and then 10 cents. Even at these lower prices, though, for working-class people the 2 cents daily price or 5 cents Sunday price of a newspaper made more economic sense because they got much more reading material—and more valuable information about their immediate communities—for their money. Newspaper historian Sidney Kobre has correctly noted, "The newspaper throughout [the nineteenth century] served the function of obtaining vicariously for the middle and working class the things [of] which the upper-class boasted." Of course, most metropolitan dailies were not read solely by working-class readers; their low price and easy availability at every street corner or even at one's doorstep made them attractive to middle-class and upper-class readers as well. The result was that everyone seemed to be reading newspapers. One 1890 report stated that in New York on Sundays, "Everywhere you see people reading [newspapers]. . . . The benches in Union and Madison Squares are occupied with readers. Central Park, on a fine Sunday forenoon, contains hundreds of students of this secular Sunday literature. In the trains, in the street-cars, in waiting rooms, and on the pleasure boats, the same spectacle meets one"; he then added, "What happens in New York takes place in other large cities." Thus one can see that in the decades before the lines of cultural stratification were more rigidly drawn at the turn of the century—so well delineated by Lawrence Levine in *Highbrow/Lowbrow: The Emergence of Cultural Hierarchy in America* (1988)—newspapers were truly where "the masses met the classes."[18]

Newspapers as Sites of Fiction Reception

Printings of fictions in newspapers represent unique sites of reader-text interaction and as such deserve much closer examination. Because these fictions were not read in the same contexts that they were when they appeared in monthly magazines and books, they were likely not understood by their newspaper readers in the same ways they were by magazine or book readers. In urban areas, where the greatest number of readers lived, newspapers (except for Sunday editions) were most often read hurriedly in trains, in streetcars and subways, on boats, in waiting rooms, and during breaks at work. According to one report, most were only "'skimmed over' in the ten minutes which the average city dweller allows himself to read the paper." An article entitled "Universal Habit of Reading Newspapers," which appeared in the *Boston Globe* in 1905, included a number of images that reveal a good deal about newspaper reading habits: two show people reading newspapers in "an Elevated Car" and "a morning train," one catches people reading newspapers standing up "At a Street News Stand," and the other eight show men—no women—reading newspapers during breaks from their work.[19] City dwellers also typically read their papers only once and then discarded them. On the other hand, in rural areas where reading materials of all kinds were less readily available, newspapers were read much more slowly and were often kept for longer periods and passed among multiple readers.

What made the act of reading fictions in newspapers so different was that fictions printed there, unlike works appearing in books and genteel monthly magazines, were almost always printed amid a smorgasbord of other printed and visual materials. Throughout the entire period under discussion, in most newspapers fictional works were inserted not only among news stories but also among advertisements, editorials, letters to the editor, features of all kinds, and so forth. Fictions were also frequently illustrated, something not nearly as common for book and magazine publication. American readers first encountered *The Red Badge of Courage*, for instance, as a text crudely illustrated with line drawings, usually amid multiple advertisements (in one case, a nearby ad promised "Manhood Restored" if one used a certain product, and some readers might have advocated Henry Fleming take it) and news items, such as one for "Missionary Progress."[20] Readers of newspapers also in general approached fiction texts printed in newspapers differently because they had different expectations of a newspaper's contents, compared to those of a magazine or book. Newspapers were commonly supposed to provide information and insights that were useful in one's daily life. Consequently, readers of serialized newspaper fictions would not have read them as reverently as they did those works printed on advertisement-free—and illustration-free—quality paper pages and sometimes bound between distinguished-looking cloth-bound covers (as, for example, *The Red Badge of Courage* was just a few months after its serialization). Yet, if the medium really is the message, as Marshall McLuhan famously asserted, fictions published in newspapers gave readers the impression that they were important for the ways they supplemented and complemented the knowledge gained through reading the other contents of the paper and thereby should be incorporated into their daily lives rather than laid aside after reading as "just another story."

To what extent, however, did all these contextual elements affect readers' perceptions of particular fiction texts, or of particular genres? Unfortunately, despite my having pored over countless editorials and letters to the editor printed in a great number of newspapers, I have yet to locate a specific reaction to an individual fiction published in a newspaper.

In the absence of empirical evidence about readers' responses to specific newspaper fictions, I have developed a new type of interpretive approach to ascertain the cultural work such texts performed among readers. In order to create more believable hypotheses about the reception of works published in periodicals—and newspapers in particular—I believe it is necessary to replicate as fully as possible the original newspaper reading experience. Although all postulations of mass historical reader response must remain speculative, situating texts more firmly in their original sites of reception enables us to construct better-informed hypotheses about how great numbers of readers might have interpreted such texts. My model is based on the ideas of Hans Robert Jauss and Stanley Fish, who both contend that readers interpret individual texts based on the assumptions and expectations that they bring to reading them. The assumptions and expectations of nineteenth- and early-twentieth-century newspaper readers, I believe, would have been strongly influenced by the "personality" of each newspaper, somewhat akin to what Fish calls an "interpretive community." In addition, as Gerard Genette, George Bornstein, Jerome McGann, and others have shown with book texts, the many printed elements that surround an individual fiction text can, even if the author has no control over them, potentially influence the reader's understanding of that text; McGann calls the interaction of the linguistic and bibliographical elements involved in a text's reception its "reading field." Following McGann and Genette, in the case of newspapers, I would suggest that scholars interested in understanding readers' responses to a particular fiction need to look at the prepublication advertising for the serialized text, the headlines and subheadlines for it, its placement on the page, its typography, the illustrations that accompanied it, and their captions, as well as other printed materials that likely appeared nearby in the newspaper, such as nonfiction articles, advertisements, and other fictions. To properly situate a serial text and recreate the original readers' experiences in a particular interpretive community, one must also take into account the editorial goals of the newspaper, knowledge about who its readers were, their expectations of the periodical as a whole, what school training taught them to look for in fiction, and the general ideological milieu of the times in which the text was read. After one gathers all this information and examines how the various contextual elements might have affected readers of a newspaper, I believe, one is prepared to make very believable hypotheses about how readers responded to an individual fiction text that appeared in the pages of that newspaper.[21]

Over the past 15 or so years, I have applied my theory to a number of newspaper fiction texts by Frank Norris, Henry James, Stephen Crane, and Sarah Orne Jewett. One important lesson learned from this research stands out: because of their reading experiences, which were very different from those of book and magazine readers, nineteenth-century readers of literary texts in newspapers were unlikely to interpret fictions as modern scholars do or how hypothetically "informed readers" supposedly did.

As I have argued in one article, for instance, because of the way Henry James's "The Real Thing" was framed in newspapers by prepublication advertising, subheadlines, and illustrations, its newspaper readers would have been prompted to read this story for its plot and to focus on the class dimensions of the relationship between its characters, not on what modern scholars contend it is about: James's theories about the best ways to represent his subjects artistically. In another instance, I have argued that, in large part because of its publication in Sunday newspapers, Frank Norris's short story "A Salvation 'Boom' in Matabeleland," in which an American missionary named Marks is killed and crucified by African tribesmen, almost certainly would not have been interpreted as a subversively anti-imperialist text, an approach modern scholars are likely to take. Instead, "because for various reasons readers of Sunday newspapers at the time generally expected their contents to support Christianity and be morally and religiously edifying, it is more likely that these readers would have interpreted the text as a parable of how a Salvation Army worker is martyred for the Christian faith by 'savages,' and as a 'lesson' that stronger—and more—such missionaries were needed to follow in his imperialist path."[22]

What is sorely needed now are more studies analyzing the interplay of fiction texts and newspaper contexts, as well as more archival work on newspaper readers' attitudes during this time. Such work might appear daunting, but the eventual result will be a much deeper understanding of how fictions functioned in the daily lives of millions of people in the late nineteenth and early twentieth centuries.

FUTURE PROSPECTS FOR RESEARCH ON LITERATURE AND NEWSPAPERS

Given all the potential benefits of studying the intersection of literature and newspapers outlined previously, it would seem natural to ask why more work has not been done on this subject and what the field's prospects are.

There are many reasons why newspapers have been underexamined by scholars. On a very practical level, newspapers from this period were (and still are) generally much more difficult to obtain and work with than books and magazines. Until quite recently, most newspapers existed only in the form of crumbling piles or volumes of newsprint, scattered throughout the country in local libraries and historical societies. In the latter decades of the twentieth century the situation improved somewhat as the US Newspaper Program, under the auspices of the National Endowment for the Humanities, performed the valuable work of collecting a great number of these papers and having them microfilmed. Important bibliographies and databases noting the paper and microfilm copies of newspapers were also created, including *Newspapers in Microform*, WorldCat, and the bibliographies of Native American and African American newspapers by James Danky and Maureen Hady. However, knowing where microfilm and hard copies of newspapers were located did not always help the researcher a great deal, for unlike with books and popular nineteenth-century monthly magazines, very often there existed only single copies of these microfilm reels, and their owners tended not to want to lend them via interlibrary loan. In addition, collections often were—and continue to be—far from complete.

Even when one *could* obtain copies of these papers on microfilm, working with them was not always the most pleasant task. Modern microfilm readers/printers, introduced in the 1980s, as well as the readers/scanners that followed, helped make this work somewhat easier, but most people could not bear looking at microfilm for very long. Another major impediment to newspaper research was that, except for the *New York Times* and a few nineteenth-century newspapers indexed by WPA workers in the 1930s or by local historians, there were no indexes available to help locate the works of specific authors.[23] If one wanted to find fictions by Stephen Crane, Mark Twain, Sarah Orne Jewett, or anyone else, there was no other option than to turn over yellowed newspapers from the era or scroll through multiple reels of microfilm.

Also contributing to the general lack of literary research using newspapers were the relatively strict disciplinary boundaries that separated literary studies, journalism, and history. Despite repeated calls for "interdisciplinarity," there simply were not many literary scholars adequately motivated or trained to conduct historical as well as literary research or who knew well the field of journalism history; when Shelley Fisher Fishkin published her groundbreaking study, *From Fact to Fiction: Journalism and Imaginative Writing in America* (1985), she was virtually alone in the field.[24] The same situation held true in reverse, with no journalism historians being interested in the literary works they undoubtedly saw while conducting their research on editorial and reporting policies of nineteenth-century newspapers.

Fortunately, these conditions have, in the past few years, begun to change rapidly in significant ways. As noted earlier, more literary scholars are beginning to follow in Fishkin's footsteps and cross disciplinary lines to look more closely at how the worlds of journalism and literature intersected in the late nineteenth and early twentieth centuries. The Research Society for American Periodicals, begun in 1991, as well as its journal, *American Periodicals*, accord full recognition to newspapers as well as magazines. A growing number of other scholarly journals are also now quite receptive to articles about newspapers and fiction. Most important, it has become much easier to search newspapers because of the digitizing revolution. The ProQuest Historical Newspaper database includes searchable texts of 36 newspapers from this period, including a number of African American and Jewish American titles; the Readex Company's *America's Historical Newspapers* database provides similar search capabilities for newspapers from 1690 to 1889. Other subscription databases such as Newspaper Archives Online, Gale Publishing's *19th Century U.S. Newspapers*, and the *Historical New York Times* also provide ways to easily search for information on literary topics in older newspapers. Nevertheless, many of these databases continue to be difficult for many scholars to access, since only the wealthiest institutions can afford subscriptions to the best of them.

Promising much more democratic access is the National Digital Newspaper Program, which recently succeeded the US Newspaper Program's microfilming efforts. Cosponsored by the National Endowment for the Humanities and the Library of Congress, the NDNP has already digitized more than 600 American newspapers from microfilm copies and made them available for free to anyone with an Internet connection via the *Chronicling America: Historical American Newspapers* website. This database is especially noteworthy for its inclusion of a great number of newspapers published by and for various racial and ethnic groups. The search capabilities of this database are impressive, yet one cannot always be certain that searches will turn up all relevant items, since most of the digitized images are being captured from microfilm copies, including some that have already deteriorated a good deal. Nonetheless, if this project continues to receive adequate funding, it will remove some of the most significant practical barriers that have kept literary scholars from studying the intersection of literary studies and journalism history. One should also note that some private digital projects are also making important materials freely available. For instance, http://www.fultonhistory.com allows researchers to search thousands of pages of New York State newspapers digitized from microfilm first created by the State of New York Newspaper Program.

Because of all these developments, I am very optimistic that a new generation of scholars will feel encouraged and empowered to conduct more extensive explorations of the important connections between newspapers and literature. The rewards for doing so can be tremendous. For instance, just a year or so ago professors Glenda R. Carpio and Werner Sollors, as part of a class project, asked their students to comb through various archives and microfilm collections in search of information about Zora Neale Hurston. As it turned out, they themselves ended up finding, buried in old, microfilmed newspaper pages, a number of previously unknown stories by Hurston from the late 1920s, stories that shed a great deal of light on a hitherto unexplored aspect of Hurston's career and provide important insights into her political affiliations within the Harlem Renaissance movement.[25]

This one group's recent success with a writer from the 1920s highlights how, even in the more modern era, newspapers can yield important information for literary scholars. It is my hope that in upcoming years numerous articles similar to those by Carpio and Sollors will be written by scholars recounting their discoveries from American newspapers from all different eras. Analyzing the materials they find in newspapers will, one may confidently assert, help with the important project of filling out, complicating, and enriching our understanding of many authors' careers and the impact of their works on American culture.

NOTES

1. Charles Johanningsmeier, *Fiction and the American Literary Marketplace: The Role of Newspaper Syndicates, 1860–1900* (Cambridge: Cambridge University Press, 1997); Karen Roggenkamp, *Narrating the News: New Journalism and Literary Genre in Late Nineteenth-Century American Newspapers and Fiction* (Kent, OH: Kent State University Press, 2005); Patricia Okker, ed., *Transnationalism and American Serial Fiction* (New York: Routledge, 2012).
2. David Reynolds, *Beneath the American Renaissance: The Subversive Imagination in the Age of Emerson and Melville* (New York: Knopf / Random House, 1988); for the newspaper article that inspired *McTeague*, see "Twenty-nine Fatal Wounds," *San Francisco Examiner*, October 10, 1893: 12; for the article that inspired this portion of *Ethan Frome*, see "Fatal Coasting Accident," *Berkshire Evening Eagle* (Pittsfield, Massachusetts), March 12, 1904, reprinted in Edith Wharton, *Ethan Frome*, ed. Kristin O. Lauer and Cynthia Griffin Wolff (New York: W. W. Norton, 1995), 86–90; for a

detailed account of Dreiser's use of newspapers in writing *An American Tragedy*, see Jerome Loving, *The Last Titan: A Life of Theodore Dreiser* (Berkeley: University of California Press, 2005), 297–315.

3. "Talk with Dr. Conan Doyle," *Boston Herald*, May 8, 1892: 24; *Boston Globe*, April 16, 1899: 33; Jewett's comments are in "A Matter of Common Justice to Woman," *Los Angeles Times*, April 15, 1894: 18.
4. "A Lincoln Man Tells of Norris," Lincoln, Nebraska *Star*, November 22, 1902: 16; Joseph McElrath Jr. and Jesse Crisler, *Frank Norris: A Life* (Urbana: University of Illinois Press, 2006), 63.
5. Charles Johanningsmeier, "A Newly-Discovered Norris Newspaper Publication Sheds Light on His Work at McClure's," *Studies in American Naturalism* 6.2, (Winter 2011): 185–96.
6. "A Talk about Authors," Galesburg, Illinois *Republican-Register*, January 2, 1892, 2.
7. For these reviews see Stephanie P. Browner, ed., *The Charles Chesnutt Digital Archive*, http://www.chesnuttarchive.org/Reviews/contemp_reviews.html.
8. Jeannette Gilder, "Among the New Books," *Chicago Tribune*, March 22, 1899, 8; see Ernest Marchand's summary, "[1899 Reviews of *McTeague*]," in Frank Norris, *McTeague*, ed. Donald Pizer, Second Edition (New York: W. W. Norton, 1997), 301–5; Kate Chopin, *The Awakening*, ed. Margo Culley (New York: W. W. Norton, 1994), 161–78; Jeannette Gilder, "Novel Leaves a Bad Taste," Rev. of Kate Chopin, *The Awakening*, in *Chicago Tribune*, April 16, 1899, 51.
9. Mary Wilkins Freeman, letter to Eliza Anna Farman Pratt, September 20, [1893], in *The Infant Sphinx: Collected Letters of Mary E. Wilkins Freeman*, ed. Brent L. Kendrick (Metuchen, NJ: Scarecrow Press, 1985), 159; "The White Witch: Her Christmas Dealings with the Children of Polaria," *Louisville Courier-Journal*, December 24, 1893, 11, and Chicago *Inter-Ocean*, December 24, 1893, 3; Joseph Conrad to Garnett, Letter, June 2, 1897, *The Collected Letters of Joseph Conrad, Volume 1, 1861–1897*, ed. Frederick R. Karl and Laurence Davies (Cambridge: Cambridge University Press, 1983), 356; for the new discoveries, see *Conrad First: The Joseph Conrad Periodical Archive*, ed. Stephen Donovan, Dept. of English, Uppsala University, Uppsala, Sweden, http://www.conradfirst.net; William Dean Howells, "The Flight of Pony Baker," *Atlanta Constitution, Jr.*, December 22, 1895, 1; Joseph Katz, "The Shorter Publications of Frank Norris: A Checklist," *Proof* 3 (1973):

165; for a complete listing of the publication information for Norris's story, see Charles Johanningsmeier, "A Newly-Discovered Norris Newspaper Publication . . ."; Jack London, "The Unmasking of the Cad," *Utica Daily Observer*, September 13, 1899, 3; "The Grilling of Loren Ellery," *Utica Daily Observer*, October 2, 1899, 3; Robert Louis Stevenson, "Weir of Hermiston," *Nebraska State Journal*, April 14 and 19, 1896, 14.

10. David Nordloh, "First Appearances of Henry James's 'The Real Thing': The McClure Papers as a Bibliographical Resource," *Papers of the Bibliographical Society of America* 78.1 (1984): 69–71; and Charles Johanningsmeier, "How American Readers Originally Experienced James's 'The Real Thing,'" *The Henry James Review* 27 (2006): 75–99; Mary R. Reichardt lists the first American publication of "The Long Arm," coauthored with Joseph E. Chamberlin, as being in *Pocket Magazine* 1.2 (December 1895): 1–76 (*A Mary Wilkins Freeman Reader* [Lincoln: University of Nebraska Press, 1997], 324); newspaper printings of "The Long Arm" include *Utica Daily Observer*, August 3, 5, 6, 7, 8, and 9, 1895, 7 (all days); *Austin Daily Statesman*, August 3, 5, 6, and 7, 1895, 4 (all days), plus August 8, 1895, 4–5; *New York Herald*, August 4, 1895, section 6, page 1, and August 11, 1895, section 5, pages 1, 4; it was also published in Britain in *Chapman's Magazine of Fiction* 1 (August 1895): 397–426.
11. Leon Edel and Dan Laurence, *A Bibliography of Henry James*, Third Edition, revised with the assistance of James Rambeau (Oxford: Clarendon Press, 1982), 339; Charles Johanningsmeier, "Henry James's Dalliance with the Newspaper World," *The Henry James Review* 19 (Winter 1998): 36–52; Richard Lancelyn Green and John Michael Gibson, *A Bibliography of A. Conan Doyle* (Oxford: Clarendon Press, 1983). As just one example of a scholar highlighting such bibliographical oversights, see John M. Freiermuth, "An Updated Bibliography of Charles Chesnutt's Syndicated Newspaper Publications," *American Literary Realism* 42 (2010): 278–79.
12. Stephen Crane, "An Experiment in Misery," New York *Press*, April 22, 1894, part 3, page 2. *The University of Virginia Edition of the Works of Stephen Crane, Volume 8: Tales, Sketches, and Reports*, ed. Fredson Bowers, with introduction by Edwin H. Cady (Charlottesville: University Press of Virginia, 1973), 283–93.
13. Joseph Katz, "Bibliography and the Rise of American Literary Realism," *Studies in American Fiction* 2 (1974): 79–80; the most up-to-date bibliographical listing of Jewett's works currently can be found at the Sarah Orne Jewett website edited by Professor Terry

Heller of Coe College in Cedar Rapids, Iowa, http://www.public.coe.edu/~theller/soj/biblio.html. Sarah Orne Jewett, "A Business Man," *Los Angeles Sunday Times,* March 8, 1885, 4; "Mrs. Blackford's Only Rose," *Dallas Morning News,* July 5, 1895, 7; "Dolly Franklin's Decision," *Boston Globe,* November 24, 1889, 17; Charles Johanningsmeier, "'Dolly Franklin's Decision': Sarah Orne Jewett's Definition of 'A Good Girl,'" *Legacy* 17.1 (2000): 95–101; Mary Wilkins, "Emma Jane's Checkerberry Lozenges," New York *World,* May 6, 1894, 43; Wilkins, "Found in the Snow," Detroit *Free Press,* December 24, 1899, Section 4, page 2; Wilkins, "My Lady Primrose," *Atlanta Constitution, Jr.*, December 23, 1894, 3; Wilkins, "Lauretta," *Washington Post,* April 7, 1901, 33; "Frisk's Rat" is reprinted in the *North Carolina Literary Review* 8 (1999): 87.

14. Sarah Orne Jewett, "A Financial Failure," *Boston Globe,* December 7, 1890, 25; for *Globe* circulation see Advertisement, *Boston Sunday Globe,* November 1, 1891, 1; for *Atlantic* circulation see *The Building of the House: Houghton Mifflin's Formative Years* (Boston: Houghton-Mifflin, 1970), 365, 453; for *Harper's Monthly* circulation see Eugene Exman, *The House of Harper: One Hundred and Fifty Years of Publishing* (New York: Harper and Row, 1967), 79; "Literature in Newspapers," *The Newspaper Maker,* August 29, 1895, 7.
15. J. Lincoln Steffens, "The Business of a Newspaper," *Scribner's Magazine* 22 (October 1897): 464; "At 4:45," Editorial, *Atlanta Constitution,* November 23, 1884, 6; Donald J. O'Grady, *The Pioneer Press and Dispatch: History at Your Door, 1849–1983* (St. Paul: Northwest Publications, 1983), 41; Laura Ingalls Wilder, *The Long Winter* (New York: Harper and Row, 1953[1940]), 168–75; Edgar Watson Howe, "Country Newspapers," *Century* 42 (1891): 782.
16. *Dictionary Catalog of Periodicals* (Denver: Carson-Harper, [1895]), 42–44; *Finding List of [the] Council Bluffs Free Public Library* (Council Bluffs, IA: Pryor Bros., Bee Job Print, 1894), n.p.
17. Richard Brodhead, "Literature and Culture," in Emory Elliott et al., eds., *Columbia Literary History of the United States* (New York: Columbia University Press, 1988), 474.
18. Sidney Kobre, *The Yellow Press and Gilded Age Journalism* (Tallahassee: Florida State University Press, 1964), 70; Robert Donald, "Sunday Newspapers in the United States," *The Universal Review* 8 (September-October 1890): 80; Lawrence Levine, *Highbrow / Lowbrow: The Emergence of Cultural Hierarchy in America* (Cambridge: Harvard University Press, 1988).

19. "Newspaper Reading," *Boston Herald*, November 15, 1885, 12; "Universal Habit of Reading Newspapers," *Boston Globe*, April 2, 1905, Sunday Magazine, 4.
20. "The Red Badge of Courage," *Rochester [New York] Herald*, December 3, 1894, 5.
21. Hans Robert Jauss, "Literary History as a Challenge to Literary Theory," *New Literary History* 2 (Autumn 1970): 7–37; Stanley Fish, *Is There a Text in This Class?* (Cambridge, MA: Harvard University Press, 1980), 318, 322, and 342; Gerard Genette, *Paratexts: The Threshold of Literary Interpretation* (Cambridge: Cambridge University Press, 1997); George Bornstein, "How to Read a Page: Modernism and Material Textuality," *Studies in the Literary Imagination* 32.1 (Spring 1999): 29–58; Jerome McGann, "The Monks and the Giants: Textual and Bibliographical Studies and the Interpretation of Literary Works," in *Textual Criticism and Literary Interpretation*, ed. Jerome McGann (Chicago: University of Chicago Press, 1985), 180–230; McGann uses the term *reading field* in his monograph *The Textual Condition* (Princeton: Princeton University Press, 1991), 56. For a more complete description of how to formulate mass readers' responses, see Charles Johanningsmeier, "Understanding Readers of Fiction in American Periodicals, 1880–1914," in *U.S. Popular Print Culture 1860–1920*, ed. Christine Bold (New York: Oxford University Press, 2011), 591–609.
22. Charles Johanningsmeier, "How American Readers Originally Experienced James's 'The Real Thing,'" *The Henry James Review* 27 (2006): 97; Johanningsmeier, "Understanding Readers of Fiction in American Periodicals, 1880–1914," 600. For a full analysis of how Sunday newspaper readers likely would have interpreted Norris's story, see Johanningsmeier, "The Devil, Capitalism, and Frank Norris: Defining the 'Reading Field' for Sunday Newspaper Fiction, 1870–1910," *American Periodicals* 14.1 (Spring 2004): 104–10.
23. *Newspapers in Microform: United States, 1948–1983* (Washington, DC: Library of Congress, 1984); *Native American Periodicals and Newspapers, 1828–1982: Bibliography, Publishing Record, and Holdings*, ed. James P. Danky, compiled by Maureen E. Hady, research assistant Ann Bowles, foreword by Vine Deloria Jr. (Westport, CT: Greenwood, 1984); *African-American Newspapers and Periodicals: A National Bibliography*, ed. James P. Danky and Maureen E. Hady (Cambridge, MA: Harvard University Press, 1998). One example of indexes compiled by Works Progress Administration workers can be found at the Indiana State Library: http://www.in.gov/library/indiana.htm.

24. Shelley Fisher Fishkin, *From Fact to Fiction: Journalism and Imaginative Writing in America* (Baltimore: Johns Hopkins University Press, 1985).
25. Glenda R. Carpio and Werner Sollors, "Five Harlem Short Stories by Zora Neale Hurston," *Amerikastudien / American Studies* 55 (2010): 557–60; Glenda R. Carpio and Werner Sollors, "The Newly Complicated Zora Neale Hurston," *The Chronicle Review*, January 8, 2011, B7.

CHAPTER 7

FAME AND THE FATE OF CELEBRITY

THE TRAUMA OF THE LIONIZED JOURNALIST–LITERARY FIGURE

DOUG UNDERWOOD

> I'm scared to death of popularity. It has ruined everyone I know.
>
> —John Steinbeck

MARGARET MITCHELL, PERHAPS THE MOST PROMINENT ONE-BOOK novelist in American literary history, was once asked by E. B. White what she was doing instead of spending her time writing a sequel to her famous bestseller. "Doing?" she reportedly responded, "It's a full-time job to be the author of 'Gone with the Wind.'"[1]

Mitchell, in fact, came to see herself as the "victim" of the very media attention that had made her a celebrity, and she liked to use this as the basis for explaining why she never wrote a follow-up to her novel of Civil War romance and suffering, which was turned into one of the iconic movies in Hollywood history. Reclusive and plagued by bouts of depression, obsessed with her status as a figurehead of popular entertainment, and struggling with an alcohol problem, Mitchell by her midthirties was engaging in bizarre behavior that helped to cement her reputation as the neurotic and melodramatic southern belle who created Scarlett O'Hara, one of the most memorably neurotic characters to grace the pages of popular literature. Once in a panic over some pending press interviews, Mitchell left her hometown of Atlanta for the nearby mountains, where she wrote vivid, pathetic appeals to journalists who had reviewed her work, describing the nightmare she believed she was experiencing in the public spotlight and asking for their sympathy. ("I'm sure Scarlett O'Hara never struggled harder to get out of Atlanta or suffered more during the siege of Atlanta than I have suffered during the siege that has been on since publication day," she wrote to one.) This was followed by years in which she avidly followed the developments in the filming of *Gone with the Wind*, criticized the casting and the script writers, and placed anonymous tips and gossip items with columnists, all the while coyly refusing to participate directly in the production. These activities—plus personally typing in duplicate nearly one hundred letters a week, often long and detailed and highly emotional, in response to her fan mail—paint a picture of Mitchell, a longtime society page reporter for the *Atlanta Journal*, as unhealthily absorbed in her image of herself as a person so ravaged by public adulation that she could never bring herself to write again for public attention.[2]

As Mitchell's experience demonstrates, celebrity has been both boon and bane to the journalist–literary figure.[3] Even before the coming of movies, television, and instantly transmitted electronic imagery, Thomas Paine, Stephen Crane, and Bret Harte all rose and fell by celebrity, and all three ended their days struggling with a variety of health and personal problems while living under a public microscope. The twentieth century saw similar spectacles of the rise and fall in public esteem of journalist-writers who became the focus of extensive media coverage of their mishaps and peccadilloes: Theodore Dreiser's arrest with a girlfriend in a small-town Kentucky hotel on a morals charge after he had arrived to give celebrity support to a miner's strike; Dorothy Parker's high-profile membership in the Algonquin Roundtable group, where gossip journalists would circulate her vinegar-witted comments (she lived at the Algonquin Hotel, she once said, because all she needed was "room enough to lay a hat and a few friends"); James Agee's late-life state of alcoholic disorder and dishevelment that became the target of complaints about his lack of hygiene by his fellow Hollywood screenwriters; and Truman Capote's incoherent performance on a television talk show, where viewers got a glimpse of the drug and alcohol addiction that had come to rule him. (When asked by the host about his "problem," Capote said, "The obvious answer is that eventually I'll kill myself.") With the coming of the "new" journalism movement of the 1960s and 1970s, a number of other prominent figures, including Norman Mailer, Hunter S. Thompson, and George Plimpton, made themselves the heroes (or antiheroes) of their own narrative adventures, and to one degree or another (Thompson and

Mailer with drugs and alcohol, Plimpton with his pranks and participatory journalism pratfalls) made their attention-seeking but (particularly in the case of Thompson and Mailer) often destructive behavior a key feature of their trademark public image.[4]

As a group, American journalist–literary figures—who as journalists often had covered other public figures and had an intimate understanding of the relationship between media and celebrity—nonetheless have been more than eager to grasp fame when their opportunities came. With each new communications development—beginning with the use of the printing press to produce the first regular periodical publications in the early 1600s to the mass production of newspapers and magazines by the steam-powered printing press in the early 1800s, the invention of the telegraph and the telephone in the mid to late 1800s, and the coming of movies, radio, television, and the Internet in the twentieth century—the media celebrity business has grown more intense and expansive in scope, and the ability to exploit the dominant communication systems for publicity and career advancement purposes has become an integral part of many successful journalistic writers' lives. Still, psychological stress is an occupational hazard for those living in the media limelight, and these writers have experienced some of the traumas that have afflicted other celebrities. As much as journalism has been their pathway to achieve success and literary renown, to a remarkable degree, fame also helped contribute to their personal ruin. "Something happens to our good writers at a certain age," Ernest Hemingway once said. "We destroy them in many ways."[5] A study of the experiences of several journalist–literary figures reveals both the causes and consequences of literary celebrity.

THE MOTIVATIONS FOR SEEKING CELEBRITY

> One of the commonest forms of madness is the desire to be noticed.
>
> —Mark Twain

One must look at the individual psyche of each celebrity journalist–literary figure to try to understand what drove him or her to the cultivation of fame and the forces that sometimes brought a fall. Nearly every one had a colossal ego, an abiding sense of personal destiny, and a powerful need for individual expression and exposure. A number of writers in this category were haunted by the feeling that life had little meaning if one did not rise above a humdrum existence and succeed on a larger-than-life scale. Many were fueled by dynamic personalities and a drive to self-mythologize. The word *charisma*, which derives from a religious concept signifying a person who has been given the spiritual gift of eloquence and the ability to charm and persuade people, has been used to describe a remarkably large number of them. But many also suffered from character weaknesses and internal turmoil that led to painful tragedies and public failures in their personal lives. It was not uncommon for them to use the "highs" of celebrity to counterbalance the lows in their lives—including their struggles with self-esteem, emotional imbalance, and difficulties in their personal relationships. Few lived lives of inner peace or tranquility, and some were noted for their less-than-charitable natures. In fact, the high regard in which posterity holds a number of these figures can be seen as an illustration of how society judges the artist by his or her art rather than by measures of morality, integrity, generosity, or self-sacrifice.

The Lure of the Byline

In the years of early commercial journalism, writers produced most of their material without identifying themselves, and their satisfactions came from having one's friends know who had penned a certain anonymous tract or from a quiet pride, as in the case of the young Benjamin Franklin, who pushed his "Silence Dogood" columns under the door of his brother's print shop. When they were published, he realized that he was the author whose identity everyone was trying to guess. But editors soon discovered that the lure of a byline or a signed column, and the ego gratification that could come with it, was a powerful attraction for ambitious writing talents. Things had changed so much that by the end of the nineteenth century newspapers were hiring celebrity journalists because of their marketing appeal and running material about them under promotional headlines, such as the one that biographer James Colvert reported was written about Stephen Crane after he survived a shipwreck on the way to reporting the Spanish American War: "Young New York Writer Astonishes the Sea Dogs by his Courage in the Face of Death." His account of the experience appeared in the *New York Press* under the simple title "Stephen Crane's Own Story."[6]

Early Glory

The precociousness of many journalist–literary figures has drawn attention from a number of observers. Writers such as Crane, Frank Norris, and Jack London completed prodigious bodies of work before succumbing to early deaths, and young talents such as Harte, Dreiser, Hemingway, Mark Twain, Norman Mailer, Willa Cather, John Dos Passos, and Erskine Caldwell produced major works—and, in the opinion of many critics, some of their best ones—while still in their twenties. In some cases, these writers spent only limited time in school before heading into journalism, where they were soon hailed as rising stars. Often forced by circumstances to mature early (at least, in professional terms), they found themselves in a young person's field that required high energy and a good deal of bravado, and it came naturally that they would discount the journalistic writing that came easily to them and set their sights on higher literary goals. By age 12, William Dean Howells, for example, worked six days a week from five in the morning until eleven at night as a print shop worker at his father's small-town Ohio newspapers. Sometimes his father would let him leave the printing office to study, write poetry, or work on his fiction—which he often slipped into the family newspaper. By the time he was in his twenties and working as a journalist on his father's *Ohio State Journal* in Columbus, he was submitting fiction to the *Atlantic*, eyeing an editorial post with the magazine, and complaining of putting his literary work into "the predatory press . . . tossed upon a newspaper sea, a helmless boat with no clearance papers aboard."[7]

Perpetual Adolescence

Journalists, and particularly reporters, can easily live in a state of "arrested development," as Hemingway described one of his journalist characters in *The Sun Also Rises*, which encourages them to externalize their frustrations in complaints about the tyranny of bosses and workplace restraints on free expression.[8] The tension produced by the clash of forceful personalities who are dispensable cogs in an industrial enterprise can make for a dynamic writing environment, but it can also leave reporters grousing like teenagers that it is unjust authority that holds them back. This professional environment has helped to turn some of the journalist–literary figures into the literary version of the "enfant terrible," and greater literary success did little to curb their unrestrained demands on life or the hunger many developed for ego gratification in the public limelight.

Professional Networks

Journalists spend much of their careers mixing with the high and mighty, but their professional culture encourages them to deal with officialdom with cynicism and even contempt. This situation can leave journalists yearning for public praise for themselves while disdaining similar ambitions in those they cover. Many journalist–literary figures profited in their careers from their connections with and exposure to powerful people, whose support and admiration proved to be instrumental to their literary rise. In the nineteenth century, Harte, Twain, and Ambrose Bierce helped to nurture one another's careers as California writers and then expanded their reach thanks to the help they gave each other through the contacts and alliances they had gained in the writing and publishing world. Even among journalist–literary figures of the twentieth century, there was still a great deal of value in what we call "networking," and it was possible to boost one's literary career by achieving a reputation in tight-knit artistic circles. This led such journalist–literary figures as Cather, Hemingway, Parker, Dos Passos, Capote, Mailer, Ring Lardner, Sherwood Anderson, Robert Benchley, James Thurber, E. B. White, and others to gather in cities such as New York and Chicago to gain the benefits that literary friendships and close proximity to the publishing powers could provide. In many cases, they were helped by people with exactly the same profile as their own—former journalists who began in newspapering or magazines and then moved onto greater artistic accomplishment—and some (such as Hemingway and Capote) were proclaimed rising stars before they had actually published much that was notable.

The Benefits of a Likable Nature

Some of these writers kept what would turn out to be a fleeting reputation afloat throughout a lifetime by impressing their contemporaries with their genial and engaging personalities. For example, Washington Irving—who was criticized in his time and ours for the superficiality of his insights as a cultural observer and the flatness of his prose—nonetheless was treated as a top-ranked figure of letters in his many travels throughout Europe and America in great part because he had such a winning way with both the public and other authors.[9] The likeability factor played an important role in the regard of their audience and their literary friends for such other affable figures as Howells, Benchley, Lardner, and Henry Adams—all of whom were treated as more important literary figures in their time than they have been by posterity.

Comfort with Public Scrutiny and Judgment

Journalists grow used to having the product of their efforts displayed for public inspection, and it can encourage some to be thick skinned when it comes to dealing with negative critical judgment. However, it is remarkable how sensitive to criticism many journalist–literary figures became after they achieved literary success, given their general resilience and ability to bounce back from failure in their early days. Although some were practically overnight successes, others—including Dreiser, London,

Thurber, Caldwell, John Steinbeck, Sinclair Lewis, James Agee, and Conrad Richter—had to overcome much early rejection by publishers, public indifference to their work, or hostile critical reaction. In some cases, such as those of London and Lewis, the early rejections only further fed a hunger for celebrity once success was achieved and a need to engage in great showmanship and bizarre public antics designed to keep themselves in the spotlight.

PERSEVERANCE

The determination to overcome odds and the belief in persevering against the world that are part of the journalist's professional self-image were notable features of these writers' careers. For many, the scorn shown by critics for their least successful literary efforts—particularly as their talents declined with age and overexposure—amounted to emotional torture, and they often developed colossal contempt for those who dispensed what was often fair and justified criticism of their more problematic literary works. Yet a sizeable number who were written off by critics as having lost the edge persisted in their writing. Some, such as London and Hemingway, became embittered at their pummeling by the critics and fought back in their public writings; others, such as Dreiser and Anderson, tended to ignore external factors and to churn out fiction long after they had become the subjects of ridicule, with some of the most savage criticism coming from their own friends and fellow artists. Steinbeck, who took a beating from critics in his late career, acknowledged that it might have been best if he had quit writing, but he persisted—including taking on many journalistic tasks and proudly taking on the mantle of the journalist, despite his detractors, who complained of his abandoning fiction for prosaic nonfictional projects. In his words, "When you do something for over thirty years, when you hardly think about anything else but how to put your experiences into the right words, you can't just turn it off and go play in the garden."[10]

THE SEARCH FOR OUTSIDE TARGETS

Many of these writers were in a state of perpetual struggle with life from their early days, and they found first in journalism and then in literature a place for working out a host of psychic stresses and emotional issues. The Freudian concept of transference—the tendency of human beings to transfer psychological needs and frustrations unconsciously onto targets outside of one's own personality—was reflected in a full range of neuroses and obsessions that they expressed in their journalism, their literature, and their quest for fame. Paine launched vitriolic and obsessive crusades against the inequities of the world (linked, one suspects, to the many failures of his early life in England). While imprisoned in France during the French Revolution, he worked on his book, *The Age of Reason*, which attacked Christian teachings, and plotted to slip it out so he could gain public attention. Bierce expressed a bitter view of life (rooted in his anger at his parents and the violence of his Civil War military experiences), which was manifested in his attack columns, where he relished drawing attention to himself by launching broadsides against preachers, patriots, and other mouthers of public pieties. Thurber gave voice to a darkly comic vision of his family and his early years (revolving around his mother's refusal to get him proper medical treatment for an eye injury that led to his blindness), and he did not mind alienating family members while building his literary reputation. All manifested huge grudges against the world and a desire for success as compensation for the emotional turbulence and disappointments of their lives.

A Grandiose Self-Image

A wag once called journalists "shy egomaniacs," which may explain why many of these writers—a number of whom were anything but shy—ultimately found themselves so out of place in the journalism profession. With its opportunity to give a journalist a "front row seat on history" and a regular forum for expression, journalism has drawn into it people with a powerful sense of personal destiny and a visionary's certainty about life's purpose. But both can prove to be difficult to satisfy in a profession circumscribed by commercial pressures, editorial oversight, the boundaries of public opinion, and a timidity about unshackled speech. The freedoms available in the conventions of fiction writing proved too alluring for many to resist. In fiction they found a place to tell a story that journalistic formulas did not have a place for, to give rein to one's imagination and lyrical talents, and to soar beyond the limitations of "the facts" as the press presented them and to let their personal vision shape their picture of the world. It also is worth noting that since society has come to value achievement in art more highly than journalism, it is no surprise that some of the profession's largest egos would reach for success on the grandest scale available to them. Tom Wolfe—despite his successes as a literary journalist—turned to fiction writing late in his career. "It is hard to explain what an American dream the idea of writing a novel was" during his years growing up, he said. "The Novel was no mere literary form. It was a psychological phenomenon. It was a cortical fever."[11]

Lack of a Future in Journalism

In exiting the journalism profession, many of these writers were only following a path taken by other newsroom hands—whether they had literary aspirations or not. The daily newspaper business has long depended on a steady flow of young people willing to work energetically but cheaply. As the loose cannons in the assembly line of the daily publication, reporters, in particular, have career spans limited by the levels of enthusiasm and endurance that they can continue to summon up for the job. Whereas journalist–literary figures left to pursue art, many of their colleagues found jobs in public relations, political consulting, teaching, and other places. Given that many journalists have faced the prospect of ending up as "gray-haired, humpbacked slobs, dodging garnishes" in copy desk jobs, as Ben Hecht and Charles MacArthur put it in their play, *Front Page*, it is no wonder that the promise of a life of literary success would look like the preferable option.[12] Still, it would be misleading to imply that all journalist–literary figures escaped frustration and found creative freedom by moving from journalism to the world of literature. Many discovered that the publishers of literary works were also dictated to by public taste and the demands of the marketplace, and a number feuded with their literary publishers with the same vehemence that they had with newsroom overseers. Even in modern times, censorship was a real threat in the book publishing field—especially for those writers who grew radicalized in their political opinions and outspoken in their sexual expression. Some established journalistic writers, including Dreiser, Sinclair, Dos Passos, Agee, Henry Miller, and James Branch Cabell, experienced periodic rejection of their books by publishers unwilling to countenance their unconventional views and mores, their graphic language and expression, or all of the above. However, many of these writers were fortunate to live at a time when family-owned publishing ventures, as opposed to the corporate-controlled publishing houses of today, were willing to take a chance on an author who was not yet established or who came recommended by other writers. This relationship worked at the other end of a career, too, as was the case when the publisher Alfred Knopf suggested to Richter that one of his later novels was not up to his usual standards and perhaps should not be published—a judgment to which Richter humbly submitted.[13] (This was advice that some other journalist–literary figures in their declining years might have been well served to receive and follow.)

Publicity to Deal with the Plight of Women in Journalism

In the tradition of Nellie Bly, with her famous stunt where she faked insanity to expose the conditions in a mental asylum and her round-the-world trip, women journalists have sometimes been attracted (or virtually forced) to project themselves into the public spotlight as a way to gain career success within a profession that traditionally has offered limited opportunities for females in the newsroom. The journalist-novelist Djuna Barnes is best known for her experimental novels of the 1920s and 1930s, but she began her career as a stunt journalist for a variety of New York City newspapers. Psychologically oriented critics have speculated that Barnes's role as a seductive stunt reporter who was fascinated with people who displayed their neuroses in public and specialized in drawing shocking material out of celebrity interviews was motivated by her own inner emotional turmoil rooted in childhood experiences of incest and psychological abuse. This fits, they say, with the willingness of news organizations to exploit women by offering them celebrity-making assignments—but only if they were willing to display their sexuality or their vulnerability in provocative ways.[14]

The Consequences of Celebrity throughout the Centuries

The benefits and the drawbacks in managing a public reputation were major preoccupations for several American journalist–literary figures, including Paine, Bly, Harte, London, Parker, Mailer, and Capote, even though they gained celebrity status in different decades with different ground rules for achieving fame.

The American colonists, with their mobile society and their recognition of the expanding importance of public opinion, made a highly receptive audience for Paine, who sought the center stage from the moment he took on the role of propagandist for the cause of American independence after arriving in Pennsylvania from England in 1774. Paine lived his life on the crest of great historic events, first helping to foment them and then taking full advantage of the international fame brought him by his role as the passionate champion of the rights of mankind. Rising to nearly instantaneous celebrity status with his bestselling pamphlet, *Common Sense,* Paine also came to understand the sufferings inherent in the fickle nature of fame. In 1792, when the mayor of Calais announced Paine's arrival and his election to the French National Convention to help write a new French constitution, a huge crowd assembled and shouted, "Vive la nation! Vive Tom Paine!" The trip to Paris took three days, and great throngs gathered to greet him in the towns on the way. However, in short order Paine was imprisoned after leaders of the convention, taking a radical turn, turned on him for his opposition to the execution of Louis XVI. When Paine was released from prison, even President Thomas Jefferson, a good friend, had to meet with him privately to avoid being associated with a man who was under constant attack for his radical views about religion and world revolution. Paine's ignominious last years—when he unsuccessfully sought remuneration from Congress for his work in behalf of the American Revolution and blasted in words and print those who circulated rumors about his private life—testify to the growing power of the media to distribute both glory and disparagement to a literary celebrity.[15]

Throughout the nineteenth century, the growing emphasis on celebrity building as a way to advance a journalist–literary figure's prospects left an increasing number of broken careers in its wake. Bly, who was probably the most famous journalist of this period to build her reputation on celebrity-building stunts, profited enormously from her public antics, but she also suffered from bouts of severe depression throughout her life. There are those who believe that her seeking after celebrity—which she pursued relentlessly throughout her career—was compensation for a troubled inner and early family life. The downward curve of Harte's writing life amply demonstrates celebrity's negative side, with intensive media attention, if not the culprit, at least a catalyst in his fall from public grace. More by luck than anything else, Harte found himself "one of the idols of Gilded Age America," as biographer Richard O'Connor put it, and an example of how the industrialized mass media could catapult someone who had written only a few lines of humorous verse and a handful of short stories into the role of the authentic new voice of the American West. Howells—as editor of *The Atlantic Monthly*, which had offered Harte a sizeable sum for his future stories—described the "princely progress" of Harte's journey when he moved east from California. Similarly, an English periodical noted how Harte's "slightest movement is chronicled in every newspaper, and where he stops for a few days, a kind of 'Bret Harte Circular' appears in the daily press." Harte relished the media attention, perhaps because he had a premonition that his good luck was about to run out. In short order, Harte failed to produce acceptable work for the *Atlantic* and other magazines that had contracted for it, fell into debt and unreliable ways, and soon dropped out of critical favor. Twain, who came to loathe the high-handed person that the easy-going Harte of San Francisco days became as a celebrity, commented that it was "a pity that we cannot escape from life when we are young" and added that Harte as a polished shell of his old self "had lived all of his life that was worth living." (In his later years, Twain also opined darkly about this pattern in his own fate: "Fame is a vapor, popularity an accident; the only earthly certainty oblivion.")[16]

Even as a famous author, London, like many other foreign correspondents of the time, wanted to emulate Richard Harding Davis, the "Great White Scribe" of the period. For his war reporting in China and Korea during the Russo-Japanese War, London built up a large entourage with hired horses, pack ponies, grooms, a manservant, and an interpreter. While covering the Mexican revolution for *Collier's*, he hardly left the bars of Veracruz and Tampico, except for two days riding with the rebels in a Baden Powell hat and white Palm Beach suit. London's movie star good looks and his "self-dramatizing style of existence," as one biographer put it, led Ford Maddox Ford to comment that he was a "Peter Pan" who could not grow up and who lived his own stories so intensely that he ended up believing them. London's self-aggrandizing ventures and his emotional instability led biographer Andrew Sinclair to say London "knew that his power of persuasion was so great that he could convince nearly anyone who met him or read his work of anything he wanted to say about himself. It was a dangerous gift for a man who liked to exaggerate and saw himself as something of a hero."[17]

By the advent of the age of television, Hollywood movies, and electronic media in the twentieth century, the intensity of celebrity life had ratcheted up to levels where it played on the psychopathologies of writers whose pursuit of fame often was inseparable from the core of their literary accomplishments. Parker, for example, was celebrated for her talent as a celebrity as much as or more than her literature. She had a genius for gaining press exposure, and her public image—witty, sophisticated, sexually free but scornful of men, a flapper-era hedonist—made her a model and an inspiration for certain women of her time. Parker showed up in all the romantic literary spots of the 1920s—including Hemingway's Left Bank cafes and the glittering Long Island parties of Fitzgerald and Ring Lardner where the flow of illegal alcohol was readily available to the rich and famous—and she fit well into the 1920s' "hysterical insistence at having fun" and the era's ethic that nothing was really worth believing in anymore. Parker was an emotional mess throughout her life, and she never tried to hide it. In fact, it is fair to say that she capitalized on the disastrous elements of her personal life for her subject matter, and it became a major attraction for those drawn to her short fiction, her celebrity journalism, and her much-circulated witticisms. With her platform as a member of the Algonquin Round Table, Parker's quips were spread nationwide in the "Conning Tower" columns of fellow Round Table member Franklin Pierce Adams. In a sense, Parker's life was her most important creation—and she played the celebrity game with the same aggressive appetite as she did everything else in her life. The spectacle that she created of herself—as a clever alcoholic helplessly attracted to worthless men—contributed to the public's fascination with her, as it often is with celebrities who are willing to display their self-destructive life choices for public inspection.[18]

Mailer, in a similar fashion, was described as someone whose "career was always in public" and "who put himself forward" in ways that demonstrated a "psychotic" need for publicity. In his desire to achieve the celebrity stature of Hemingway and Twain, in his habit of subconsciously mimicking the accents of other writers, in his fear that his writing could not stand on its own, Mailer was a "kind of intellectual hermit crab, looking for the cast-off shell of other animals to throw himself into," said one fellow novelist, a figure of "emptiness [walking] on two legs" whose needs were fed by the "psychopathology" of his times, where people were desperate for a cultural hero and notoriety had become an entertainment for the masses. "One of [Mailer's] darkest secrets was that a large part of him belonged more to the performing arts than to literature," wrote biographer Peter Manso. As a professional public figure, Mailer never let good taste, dignity, or self-restraint deter him from brazen displays of self-promotion (or *Advertisements for Myself*, as he titled one book). Mailer became an instant literary star with the publication of *The Naked and the Dead*, which was based on his experiences as a soldier in the Pacific theatre in World War II. But his failure to follow it up with another blockbuster novel gnawed at him, and he spent the 1950s obsessed with his faded public image. By the 1960s he had come up with the formula to launch himself back into the literary limelight: the writer as the hero of his own story, as he came to develop it in *The Armies of the Night*, his account of his involvement in the Vietnam War protest march to the Pentagon. Mailer demonstrated a flagrant egotism, and the press rewarded his behavior, both good and bad, with relentless attention. His style—pushing the boundaries, living on the edge, always seeking opportunities to be provocative—became the benchmark for a new kind of manic celebrity figure in a media age where no self-aggrandizing stunt goes unrewarded. In raising narcissism to a public art, Mailer believed in the idea of the writer as an outsized personality who can change the current of the culture. In this context, Mailer's career can be seen as a phenomenon in itself, a triumph of the "star system in literature," as critic Pauline Kael said of his biography of Marilyn Monroe, where "you can feel him bucking up for the big time . . . (when) he starts flying it's so exhilarating you want to applaud."[19]

Like Mailer, Capote was a legend in his lifetime, beginning when he began hanging out at bars and cultivating the New York City high life as a teenager and then earning praise as one of the country's rising novelists before he had anything serious published. For some New York socialites, his greatest accomplishment was a celebrity gala he threw in 1966 for the *Washington Post*'s Katharine Graham, an event that some members of the press dubbed the social event of the decade. As the most prominent openly gay personality of his generation, Capote cut a fascinating figure to many; he gained widespread exposure as a regular guest on television talk shows, and his high voice and flamboyant mannerisms made him a national star well before the publication of *In Cold Blood* made his literary reputation. His death from drug and alcohol abuse (while staying at the home of the ex-wife of television host Johnny Carson in Hollywood) was widely interpreted as the result of the pressures that American public life could put on a gay person and someone who lived too much in the media spotlight. Capote blamed many of his problems on his literary tribulations in finishing *In Cold Blood*, and he was prone to saying that the writing of the book would kill him. He regretted a ruse he employed to get access to the murderers' stories, appearing to side with them to earn their confidence. Along the way, he came to like one of them, Perry Smith, and wrestled with conflicted feelings as the death sentence drew near. But Capote's hunger for success was too great to let his qualms deter him, and he recognized that his "real life" novel would have greater impact if the killers were executed. Although he often flaunted it, Capote used alcohol and drugs in the same way as many other journalist–literary figures—to self-medicate and to blunt the distress of a painful upbringing and the abandonment anxieties it engendered in him. Even as a young man, when Capote was fired from his job as a copy boy at *The New Yorker*, he had a flair for the dramatic and a habit of turning his victimhood into positive gain. After Robert Frost accused Capote of snubbing him during a reading at a writers' conference, the magazine released the copy boy for allegedly passing himself off as a writer for the magazine. Although Capote insisted that he had been misunderstood, he came to see the incident as a boon to his career, since it ultimately allowed him to develop as a writer outside the strictures of a journalistic organization.[20]

Not all the journalist–literary figures wrote their finest literary works in their early careers or in the days closest to their journalistic experiences, but a large number did. Critics have sometimes tried to explain this phenomenon—both with journalist–literary figures as well as other artists—by pointing out how the experiences of real life make for the best material for a writer. But as artists move into circles of the literary elite, they can lose touch with what is authentic in their lives. This was something that worried a number of these writers. Norris, for example, wrote a number of stories and articles explaining how a writer might hope to fend off being ruined by success. (Norris, unfortunately, did not have time to test his theories; he died at age 32 before he could fully experience a life of fame.) Lewis, too, always feared success would ruin him and—after *Main Street* became a critical and popular success—reportedly said, "This will change me. This will change everything!" After winning the Nobel Prize, he also is said to have exclaimed, "This is the end of me. This is fatal. I cannot live up to it."[21]

Fame is often a mixed blessing, particularly for people who must manage difficult interior lives in an appearance-driven world that has become dominated by the combined forces of media, marketing, and public relations. The drive for success and the love of the center stage among the literary figures who emerged from a journalistic background was often a function of pain they had endured and an attempt to fill the empty emotional space left by early life traumas, the inheritance of psychological disorders, and an attraction to lifestyles that substituted intensity of experience for dealing with emotional wounds. The lives of many of the best-known and most successful of the journalist–literary figures can be seen as the embodiments of the lesson that in a capitalistic society artistic vision—and the life forces that produce it—rarely remain untouched by the seductions of the marketplace. Unfortunately, these figures found that the existence to which literary triumph led them could not always sustain the vitality, the authenticity, and the determination of their early careers, nor did their bodies and their nervous systems hold up as they aged under the strain of damaged psyches living within larger-than-life public personas. The celebrity collapsing under the load of his or her accumulated emotional "baggage" has become an archetype in an age where the disastrous personal events that can befall the famous fascinate us as much as do the artifacts of their success. Journalism's contribution to the pantheon of celebrities who have both risen and fallen in the crucible of artistic accomplishment has been considerable and proven in innumerable instances that life in the spotlight seldom cures the pain of a traumatic past or the emotional residue of a troubled career.

NOTES

1. Scott Elledge, *E. B. White: A Biography* (New York: Norton, 1986[1984]), 324.
2. Anne Edwards, *Road to Tara: The Life of Margaret Mitchell* (New Haven, CN: Ticknor and Fields, 1983), 212, 216–25, 256, 263, 273–81, 316.
3. See Doug Underwood, *Journalism and the Novel: Truth and Fiction, 1700–2000* (Cambridge, UK: Cambridge University Press, 2008) for a discussion of what is meant by the term *journalist–literary figure* and an appendix of more than three hundred figures who are described as writers of fiction and/or literary nonfiction who had an important career in journalism and built their literary work on a foundation of journalistic research, reporting, and professional experience.
4. Jack Fruchtman Jr., *Thomas Paine: Apostle of Freedom* (New York: Four Walls Eight Windows, 1994), 269, 275–76, 293–331; Linda H. Davis, *Badge of Courage: The Life of Stephen Crane* (Boston: Houghton Mifflin, 1998), 291–330; Richard O'Connor, *Bret Harte; A Biography* (Boston: Little, Brown, 1966), 125, 128–33; W. A. Swanberg, *Dreiser* (New York: Scribner's, 1965), 387–88; Marion Meade, *Dorothy Parker: What Fresh Hell Is This?* (New York: Penguin, 1989[1988]), xvii, 345; Gerald Clarke, *Capote* (New York: Ballantine, 1989[1988]), 513; Doug Underwood, *Chronicling Trauma: Journalists and Writers on Violence and Loss* (Urbana: University of Illinois Press, 2011), 173–74, 178, 190–91, 183–84.
5. Ernest Hemingway, *Green Hills of Africa* (Middlesex, UK: Penguin, 1972[1935]), 23, 26.
6. James B. Colvert, *Stephen Crane* (San Diego, CA: Harcourt Brace Jovanovich, 1984), 61.
7. Underwood, *Journalism and the Novel*, 103–4.
8. Ernest Hemingway, *The Sun Also Rises* (New York: Scribner, 2003[1926]), 51.
9. Richard Dilworth Rust, "Washington Irving," in *Dictionary of Literary Biography, Volume 250: Antebellum Writers in New York: Second Series* (Detroit: Gale, 2002).
10. Jackson J. Benson, *John Steinbeck, Writer: A Biography* (New York: Penguin, 1990[1984]), 1024; Underwood, *Journalism and the Novel*, 171.
11. Underwood, *Journalism and the Novel*, 164.
12. Ben Hecht and Charles MacArthur, *The Front Page: From Theatre to Reality* (Hanover, NH: Smith and Kraus, 2002), 86.

13. David R. Johnson, *Conrad Richter: a Writer's Life* (University Park: Pennsylvania State University Press, 2001), 305.
14. Underwood, *Chronicling Trauma*, 33–34, 166, 170.
15. Fruchtman, *Thomas Paine*, 15–16.
16. Underwood, *Chronicling Trauma*, 63, 170; Richard O'Connor, *Bret Harte; A Biography* (Boston: Little Brown, 1966), 124–25, 129, 137, 146; Twain is quoted in Albert Bigelow Paine, *Mark Twain: A Biography* (New York: Harper & Brothers, 1912), 373.
17. Andrew Sinclair, *Jack: A Biography of Jack London* (New York: Pocket, 1977), 109, 123, 210–11.
18. Meade, *Dorothy Parker*, 80, 84, 86.
19. Mary V. Dearborn, *Mailer: A Biography* (Boston: Houghton Mifflin, 1999), 7–8, 109, 142, 321, 325; Peter Manso, *Mailer: His Life and Times* (New York: Washington Square, 2008[1985]), 274, 310, 327–28, 335, 700. Quotations all appear in Manso biography, including from the critic Alfred Kazin, novelists Alan Kapelner and Chandler Brossard, and Rhoda Lazare Wolf.
20. Clarke, *Capote*, 76–77.
21. Richard Lingeman, *Sinclair Lewis: Rebel from Main Street* (New York: Random House, 2002), 163; Mark Schorer, *Sinclair Lewis: An American Life* (New York: McGraw-Hill, 1961), 543.

Chapter 8

Ernest Hemingway in *Esquire*

Contextualizing Arnold Gingrich's Posthumous Portrait(s) of Man and Artist, 1961–73

John Fenstermaker

In April 1965, Arnold Gingrich, publisher and editor of *Esquire* and a major figure in contemporary magazine publishing, helped design *Esquire*'s Seventh Literary Symposium as part of the Fine Arts Festival at the University of North Carolina. The magazine's program responsibility was "The Novelist as Journalist," this keynote idea coming from Norman Podhoretz: "We may be looking in the wrong place for the achievements of the creative literary imagination when we look for them only where they were last seen—in novels and plays."[1]

Gingrich had long recognized this general truth, Ernest Hemingway embodying for him a singular instance of a writer talented both as novelist and journalist. Founding editor of *Esquire* in 1933, Gingrich published 16 Nobel Laureates over forty years, beginning with Hemingway in the magazine's premiere issue. He appreciated and consistently affirmed Hemingway's creative literary imagination and fine writing beyond his fiction: evident early in *Esquire* (27 journalistic essays, 1933–39) and in *Death in the Afternoon* (1932) and *Green Hills of Africa* (1935); and, posthumously, in the poetic moments of *A Moveable Feast* (1964). From the author's death in 1961 until Gingrich's retirement in 1973, *Esquire*, alone among American periodicals, continually published (in 34 issues) wide-ranging professional commentary and assessment of Hemingway, the man and his work. Thus, in two very different decades, Arnold Gingrich, working in the first primarily with the journalism but in both exclusively within *Esquire* magazine, acted deliberately and prominently to energize and shape debate over Ernest Hemingway's critical reputation.

Following July 2, 1961, journalists worldwide reacted to the death of Ernest Hemingway—renowned author and celebrity, and more recently, hero-avatar in men's magazines. (The latter featured a new postwar masculinity believed to be epitomized in this writer.[2]) Throughout the 1950s, the media had published, reprinted, and discussed Ernest Hemingway, man and artist. At his death, as Matthew Bruccoli has wryly observed, Hemingway's roles as man of letters and public figure encompassed "divergent personae—hunter, fisherman, soldier, aesthetician, patriot, military strategist, yachtsman, drinker, womanizer, gourmet, sportsman, philosopher, naturalist, intellectual, anti-intellectual, traveler, war correspondent, boxer, big-game hunter—and author."[3] Across the mainstream media, from intellectual journals to weekly magazines and daily newspapers, Hemingway's suicide produced widespread reverberations—initiating, often defining, the earliest critical assessments of his life and work. Uniformly, these first postmortems addressed Ernest Hemingway, fiction writer; they ignored his "divergent personae" in periodicals and the press—both as writer and subject.

***

Ernest Hemingway began his career as a journalist—publishing 15,000 words in the high school *Trapeze*, 1916–17, and more than 170 items for the *Toronto Star*, 1920–24. He ended his career as a journalist—chronicling for *Life* magazine the competition between Spain's finest matadors, brothers-in-law Miguel Ordonez and Luis Miguel Dominguin, in the summer of 1959.[4] Midcareer, he reported on "war and war's alarms" in Spain, China, and Europe for the *North American Newspaper Alliance, Ken, PM* (1937–41), and *Collier's* (1944). More important, during the 1930s, he developed a personalized nonfiction/journalism, a mode he initiated in *Death in the Afternoon,* a history of and an apologia for the Spanish bullfight tradition (1932), and *Green Hills of Africa*, a "nonfiction" novel about a month-long African safari (1935); he perfected this subgenre in letter-essays in *Esquire* (1933–36). With this latter work encouraged and facilitated by editor Arnold Gingrich, Hemingway appeared in 30 of *Esquire*'s first 33 monthly issues—effectively guaranteeing the magazine's successful launch in October 1933 and its initial staying power. In the heart of the Depression, from 1934 through 1937, the magazine sold more than 10 million copies—at 50 cents a copy.[5] Equally important, Hemingway regularly appeared before an audience of extraordinary size as the complete "man of letters": insider, sportsman, celebrity, connoisseur, literary artist, and, not least, journalist.

Over 40 years (1933–73), Arnold Gingrich served *Esquire* variously as editor, publisher, and senior vice president. Hemingway's relationship with *Esquire* in the 1930s has been variously commented on. Unexamined has been the author's posthumous presence in the magazine during Gingrich's later years: more than 60 separate appearances in 34 issues over the 12 years from 1961 to 1973, including 9 in *Esquire*'s fortieth anniversary issue (October 1973). Roughly half of these pieces are article length: critical assessments of Hemingway's art; anecdotes analyzing his character; reprintings of his *Esquire* writings; mentions of him on broad cultural topics in essays by various hands. Readers' responses to this continually emerging figure enliven "The Sound and the Fury" letters section, and Hemingway appears on the "Publisher's Page" and in "Editor's Notes." Collectively, these voices in *Esquire* effect the most extensive commentary on Hemingway's life and work (here also including the journalism and nonfiction) to be found in any American periodical in the first decade following his death.

***

After graduating Phi Beta Kappa from the University of Michigan in 1925, Arnold Gingrich joined Men's Wear Service Corporation. In 1931, he created *Apparel Arts* to rival the trade publication *Men's Wear*. Plans for *Esquire*, "The Magazine for Men," a male counterpart to *Vogue* and *Harper's Bazaar*, followed in 1932: "Conceived at the darkest moment of the depression . . . born at the dawn of the New Deal," it targeted men unimpeded by financial worries, the "first to buy the new styles . . . new models . . . to take up new vogues."[6] Additionally, it assumed a cultured cachet to attract the "serious reader, interested in *Esquire*'s lettered side."[7] Gingrich soon became renowned as a "headhunter of famous authors."[8] First among this elite was Ernest Hemingway.

Collecting his books and corresponding with Hemingway for some months before a chance meeting in New York, Gingrich, confident about the prospective magazine, persuaded Hemingway to become its pre-eminent and principal contributor. Additionally, Hemingway volunteered use of his name to recruit others.[9] For payment double that given others, beginning with the first issue (October 1933), Hemingway would write a letter (roughly 1,500 words) from wherever he was on any subject he wished. Through 1939, he contributed 27 essays and six stories, including among the latter what may be his finest: "The Snows of Kilimanjaro" (August 1936).

Hemingway's essays ranged from sport and travel to subjects conspicuously more serious: angling for marlin and the wonders of deep-sea life—from Key West, Bimini, and Cuba; the artistry and thrill of big-game hunting in Africa and the beauty of the country's wildlife and terrain—from Tanganyika; politics in Washington and abroad and fear of the inevitable next war in Europe—from Paris and Spain; and reflections on art and writing—from New York and Key West—including his quarrel with professional critics—William Saroyan, Alexander Woollcott, Heywood Broun, Gilbert Seldes, and Westbrook Pegler—who had been assailing him particularly for selling out his talent and ignoring the country's economic woes. Throughout, in the unflinching first-person voice of teacher and insider, world traveler, sportsman, and hardworking professional, he defended a personal vision of the man of letters—and of himself in that role. After 1936, Hemingway's activities—covering the war in Spain, divorcing second wife Pauline and marrying third wife Martha, moving to Cuba, extensive travel, and beginning *For Whom the Bell Tolls* (1940)—caused him to cease writing for *Esquire* in 1939. Hemingway's last contact with Gingrich in this period occurred in 1940.[10]

***

Journalistic coverage of Hemingway during the transition from the forties to the fifties featured two important profiles: Malcolm Cowley's upbeat, biographical "A Portrait of Mr. Papa" in *Life* magazine in January 1949 and Lillian Ross's more personal and controversial "How Do You Like It Now, Gentlemen?" in the *New Yorker* in May 1950. Ross amply recorded an informal Hemingway speaking spontaneously—remarks never humble, and not always serious, mature, or grammatical—producing a mixed assessment of man and artist, even some negative media reception in 1950 of Hemingway's *Across the River and into the Trees.*[11] Positive press returned with *The Old Man and the Sea* (1952), which brought Hemingway a Pulitzer (1953) followed by the Nobel Prize (1954).

At *Esquire*, Arnold Gingrich became publisher in 1952, the year of *The Old Man and the Sea.* By 1958, that novel and Hemingway's Pulitzer and Nobel prizes—particularly given the writer's earlier successful association with *Esquire*—made Hemingway uniquely attractive to the magazine.

When planning *The Armchair Esquire*, a collection from the magazine's first 25 years, Gingrich acted. He selected the last three of Hemingway's six *Esquire* stories: "The Denunciation" (November 1938), "The Butterfly and the Tank" (December 1938), and "Night Before Battle" (February 1939), the three connected by the Spanish Civil War and Chicote's Bar in Madrid. When approached, Hemingway balked, wanting to rewrite two of the stories, even briefly initiating a lawsuit. Only "The Butterfly and the Tank" appeared in the *Armchair* collection (1958). Thus ended the personal interaction of author and editor, and Hemingway was dead within three years. Gingrich waited eight years before bringing this flap to the magazine, even then doing so without rancor, in a manner lighthearted and humorous.[12]

Regarding Hemingway, Gingrich pressed on carefully. In 1959, *Esquire* published Eric Sevareid's "Mano-a-Mano," recording Hemingway's involvement with the bullfighting competitions between Antonio Ordonez and Luis Dominguin.[13] Hemingway's reporting on these competitions was a project for *Life* magazine (1960), and, finally, for Scribner's in the posthumous *The Dangerous Summer* (1985). To a degree, Gingrich pre-empted both publishers with Sevareid's piece. Nor does this portrait conclude Hemingway's presence in *Esquire* in the 1950s. In the wide-ranging "The Flowering Dream: Notes on Writing" (December 1959), Carson McCullers praises Hemingway, "the most cosmopolitan of all American writers."[14] (A year later, adjusting to a new decade in December 1960, Gingrich may have wondered whether Lester Cohen's ". . . And the Sinner: Horace Liveright" would upset Hemingway. In 1925, Boni and Liveright was publisher of, among other successful writers, Anderson, Dreiser, Faulkner, O'Neill, and Hemingway. Fortunately, the article's attention to Hemingway proved less than fleeting. He and Faulkner received the identical, lone sentence: "Mr. Hemingway had a flop and was dismissed." "Mr. Faulkner had a flop . . ."[15])

Hemingway's death in July 1961 unfettered Gingrich, and he committed to early and continuous Hemingway coverage: professional voices, various perspectives, even multiple pieces in a single issue. In the beginning, Gingrich wanted Hemingway; from the author's death to the editor's retirement in 1973, Gingrich wanted Hemingway. He made a matter-of-fact rationale explicit in June 1967: "There are people about whom anything new is news. Ernest Hemingway dead is still far more newsworthy than almost any writer you can think of who is still living."[16]

***

Gingrich's personal assessments first appeared in *Esquire* February and June 1937, after Hemingway stopped appearing regularly in the magazine. Gingrich rebutted certain virulent personal criticism: "They can't forgive his fishing and hunting. They wish he would grow up and face the ugly facts of our changing times . . . season his literary soup to the moment's taste with a sprinkling of class-consciousness, of politico-sociological salt. They forget that politics, as such, is the death of art." Regarding Hemingway's art, "Like Cezanne, Hemingway not only worked out a new way of setting things down but, far more important, he worked out a new way of looking at things before setting them down."[17] Hemingway's professionalism, critical to the magazine early in its existence, drew praise from his editor: "For the first two years he was . . . [*Esquire*'s] most conscientious contributor. He had to send his copy in from all over the world and he never let us down. He more than once chartered planes to reach a point where he could dispatch his piece in time to make a deadline. . . . He was there when we needed him and as long as we needed him. He never needed us."[18]

Esquire reprinted "The Snows of Kilimanjaro" in September 1949, Hemingway's only appearance in the magazine in the 1940s. The editorial introducing "Snows" again emphasized the responsible professional. In 1936, Hemingway owed *Cosmopolitan* and *Esquire* stories. Because the former's deadline came first, "The Short Happy Life of Francis Macomber," intended for *Esquire*, went to *Cosmopolitan*. Regardless, Hemingway honored *Esquire*'s deadline, impressively presenting a second African story, "The Snows of Kilimanjaro"—by 1949, already a classic. Gingrich's memorializings in 1937 and the praising note of 1949 join with Sevareid's and McCuller's pieces in 1959. Together, they constitute a positive, albeit fortuitous, portrait of Hemingway in *Esquire* drawn during the first 12 years after his leaving the magazine: Hemingway is a conscientious professional; he is a literary artist ("Macomber," "Snows"); he is a sophisticated sportsman and man of the world (master of the African savannah and an authority on Spanish taurine culture).

The 12 years from 1961 to Gingrich's retirement in 1973 produce fuller sketches, creating multiple Hemingway likenesses. Important discussion appears over three periods. Each features "authorities," in addition to Gingrich: Andrew Turnbull, Norman Mailer, and Gay Talese, 1961–63; Malcolm Muggeridge, Jerome Beatty, Malcolm Cowley, Scott Fitzgerald, and Matthew Bruccoli, 1966–68; and Lillian Ross, A. E. Hotchner, Malcolm Cowley, Truman Capote, Carlos Baker, George Plimpton, and

Mary Hemingway, 1969–73. The first years focus primarily on Hemingway the man, only secondarily on the literary artist; the later years focus on man and artist, Malcolm Cowley's "Papa and the Parricides" constituting a major critical statement. Each contributor speaks freely. Among the variety of viewpoints, patterns arise and subjects recur—one such: F. Scott Fitzgerald.

Fitzgerald was young Arnold Gingrich's "idol." Between February 1934 and July 1941, *Esquire* published 45 Fitzgerald pieces, and in 1962, Gingrich edited a volume of Fitzgerald's Pat Hobby stories for Scribner's. Inevitably, comparison of Fitzgerald and Hemingway comprises a primary pattern. Clear when Gingrich expresses his own judgments is the tension he feels touching mutual justice. Despite preferring Fitzgerald, he communicates genuine gratitude for Hemingway—in the author's own right and for his role in giving the magazine an early history. Gingrich undoubtedly considered Andrew Turnbull's authoritative *Scott Fitzgerald* (1962) crucial to reassessing both authors, especially Fitzgerald; he asked Turnbull to describe their relationship.

Gingrich began *Esquire*'s posthumous portrait(s) with his own affirmative "E. H.: A Coda from the Maestro" in October 1961, recapitulating his sentiments of 1937. He offers characteristic passages from Hemingway's essays of 1933–36: "Any good man would rather take chances any day with his life than with his livelihood and that is the main point about professionals that amateurs seem never to appreciate." He concludes with a comment sent him by Arnold Samuelson, the Maestro of Hemingway's "Monologue to the Maestro" (October 1935). Young Samuelson played the violin and worked a year for Hemingway in exchange for writing instruction. His coda constitutes a brief eulogy: "Ernest lived as long as he could. His last act was the most deliberate of his life. He had never written about his own suffering. He did it all without words in the language any man can understand."[19]

Robert Emmett Ginna's "Life in the Afternoon" in February 1962 captures Hemingway at home in Cuba in 1958. Ginna, hoping to film an interview, appears at the Finca with a magnum of Chateau Latour 1937 and his filmed interview with Igor Stravinski. A cordial Hemingway is initially noncommittal. When Ginna demonstrates knowledge of Hemingway's favorite books, authors, and ports of call, warmth grows. This essay reveals a celebrity, relaxed and unguarded. Hemingway calls Joyce "nasty" but soon retracts this epithet; he judges Mailer's general in *The Naked and the Dead* "crap," but again, he relents: "I ought to read it again. I might feel different, huh?" Ginna mentions *Esquire*. Hemingway expatiates: "I used to write for them. In the beginning for about two years. Gingrich . . . came down and conned me. He's a pretty good con man." Then, a courteous afterthought, "A nice guy, too. They paid me $1,000 for 'The Snows of Kilimanjaro.' . . . Do you know how they used to get me? They used to print the cover and put me—my name—on it, then leave the form open. That's how they got ['The Snows of Kilimanjaro']. What a con man gimmick! But I don't feel bitter."[20] Conversation and drinks further humanize the "great writer."

The next month Andrew Turnbull's excerpt from his *Scott Fitzgerald* radically alters the Hemingway portrait. Turnbull does not blink at Fitzgerald's peccadilloes, nor at Hemingway's often unconscionable behavior regarding his early friend and benefactor. Sensitive, comparative portraits develop in discussion of Fitzgerald's "Crack-Up" articles:

> Fitzgerald's attitude toward Hemingway was resignation tinged with jealousy. . . . Remembering the early days, Fitzgerald thought Hemingway a little lean on gratitude, but he half expected it in a man of Hemingway's pride and independence. . . . Hemingway's attitude toward Fitzgerald was a mixture of condescension and scorn. People . . . remember his saying that Fitzgerald was a 'rummy,' that he was washed up, that he had 'gone social' and hung around with the rich. *The Crack-Up* merely confirmed this view. On reading the first installment Hemingway wrote Perkins that it was so miserable—this whining in public. A writer could be a coward, but at least he should be a writer. Fitzgerald had gone from youth to senility without manhood in between. Nevertheless, it made Hemingway feel badly and he wished he could help. . . . Right up to the end, Fitzgerald peppered his letters to Perkins with questions about Ernest: where was he?—what was he doing?—how did he feel about the war? And Hemingway, for all his condescension, sent Fitzgerald a copy of *For Whom the Bell Tolls* inscribed: 'To Scott with affection and esteem.' 'It's a fine novel, better than anybody else writing could do,' Fitzgerald wrote back, and signed himself, 'With Old Affection.'[21]

Sally Belfrage's "The Haunted House of Ernest Hemingway" in February 1963 personalizes Hemingway by sketching in broad strokes materials and markings he left behind:

> [D]rawers are stuffed with prints of various wives, Gary Cooper, Ingrid Bergman, atrocity pictures from the Spanish Civil War, Antonio Ordonez, and African safari scenes. But relatively absent, despite the

> five thousand books spread throughout the house, are words of his own to indicate a man whose first importance was words. . . . His stone steps are crumbling, attacked by the roots of a ceiba tree which paradoxically shelters the roof. His books lie just as he left them, except for the worms; the penciled record of his weight, plus some comments on his days off diet and a few bullet holes remain on the dank bathroom wall. . . . There is a process of decay at work on the house that its master liked; and its master's likeness is what continues.[22]

Norman Mailer's "The Big Bite" (November 1962) and Gay Talese's "Looking for Hemingway" (July 1963) add little to Ginna, Turnbull, and Belfrage. Nevertheless, theirs are major voices, their portrait strokes deft. Mailer writes, "Ernest, so proud of his reputation. So fierce about it. His death was awful. Say it. It was the most difficult death in America since Roosevelt. One has still not recovered from Hemingway's death. One may never." Talese, contrasting Paris in the 1920s with Paris in the early 1950s at the inception of the *Paris Review*, paints in sharp images: "Once there was Ernest and Scott and Gertrude, and the wine flowed and the talk was good. But now there is Doc and Jimmy and George and Patsy, and the Scotch is light and the gossip is gossip."[23]

Esquire offered six partial portraits of the man Hemingway from 1961 to 1963—mostly, and finally, positive, despite his treatment of Fitzgerald. The six evaluative essays of 1966–68 balance man and artist. Journalist Malcolm Muggeridge and academic Jerome Beatty speak briefly. More substantive are Gingrich, Fitzgerald, Malcolm Cowley, and Matthew Bruccoli. Cowley, Fitzgerald, and Gingrich knew Hemingway. Cowley explores the art, and Gingrich reflects on the man; each shapes major judgments, and each raises significant questions. Bruccoli claims to add a front-page newspaper story to the Hemingway canon. Amid these contemporary viewpoints ring out striking previously unpublished words of Scott Fitzgerald from the thirties: "My Generation."

The first step is a misstep. Malcolm Muggeridge's piece stuns but, as a mode, proves singular. Purporting to review A. E. Hotchner's *Papa Hemingway* in June 1966, he savages Hemingway in a critique similar to certain anti-Hemingway rants in the thirties: "Hemingway destroyed himself as our world is destroying itself, by excessive indulgence in fantasy and self-delusion; by coming to believe in the ravings of his own ego as it strove with increasing hysteria to maintain itself against the ravages of flagging appetites, tired vanity and the flesh's weariness. The gunshot only completed the job. It was an act of final surrender, the ultimate succumbing to an irremediable hangover."[24]

Opposite in purpose and tone is Jerome Beatty's "Hanging Up on Hemingway" in February 1967, a half-page anecdote dating from the 1958 *Armchair Esquire* imbroglio. It is light and slightly unflattering to Hemingway, who talks nonstop over the phone about the stories Gingrich wants to republish. Hemingway is in a bar in Cuba, Beatty at home in Connecticut being repeatedly summoned to dinner by his wife, unaware of his interlocutor. Hemingway rambles on: "'When I looked over those stories,' he was saying for the umpteenth time, 'I told myself, I can write better than that.'" Beatty effects a none-too-graceful exit by rattling his pen against the phone, "making what I thought was the sound of an undersea cable breaking," then hanging up and rushing to dinner.[25]

The first substantive assessment of the second period appeared in December 1966: Arnold Gingrich's "Scott, Ernest, and Whoever," subtitled, "When Fitzgerald and Hemingway both sat at the movable feast, where was the head of the table?" Gingrich moves quickly to the "Crack-Up" essays: "After an article of Scott's had appeared that Ernest thought was too cry-babily self-revelatory, he wrote Scott a note about it in the most brutal way, using language you'd hesitate to use on a yellow dog. . . . The most that Scott ever let himself say against Ernest, and I know how strong the provocation must have been, was that 'Ernest was always ready to lend a helping hand to the one on the rung above him.'"[26]

Gingrich narrates further a negative personal experience with Hemingway unrelated to Fitzgerald. While fishing off Key West in 1937, Gingrich warned the novelist that the early part of the *To Have and Have Not* manuscript libeled John Dos Passos and wealthy socialite friends Grant and Jane Mason. (Hemingway had asked Gingrich to read the manuscript; the editor knew personally Dos Passos and the Masons.) Hemingway stumbles badly on the issue of his employing real people as models:

> "It's a little like having Cezanne include your features in a village scene," he pointed out modestly.
>
> I thought he was kidding, so I asked, "you aren't mixing your métiers, by any chance?"
>
> "Not really," he went on evenly. "After all, what I can't get through your Pennsylvania Dutch skull is that you're not dealing with some little penny-a-liner from the sports department of the *Chicago Daily*

> *News*. You're asking for changes in copy of a man who has been likened to Cezanne, for bringing a 'new way of seeing' into American literature."
>
> I almost fell out of the boat. This outsize ham was quoting *me* to my face, and without giving me any credit.[27]

Gingrich reminded Hemingway of the source of the Cezanne comparison. Hemingway effected excisions.

Gingrich strove to be fair: "Ernest was a far better friend to me, if I keep the scorecard absolutely straight, for many years than Scott ever was." Nor did his feelings blind him to Hemingway's artistic commitment: "[Scott] wanted to live his best stories more than he wanted to write them. And in a sense he almost always wrote for his living, at least whenever it came to a choice between that and living for his work." Yet, wondering whether there "may yet have to be a Hemingway revival," he concludes confidently, "there will never have to be another Fitzgerald revival, as he's had as many by now as he will ever need."[28]

Gingrich's honesty produces a remarkable admission: he fully expected Hemingway's portrait of Fitzgerald in *A Moveable Feast* to be "vicious." Instead, "I felt that Hemingway's portrait of Fitzgerald was the best portrait ever done in print, for as I read it there Scott stood again alive, at his inimitably exasperating best and worst. It simply *is* Scott, to the last breath and the last bat of an eyelash, and Scott would have recognized himself in every line."[29]

Turnbull and Gingrich focus heavily on the man. Malcolm Cowley's "Papa and the Parricides" in June 1967 responds to the first wave of literary criticism. Specifically, he criticizes efforts at "canoneering"—"posthumous assaults on his reputation"—by, among others, Vance Bourjaily, Stanley Edgar Hyman, Leslie Fiedler, and Dwight Macdonald. Their arguments for permanence among Hemingway's works range from as many as two novels and 15 or 20 stories to as few as a handful of stories. Cowley speaks of subjects, artistry, and Hemingway's place in American letters:

> Hemingway's real subject is the barriers that can be erected against death and loneliness and the void. . . . The discipline of one's calling and the further discipline required of every human being if he is to live as a man, not collapse into a jelly of emotions, is the strongest of those barriers. . . . Landscape, the weather, fishing and hunting, eating and drinking, talking around the fire and making love: those are the

> wonderful things in Hemingway. The ideas are interesting too, even though merely implied, for he was always more of an intellectual than he pretended to be . . . (103). With the necessary subtractions made, Hemingway's work as a whole is so clearly permanent, that, even if his reputation were destroyed for the moment, and the work buried, it would be exhumed after a hundred years, as Melville's was.[30]

Cowley's vision of discipline, in art and in facing the nada, underscores the central issues of Fitzgerald's "My Generation" (October 1968). Written in the thirties, it features American writers born at century's turn. Fitzgerald praises Hemingway, beginning by quoting noted critic Edmund Wilson on optimism in the previous generation: "[T]he force of the disillusion in *A Farewell to Arms* derives from Hemingway's original hope and belief. Without that, he could not have written of the war: 'Abstract words such as glory, honor, courage, or hallow were obscene besides concrete names of villages . . . of regiments . . . of dates.'" Postwar disillusion upends that earlier faith and hope. Nonetheless, Fitzgerald's disciplined postwar Hemingway at work shows him among the best: "George Gershwin was picking out tunes . . . in Tin Pan Alley and Ernest Hemingway was reporting the massacres in Smyrna."[31]

Cowley's worry over the Hemingway canon led naturally, if fortuitously, to Matthew Bruccoli's "Ernest Hemingway As Cub Reporter" in December 1968. Bruccoli argues that 18-year-old Hemingway, hiding under a Ford, witnessed a drug raid in which detectives shot two IRS agents (in action later much disputed). He reported the incident in an unsigned front-page story in the *Kansas City Star* (January 6, 1918). Bruccoli's most important observations ignore the subsequent disputes over the historical who, what, when, where, and why; like Cowley, his interest is Hemingway the artist: "[The article] presages not his style, but his fundamental approach to fiction—his distrust of anything he had not experienced—his commitment to describing things as they really happened, and not as they were supposed to happen."[32] This canonical "addition" completes the 1960s *Esquire* Hemingway portraits, but issues of canon open the Hemingway re-evaluation of the 1970s, spurred by the publication of a new novel.

Gingrich's "Publisher's Page" in October 1970 touted *Esquire*'s 34,000-word "Bimini," an excerpt from Hemingway's first posthumous novel, *Islands in the Stream.* He describes the Bimini he experienced with Hemingway in 1936 and identifies "real-life" models for major characters. He actively engages, also, the literary quality of *Islands.* He regrets the weak, unrevised parts two and three: in the first, the mother of Hudson's two sons—"transparently constructed of adolescent male wish-fulfillment"; in the second, "an endless and fruitless . . . chase of a U-boat crew." On the other hand, Paris reminiscences suggest *A Moveable Feast*, and two fishing scenes rival in quality *The Old Man and the Sea*. Gingrich concludes:

> As a short-story writer, Hemingway was remarkably consistent. As a novelist, he was an in-and-outer. His big book was not this, which he always called his big book, and which it might have become. But his big book, as his work now stands and must stand, is *For Whom the Bell Tolls*. His best book is still his first one, *The Sun Also Rises* because it is the most perfectly realized. . . . So what is left? Some of the best writing, in the non-fiction books: *A Moveable Feast, Death in the Afternoon*, always terribly underrated because it was about bullfighting, and *Green Hills of Africa*, given similar short shrift because it had to do with big-game hunting on safari. That Hemingway could still write on the master virtuoso level is proved by *A Moveable Feast*.[33]

Gingrich abandons all seriousness in the "Publisher's Page" introducing Denis Brian's "The Importance of Knowing Ernest" (February 1972), interviews with professionals who covered Hemingway. Gingrich believes that they "show an astonishing resemblance to the proverbial six blind Hindus describing an elephant from firsthand acquaintance with the object." He calls the results "a *Rashamon* vision of the author."[34] Brian asked each to respond to Ross's famous/infamous *New Yorker* interview, and their responses ranged:

Lillian Ross on her *New Yorker* profile: "Everybody found in it what he was looking for. It was sort of a Rorschach test on Hemingway."

A. E. Hotchner on why he wrote *Papa Hemingway*, a book that angered Mary Hemingway, producing a lawsuit: "Mary, you mean you've come to the point that you're going to have it told, but you're going to have it told third hand by somebody [i.e., Carlos Baker] who knows nothing about it?"

Malcolm Cowley on Carlos Baker as an unsympathetic biographer: "At times there were good stories and bad stories about what Hemingway did. And I caught Carlos Baker using the bad stories and leaving the good stories out, in cases where I knew that both were accessible to him."

Truman Capote, who could not stand Hemingway ("a total hypocrite. And he was mean"), on Baker's biography: "I never read a book in which I came away more with the feeling that the author hated the man he was writing about."

Carlos Baker on not liking Hemingway: "People will say anything, as you know, whether it's true or not. I'm rather thick skinned about this sort of thing. I just don't give a damn."

George Plimpton on Hemingway and Fitzgerald (where he invokes filmmaker Howard Hawks): "Hawks's films very often seem to be about very strong relationships between men, not homosexual, but friendships that are based on admiration and appreciation of skills, and that's why I think Hemingway and Fitzgerald were attracted to each other. . . . I think in his own private life he had these strong attachments with a whole succession of males. And then he had these almost petulant fallings-out with them. . . . Archibald MacLeish . . . Ford Madox Ford . . . Peter Viertel."

Mary Hemingway on Baker: "[T]hey had never fished together or hunted together or chatted together, or any of that sort of thing. Baker did, I thought, a marvelous job of research, but obviously couldn't, didn't know Ernest, and could not view him as a creature" (169); and on Hotchner, who Brian tells her was really fond of Hemingway: "I guess you're always fond of someone who can make you a million dollars."[35]

***

A transition in quality and kind follows in October 1973. *Esquire*'s fortieth anniversary issue reflects enormous energy—a "huge jamboree"; at 564 pages, it was then the largest-ever single issue of an American magazine. It features a foldout cover with color drawings of 39 contributors, including Arnold Gingrich. On a special sticker attached to the cover—"The Greatest Magazine Ever"—15 are singled out: "Hemingway, Fitzgerald, Steinbeck, Nabokov, Talese, Capote, O'Hara, Dreiser, Bellow, Updike, Wolfe, Faulkner, Saroyan, Dos Passos, Camus . . . plus: 50 More Top Writers."

This issue of the "magazine's bests" completes Arnold Gingrich's collection of posthumous Hemingway portraits. His personal finishing strokes effect both nostalgia and melancholia, capturing an epoch's two principals in tableau: "In 1936, within a period of six months, both men published in *Esquire* some of their finest writing [i.e., the three "Crack-Up" essays and "On the Blue Water" and "The Snows of Kilimanjaro"], curiously, in each case, reflecting his measure of the other—envy on Fitzgerald's part, contempt on Hemingway's. . . . [A]t no other time in their respective careers did their talents so sharply intersect as in those six months."[36] For Fitzgerald, Gingrich reprints "Pasting It Together" (March 1936), a follow-up to "The Crack-Up"; "My Generation" (October 1968); and Gingrich's "Scott, Ernest, and Whoever" (December 1966). For Hemingway, he reprints "On the Blue Water" (April 1936) and "The Snows of Kilimanjaro" (August 1936).

With poignant simplicity, Gingrich closes by reprinting "On the Blue Water." One of Hemingway's finest and most popular *Esquire* letters, it explores the exhilaration of marlin fishing in the Gulf Stream, contains—unmistakably—the germ of *The Old Man and the Sea*, and expresses the creative literary imagination of this talented novelist as journalist.

Arnold Gingrich preferred Scott Fitzgerald as a person, and he preferred *The Great Gatsby* as a novel. Even so, reading the thousands of words in *Esquire* devoted to Hemingway throughout the Gingrich years, including the editor's own firsthand testimony, most readers would place Ernest Hemingway's portrait at the head of any table set to commemorate that now long-past but once-magnificent movable feast. *Esquire*'s portraits shadow forth Matthew Bruccoli's man-of-many-parts, absent the caricatures painted by the men's magazines. The composite likeness is nuanced, but from whatever angle, carefully observed, it clearly images a complex man with a singular creative imagination: Ernest Hemingway, dedicated professional writer; sophisticated and cultured man of letters; Nobel Laureate, who changed the manner and matter of modern English narrative.

Gingrich consistently praised the talent of writers he published in *Esquire*, well beyond the 16 Nobel Laureates. Moreover, he was himself an award winner, honored by the Magazine Publishers' Association in 1968 with the Henry Johnson Fisher Award, its highest recognition for "Individual Achievement"—indisputably, *Esquire*'s first forty years.

And Ernest Hemingway? By Gingrich's choice and at his direction, Ernest Hemingway dominated *Esquire*'s early years, appeared as subject and in reprintings during the middle period, and returned as a major focus in Gingrich's final decade—a motif and, even more, a *presence* throughout.

NOTES

1. Arnold Gingrich, "Publisher's Page," *Esquire,* April 1965, 6.
2. David M. Earle's *All Man! Hemingway, 1950s Men's Magazines, and the Masculine Persona* neatly fits Hemingway into the larger history of men's magazines, especially the pulps. Earle relates the 1950s particularly to the late 'teens and the 1920s and 1930s while capturing Hemingway's broad presence in such publications. At their worst, they created lurid visual formats and sensational texts dramatizing a Hemingway figure acting as the new hypermasculine, often misogynist, ideal male. Frequently, Hemingway's image was exploited in unrelated texts: "Hemingway's Private War with Adolph Hitler" ("Task force Hemingway wine, women, and songed its way through France") in *Man's Magazine,* September 1959. In slick "bachelor" magazines, enterprising editors often collected and shaped Hemingway's words into compendiums of advice, as Hugh Hefner did in "Life, Love, and Leisure" for *Playboy,* January 1960. More positively, Hemingway contributed "The Shot" (article) to *True: The Man's Magazine,* April 1951; he permitted *Argosy* to excerpt *Green Hills of Africa,* June 1954; and he gave interviews as a sportsman on guns for *GUNsport,* April 1958.
3. Matthew Bruccoli, with Judith Baughman, ed., *Hemingway and the Mechanism of Fame* (Columbia: University of South Carolina Press, 2006), xix.
4. In his last decade, Hemingway's appearances in periodicals were many and varied: he serialized *Across the River and into the Trees* in *Cosmopolitan* (1950) and published *The Old Man and the Sea* in a single issue of *Life* (September 1952); his last two published stories, "Get a Seeing-Eyed Dog" and "A Man of the World," appeared in *Atlantic* (December 1957); he contributed multiple times to *Holiday, Life, Look, The New York Herald Tribune Book Review, The New York Times Book Review, Time,* and *Sports Illustrated*; *Field and Stream* reprinted "Big Two-Hearted River" (May 1954); occasionally, in Cuba, he granted magazine interviews, and, in New York, he appeared frequently in stories by *New York Post* columnists Leonard Lyons and Earl Wilson.
5. A. J. Kaul, "Arnold Gingrich," in *American Magazine Journalists, 1900-1960, Dictionary of Literary Biography,* Second Series, Vol. 137 (Detroit: Gale, 1994), 106.
6. Arnold Gingrich, "Introduction," in *The* Esquire *Treasury* (New York: Simon and Schuster, 1953), xi.

7. Arnold Gingrich, "Preface," in *The Armchair Esquire* (New York: G. P. Putnam's Sons, 1958), 21. *Esquire*'s targeting everything of interest to men raised a spectrum of criticism. For some, a cultural disjuncture resulted from the "Ziegfeldian sex and comedy" in texts and in cartoons, illustrations, and photographs (Hugh Merrill, *ESKY: The Early Years of* Esquire [New Brunswick, NJ: Rutgers University Press, 1995], 11). This material jarred against sophisticated pieces by recognized experts on literature, fashion, sports, and entertainment. In one example, among many, Henry F. Pringle in *Scribner's Magazine* saw *Esquire* as a "publishing phenomenon" developed for "people who cannot or don't read," and he compared *Esquire*'s fare "to having Thomas Mann or Ernest Hemingway read aloud from their works at a burlesque show" (Henry F. Pringle, "Sex, Esq.," *Scribner's,* March 1938, 33). Periodically, Gingrich responded to such criticism: In 1940, in the "Introduction" to *The Bedside Esquire* (New York: Grosset and Dunlap, 1940; seventy-plus texts, nothing pictorial), Gingrich concedes that the "Petty Girl" face "has launched a thousand quips," but he wearies of "hearing the cartoons talked about as if they characterized the content as a whole . . ." (6). Nearly thirty years later, he spoke at greater length in the "Preface" to *The Armchair Esquire*. This volume contains 29 "milestones" from the magazine's first 25 years: texts by D. H. Lawrence, Thomas Mann, Hemingway, Scott Fitzgerald, H. L. Mencken, Thomas Wolfe, Aldous Huxley, Henry Miller, J. D. Salinger, Norman Mailer, and Saul Bellow. The collection concludes with a stunning appendix: a "Check-List of Contributions of Literary Import to *Esquire* 1933–1958"—22 double-column pages. Taking the long view, Gingrich observes, "The sad truth that brains wear better than beauty was never more evident than in looking back over old issues: the pictures . . . reflections of the passing moment, the fads and foibles and the fleeting fancies of the stage and screen, whereas the words . . . concerned, in major part, the verities that are eternal" (17–18).
8. Kaul, "Arnold Gingrich," 104.
9. Arnold Gingrich, *Nothing But People: The Early Days at* Esquire (New York: Crown, 1971), 86. Gingrich insisted that *Esquire* always offer intelligent and literate writing from name contributors. Regardless how instrumental Hemingway's name may have been in attracting such quality during his *Esquire* years, Gingrich's hopes were realized: From the "lead off" position each month, Hemingway shared space with, among others, Fitzgerald, Huxley, Mann,

Erskine Caldwell, Ring Lardner, Clarence Darrow, John Dos Passos, Theodore Dreiser, Havelock Ellis, Dashiel Hammett, and Ezra Pound. Later, in the 1950s, new authors in the magazine included Mailer, William Styron, William Burroughs, Kurt Vonnegut, and John Updike, and Gingrich published Ray Bradbury's "Illustrated Man" and Truman Capote's "Breakfast at Tiffany's." In his "Publisher's Page" for December 1966, Gingrich updated (from 1958) the list of distinguished writers. He opens with a telling recollection from *Esquire*'s fight with the United States Post Office in 1943 over the legal propriety of sending *Esquire* through the mails. H. L. Mencken testified for *Esquire,* asserting that the magazine "had printed virtually every author of significance in this century, 'headed by Dreiser'" (8). Indeed, when Gingrich retired in 1973, he had published in *Esquire* hundreds of renowned writers and thinkers, among them 16 Nobel Laureates.

10. Hemingway's writing occasionally produced strain: his attack on cultural critic Gilbert Seldes following the latter's defense of the recently deceased Ring Lardner ("The Prizefighter and the Bull," November 1934) against Hemingway's downplaying of Lardner's achievement ("Defense of Dirty Words," September 1934); his belittling reference to Scott Fitzgerald by name in "The Snows of Kilimanjaro" (August 1936); in 1949, his justified anger, when, after being a decade away from the magazine, *Esquire* reprinted "The Snows of Kilimanjaro" without consulting him or Gingrich, then in Switzerland. Unknown to both men at the time, *Esquire* reprinted the original version—with the Fitzgerald insult—and not the corrected text changing "Scott" to "Julian" (Gingrich, "Publisher's Page," *Esquire,* September 1972, 6).
11. John Raeburn, *Fame Became of Him: Hemingway as Public Writer* (Bloomington: Indiana University Press, 1984), 130.
12. Arnold Gingrich, "Scott, Ernest, and Whoever," *Esquire,* December 1966, 186–89, 322–25. Among his "remembrances of things past" here, Gingrich takes up Hemingway's "arrogance" when refusing to allow reprinting of his two stories. Gingrich quotes the *Wall Street Journal* parody of Hemingway's style in its coverage of the lawsuit in 1958; *The Old Man and the Fee* alludes to eight Hemingway titles: "The writer has served with honor in many wars and he does not care what people think about his politics. [He] wants to revise . . . to protect his reprint rights . . . a mistake [which] reflects badly on his courage. What a way to be wounded! . . . The publisher wondered if he was to have or have not. But the author did not bid farewell to

the *Armchair Esquire.* One Spanish war story will be printed in the book by a magazine not noted for men without women . . . .The publicity is not too bad. The people now know the book and many will buy it. Do not believe the winner takes nothing. When you hear the bookstore cash registers ring, don't ask for whom the bell tolls. Just know that the sum also rises" (324). The *Wall Street Journal* parody underwrites the editor's position and effects valuable publicity for the *Armchair* volume, the number of Hemingway stories reprinted now moot.

13. Eric Sevareid, "Mano A Mano," *Esquire,* November 1959, 40–44.
14. Carson McCullers, "The Flowering Dream," *Esquire,* December 1959, 163.
15. Lester Cohen, ". . . And the Sinner: Horace Liveright," *Esquire,* December 1960, 108. Hemingway did not respond to Cohen's essay. But Edith Stern—first reader at Boni and Liveright of Hemingway's *In Our Time* manuscript—did ("The Sound and the Fury," *Esquire,* February 1961, 22). She agrees that Hemingway's collection was a "flop" ("initial sales 475"). But the publisher had first-refusal on his next two manuscripts. "Liveright and all the rest of us in the editorial office decided we must continue to publish this author; he was so good. The next book Hemingway submitted was *The Torrents of Spring,* a parody on Sherwood Anderson one of our best sellers. Horace said he'd publish it if Anderson didn't object. Anderson did object, violently." Stern recognized Hemingway's right to move to *Scribner's* when Boni and Liveright refused *Torrents.* More interesting is her final claim: Donald Friede pressed Hemingway to stay, offering him $1,000 to abandon *Torrents*: "That's more than you could possibly make on this book." Hemingway, eager to break with his publisher for personal reasons unknown to Friede then, or Stern later, refused.
16. Arnold Gingrich, "Publisher's Page," *Esquire,* June 1967, 6.
17. Arnold Gingrich, "Reviving the Practice of Salutes to the Living," *Esquire,* February 1937, 5, 28.
18. Arnold Gingrich, "A Farewell to the Lead-off Man," *Esquire,* June 1937, 5.
19. Arnold Gingrich, "E. H.: A Coda from the Maestro," *Esquire,* October 1961, 8.
20. Robert Emmett Ginna, "Life in the Afternoon," *Esquire,* February 1962, 104–5, 136, 106.
21. Andrew Turnbull, "Scott Fitzgerald and Ernest Hemingway," *Esquire,* March 1962, 121–23.

22. Sally Belfrage, "The Haunted House of Ernest Hemingway," *Esquire,* February 1963, 67.
23. Norman Mailer, "The Big Bite," *Esquire,* November 1962, 134; Gay Talese, "Looking for Hemingway," *Esquire,* July 1963, 44.
24. Malcolm Muggeridge, "Books," *Esquire,* June 1966, 34.
25. Jerome Beatty, "Hanging Up on Hemingway," *Esquire,* February 1967, 116. This reconstruction of an awkward conversation nearly a decade earlier is humorous, in the manner of Gingrich's own presentation of the *Armchair* dispute (deflating Hemingway via a *Wall Street Journal* parody). Beatty wrote of this phone conversation at the time in *The Saturday Review* (August 1958), focusing more on the artist's rationale than on the man's foibles. He allowed Hemingway to speak in detail about datedness of language and the simple desire to revise for overall improvement; about the appropriateness of the publisher wanting three stories (20,000 words) from him alone; about copyright. Beatty argued the question "Who owns the past?" Removing the 1938 Hemingway from these stories is "decidedly unconstitutional; it's *ex post facto*; it's nonsense" (36). Aware of Beatty's *earlier* article, Gingrich might have expected fuller representation in *Esquire* of Hemingway's defense of his art.
26. Arnold Gingrich, "Scott, Ernest, and Whoever," *Esquire,* December 1966, 187.
27. Ibid., 322.
28. Ibid., 324, 188.
29. Ibid., 325, 188.
30. Malcolm Cowley, "Papa and the Parricides," *Esquire,* June 1967, 101, 103, 162.
31. F. Scott Fitzgerald, "My Generation," *Esquire,* October 1968, 119, 120.
32. Matthew Bruccoli, "Ernest Hemingway as Cub Reporter," *Esquire,* December 1968, 207. This article produced letters touching both Bruccoli and Hemingway. Current *Kansas City Star* staffer Mel Foor quotes the newspaper's police reporter in 1918: "Hemingway worked the police beat for only one week in March 1918." Nat Fritz takes on Bruccoli regarding art, believing that Hemingway's story is hardly a credit to the *Kansas City Star* "'Style Book'—the proofreader—the Editor or himself. . . . The 'Style Book' notwithstanding, [Hemingway] was never a topflight journalist" ("The Sound and the Fury," *Esquire,* February 1969, 11–12).
33. Arnold Gingrich, "Publisher's Page," *Esquire,* October 1970, 6, 12. An upset Mary Hemingway responded in December 1970 (in a

letter published in *Esquire*), not to Gingrich's piece but to a blurb by another, her feelings unmistakable: "With such falsities as 'number of changes which he had been unable to make by the time of his death.' Rot. He simply wasn't thinking over nine or ten years, of making them. . . . With such stupidities as '*Islands in the Stream* will stand as one of the few completed novels by Ernest Hemingway' . . . You think *For Whom TBT* was not completed? Or *A Farewell to Arms*? . . . As you may gather, I'm angry at you and ashamed for you" (108).

34. Arnold Gingrich, "Publisher's Page," *Esquire,* February 1972, 6, 98.
35. Denis Brian, "The Importance of Knowing Ernest," *Esquire,* February 1972, 98–102, 165, 170.
36. Arnold Gingrich, "Fitzgerald/Hemingway Epoch," *Esquire,* October 1973, 139.

CHAPTER 9

STEPHEN COLBERT'S *HARVEST OF SHAME*

GEOFFREY BAYM

ON THANKSGIVING DAY, 1960, THE CBS TELEVISION network offered an unlikely hour of holiday programming: the commercial-free, hour-long documentary *Harvest of Shame*. Intended to confront an audience basking in the glow of the customary Thanksgiving feast, *Harvest* offered a gritty and often heart-wrenching exposé of the plight of migrant farmworkers—"the men, women, and children," proclaimed a somber Edward R. Murrow, "who harvest the crops in this country of ours, the best-fed nation on earth." By now considered a seminal work in television news, *Harvest* was simultaneously investigative journalism, poetry, and social advocacy. Under the banner of CBS News Reports, it championed the rights of "the forgotten people, the under-protected, the under-educated, the under-clothed, the under-fed," who toiled "in the sweatshops of the soil, the harvest of shame."

Ending with an explicit appeal for the affluent audience to "influence legislation" on behalf of those who "have no voice in legislative halls," *Harvest* may be unimaginable today. In a hypercommercialized, corporate-dominated media environment, it seems the stuff of fantasy that a major television network would take an aggressive stand on behalf of workers' rights, let alone do so advertisement-free on a holiday whose standard television fare is given over to pageantry and NFL football. Indeed, Edward R. Murrow himself has become mythologized, his name an evocation of a distant past when "broadcast journalism" was less of an oxymoron, and major American institutions, such as network news and perhaps Congress itself, saw themselves in the business of public service—of giving voice to the voiceless.[1]

And yet, fifty years after the airing of *Harvest of Shame*, as the fruit and vegetable harvest of 2010 made its way to market, the issue of farmworkers' rights would once again command national attention, this time due to unlikely advocacy from the faux pundit and real comedian Stephen Colbert. There he was, like Murrow before him (or, as we'll see, maybe not so much like Murrow), standing in the fields, calling our attention to the low pay and harsh working conditions of those who pick the corn and the beans that, as Colbert noted, have yet to figure out how to "pick themselves." And there he was, too, both in and out of character, testifying before a very real congressional subcommittee and the attending C-SPAN cameras, calling for legislative action on the question of illegal immigration and migrant farmwork.

Appearing before Congress as concerned citizen, celebrity activist, and performance artist, Colbert offered a provocative and perhaps unprecedented form of truth telling. Like much of his work on his hybrid program *The Colbert Report*, where he plays the profoundly ironic role of a right-wing blowhard, his testimony before Congress occupied a novel space in the contemporary gray areas between journalism and art, politics and performance, and fact and fiction. Struggling to make sense of it, the journalistic and political establishment largely condemned the testimony—even the Democratic Majority Leader in the House called it an "embarrassment." Colbert's fans, however, celebrated the performance, while video of his opening statement circulated widely online, registering a million views in slightly more than two weeks.[2]

Although the testimony itself gained the vast majority of attention, Colbert's appearance in Congress was the final installment in a complex intervention in the politics of farm labor performed in four parts. First, on *The Report*, Colbert would interview Arturo Rodriguez, the president of the United Farm Workers, primarily about the UFW's "Take Our Jobs" campaign that sought to raise awareness of the plight of today's migrant workers, particularly in the context of the wider debate over illegal immigration. Agreeing to try out migrant farmwork for a day, Colbert would then interview Zoe Lofgren, the chairwoman of the House Subcommittee on Immigration, before heading out to the fields to see firsthand the struggles of migrant labor. Then, and finally, at the bequest of Congresswoman Lofgren, he testified before her committee about the so-called AgJobs bill, the Agricultural Job Opportunities, Benefits, and Security Act designed to facilitate greater legal protections for migrant farmworkers.

Taken as a whole, Colbert's four-part engagement with the issue of farmworkers' rights presents intriguing ground to explore the contemporary confluence of journalistic inquiry, aesthetic performance, and political voice in an age marked by shifting paradigms of public speech and the breakdown of assumptions that guided an earlier age. Colbert certainly is no Murrow—at first blush the comparison seems absurd—but with his version of *Harvest of Shame*, the pretend pundit and increasingly real political activist offered a new, and in some ways quite serious, approach to old problems. To understand this unlikely affair, this chapter proceeds in three stages. First, I examine the three television segments aired on *The Colbert Report*: the Rodriguez and Lofgren interviews and the satirical piece in which Colbert tries out migrant farmwork as a potential "fall-back position" should he lose his job in television. Second, I consider his multivoiced testimony before Lofgren's committee. Third, I offer a reading of the journalistic establishment's reaction to the testimony—the mainstream news media's efforts to make sense of something they struggled to grasp. Ultimately, I conclude that Colbert's *Harvest of Shame* presented an alternative mode of public voice, a thoroughly hybrid or *discursively integrated* blend of rational-critical and aesthetic-expressive forms of speech. Fundamentally avant-garde, Colbert's experiment in political performance profoundly challenged the boundaries of public discourse, simultaneously offering new modalities of argument and a powerful critique of the status quo.

TRANSFORMATIONS

For scholars of documentary film, Murrow's *Harvest of Shame* was long-form broadcast journalism at its best, the exemplar of a television form steeped in the Griersonian tradition of art in the service of the public good.[3] Residing at the nexus of narrative and news, *Harvest* told "an American story . . . a 1960 *Grapes of Wrath*" that wound its way from Florida to New York and from "the Mexican border in California" to Washington state. "They travel in buses, they ride trucks," Murrow tells us, as the camera reveals disturbing images of men, women, and children packed like livestock, "they follow the sun." *Harvest* is the story, Murrow explains, of "the migrant, the lonely wanderer, the outcast . . . trapped in the stream." Intercutting among personal anecdotes and social statistics, vérité footage and interviews with both the weak and the powerful, *Harvest* tackles questions of wages, labor conditions, housing, education, child labor laws, and the possibilities of unionization. Appealing directly to the audience's morality, a chaplain who works with the migrants and who, Murrow suggests, "speaks for all of us," asks whether one can have "love without justice" and whether we might "think too much in terms of charity, in terms of Thanksgiving Day baskets . . . and not in terms enough of eliminating poverty." Finally, Murrow concludes with a direct call to action: "Only an enlightened, aroused, and perhaps angered public opinion can do anything about the migrants. The people you have seen have the strength to harvest your fruit and vegetables. They do not have the strength to influence legislation. Maybe we do. Good night, and good luck."

Intended to disturb complacency, to force its audience to see that which most would rather ignore, *Harvest* was controversial. The historian Eric Barnouw noted that the film represented the migrant workers' plight "so vividly that many people simply rejected its truth. Such poverty and human erosion could not easily be fitted into the world as seen in prime time."[4] Exposing the exploitation of those who stood among "the poorest of the poor," *Harvest* was a seminal journalistic work dealing with what has come to be called *food justice*—an umbrella term increasingly used to describe a range of concerns and interventions intended to reform an industrial, vertically integrated, and largely unsustainable food system that treats both the environment and agricultural workers as resources to be exploited in the pursuit of economic efficiencies and corporate profit.[5]

For the compelling nature of its narrative and its power in exposing one of the worst of American injustices, *Harvest* eventually was named as one of the most influential works of twentieth-century journalism.[6] So too is Murrow's work now remembered as the epitome of what another pioneer of broadcast journalism would call the "Brief, Wonderful Life of Network News."[7] As I have argued elsewhere, Murrow and his colleagues were engaged in what one could call a *high-modern* approach to television news and public affairs programming.[8] Products of the network age, they saw journalism as a kind of institutionalized public service, a noncommercial and infinitely important discourse of politics and public issues. Intended to offer citizens the resources they needed to be engaged citizens in a democracy, high-modern journalism arose hand in hand with the progressive era in US history and its belief that technocratic expertise—and the network newsmen saw themselves as experts in information—could engineer a better society.

Ten years after *Harvest*, NBC would offer its own long-form journalistic exploration of food justice with the 1970 documentary *Migrant*, an exposé of the treatment of citrus workers employed in the Minute Maid / Coca Cola food chain.[9] Although that piece forced slight changes in the

Minute Maid–supported farms, the issue of food justice would disappear from network television. Indeed, the very high-modern ideals of network news that motivated the production of *Harvest* and *Migrant* could not survive the transformations of the 1980s and 1990s, a time in which the television networks, faced with increasing competition for audiences, would be bought out by corporate interests and their news divisions reoriented toward commercialized entertainment and the raw pursuit of profit. The serious news of Murrow and its concurrent concern for social justice would devolve into a kind of *postmodern* spectacle, another form of reality television, packaged for public appeal, not for democratic service.[10]

Today, despite the fact that environmentalism has become trendy (green, they say, is the new black) and an entire cable channel is devoted to food, the food justice movement is largely invisible on mainstream television, particularly regarding its concern for labor conditions.[11] That is, except on the Comedy Channel, where, in a marker of our times, food justice advocates and issues have found an unlikely media platform. The ostensible "fake news" programs *The Daily Show* and particularly *The Colbert Report* have demonstrated a consistent interest in the various concerns that constitute the food justice movement, including labor conditions, sustainability, and the economics of food production and consumption.

Elsewhere, I have argued at length that the label *fake news* fails to adequately characterize the project in which those two programs are engaged.[12] Against the decline of mainstream journalism and the loss of high-modern ideals, *The Daily Show* and *The Colbert Report* represent an alternative approach to public affairs programming, one marked by a blend of styles, techniques, modalities, and voices. Simultaneously serious and silly, rational and rambunctious, critical and commercial, the two programs have become influential sites of democratic information, commentary, and conversation.[13] I have argued that they are better understood as a *neo-modern* approach to broadcast journalism, one that uses postmodern style to advance a modernist agenda of fact and accountability, and turns to parody, irony, and satire as means of presenting democratic information and rational-critical argument.

COLBERT'S *HARVEST*

Most unlike Murrow, Colbert's engagement with food justice is marked throughout by his fundamentally ironic approach to public affairs. As regular viewers of Colbert know, although much of what he says (and does) is outrageous, he rarely ever says what he means and quite often means the opposite of what he says. Colbert—at least in his character of the deeply egotistical, opinionated, and overly outspoken conservative pundit—is *double voiced.* His point never lies in the literal meaning of his words; to understand Colbert requires one to read between the lines.[14]

This is well on display in the first segment in Colbert's *Harvest,* his studio interview with Arturo Rodriguez, the president of the United Farm Workers of America. Borrowing the format from late-night television, *The Colbert Report* always features a studio interview in its third act. Unlike the traditional late-night talk show, however, Colbert only sometimes interviews actors and celebrities; more often he hosts authors and activists—such as Rodriguez—who speak to a range of issues rarely given a hearing on mainstream television. With his more progressive guests, Colbert usually begins as the antagonist, attacking them for their liberal convictions and concerns. Thus, with Rodriguez, he starts by noting, sternly, that the UFWA was founded by Cesar Chavez, who has become an iconic, if not entirely well-understood, figure for young progressives and a common straw man for the right. From there, Colbert continues in his seemingly critical stance, challenging Rodriguez's work on immigration reform with the common conservative talking point that "illegal immigrants are taking our jobs." When Rodriguez counters that Americans don't want to do farmwork because of the difficult working conditions, Colbert twists his words, as he so often does, and asks pointedly, "Are you saying illegal immigrants are better than Americans?"

In the Rodriguez interview, Colbert plays the role of what I have described as the *false foil.*[15] Pretending to oppose him, in actuality he gives Rodriguez a platform to address questions of immigration and farm labor. Colbert pivots to an explicitly sympathetic posture, asking if migrant workers will continue to "winter in Yuma" following the passage of Arizona's aggressive anti-immigration law, a measure of which Colbert has been continuously critical. From there, Colbert turns to the core point of the interview, the UFWA's "Take Our Jobs" campaign, which invited Americans to spend a day working as laborers in order to understand the realities of migrant farmwork. When Rodriguez explains that at that point only three people had actually signed up for a day of farmwork, Colbert enthusiastically volunteers to be the fourth. To that, Rodriguez tells him, "Stephen, we look forward for you to come out and work in the fields so you can share with everyone what it's like to work as a farmworker." Anticipating what would become the theme of his day in the fields, Colbert concludes by asking, "Is there air conditioning?"

Colbert's efforts to learn if farms are indeed air conditioned makes up the next stage of his engagement with food justice, packaged in two parts under the title "Fallback Position," his on-going series in which he playfully explores other potential career opportunities such as astrophysicist or Olympic athlete. This time, chronicling his involvement in the "Take Our Jobs" campaign, he says he wants to "test my mettle as an immigrant farmworker." His first step in learning about the nature of migrant farm labor (as he gingerly steps through the mud in suit and dress shoes) is an interview with Democratic Congresswoman Zoe Lofgren, then the chair of the House Subcommittee on Immigration, an ally of Rodriguez, and as Colbert explains, a "notorious Mexican coddler."

Lofgren, of course, is not the first sitting member of Congress to be interviewed by Colbert. Indeed, Colbert has for several years pursued the admirable goal of interviewing every member of Congress for his "435-part series" "Better Know a District."[16] The pieces in this series differ notably from Colbert's studio interviews, often shot on location (the Lofgren interview appears filmed in a barn) and heavily edited for comedic effect. Colbert, furthermore, performs in a different voice—appearing less as a belligerent pundit and more as a befuddled and entirely unreflective bozo, who, in this case, struggles to understand why Lofgren is "so passionate about the rights of migrant farmworkers." For her part, given the opportunity to publicize the issue, Lofgren explains that she hopes the attention Colbert would generate for the "Take Our Jobs" campaign would encourage millions more to volunteer.

As the conversation unfolds, Colbert's Better Know a District persona takes on a finer edge. He becomes something more than just a clown, now occupying a truly ironic stance in which he embodies the role of the soft and affluent American, who, perhaps like Murrow's audience in 1960, enjoys the harvest of plenty but turns a blind eye to its human cost. Thus he proclaims to Lofgren that the concern for workers' rights "seems archaic to me. We don't get our food from farms anymore," he argues, "we get it from the grocery store." Here Colbert enacts the willful ignorance—encouraged by agribusiness and adopted by many Americans—of the connections among the consumption, distribution, and production of food. Colbert then enacts the lack not just of understanding but also of empathy for migrant labor—the empathy that Murrow's *Harvest* so skillfully encouraged. "How hard is it really, to be a migrant farmworker?" he asks Lofgren. "Beautiful location, plenty of exercise, all the vegetables you could eat. Sounds more like fat camp." To that, Lofgren explains how challenging the work really is, but Colbert again postures as the uninterested and out of touch. "I love a challenge," he proclaims. "I do Sudoku."

Expecting farmwork to be something like a Sudoku puzzle, Colbert eagerly sets out in the second segment of "Fallback Position" to "get my farm on." Here he takes to the fields of Gill Farms in Hurley, New York, to pack corn and pick beans. Whispers of Murrow follow Colbert as he confronts the realities of migrant labor. Quite unlike Murrow, however, who stood in the fields as the observer, narrating what he saw, Colbert performs as an engaged participant. But as with all his performances, this one is deeply ironic, down to the very clothes he wears. He appears entirely unprepared for the labor confronting him, wearing an outfit better suited to Sunday suburban gardening than actual farmwork: a sunhat, an apron over his polo shirt and khaki slacks, and Croc sandals on his feet.

Thus established, Colbert enacts his incompetence—representative perhaps of *our* incompetence?—throughout the piece. He can neither keep up with the pace of the corn packing assembly line, nor tolerate the physical exertion of picking beans in the sun. "Aren't there any beans in the shade?" he asks his supervisor. Then, again implicating the audience, for whom farm labor exists only in the imagination, Colbert explains to his supervisor that he's too busy playing the Facebook game Farmville on his smart phone to do any actual work on the real farm. Later in the segment he rides around the fields in a shaded golf cart, his unwillingness or inability to do the work juxtaposed with video of the very real (and all Hispanic) workers engaged in their very difficult labor. Finally, at the end of the segment Colbert asks his supervisor if he does indeed "have what it takes to be a migrant farmworker." When the supervisor inevitably rejects him (every "Fallback Position" ends with rejection), he cheers. "Oh thank God," he exclaims, "can I go home now?" With point made, the segment finishes on a final satirical twist. Invoking the specter of both class and ethnicity that run through the issues at hand, Colbert calls for his driver, "Pablo," and as a Mariachi band is heard in the background, he climbs into his luxury SUV and is driven off the farm.

The televised segments of Colbert's *Harvest* are deceptively layered. At the least, the attention paid to food justice is remarkable in a corporate television landscape that elides the topic while at the same time readily receiving billions of dollars in annual revenue from fast-food advertising.[17] Even more remarkable is the fact that it appears not on the network news or the 24-hour cable news channels, but on Comedy Central, which, as Jon Stewart once argued, is more likely to feature puppets making crank calls than it is to air interviews with sitting congressional representatives.

Colbert's engagement with food justice, in turn, is complex, straddling divides between journalism and art. As a form of public inquiry, it is fundamentally *ironic*, its meaning always suggested but never quite said. So too is it *performative*.[18] Colbert plays a nuanced character who advances argument less through logic and more through situational humor and the juxtaposition between the foolishness of his persona and the gravity of the people and the issues with which he interacts. Ultimately this illuminates the detachment of Americans on the one hand and the disturbing reality of migrant farmwork on the other. As such, Colbert's *Harvest* is profoundly *playful*, but here pleasure and play are harnessed as serious means of entertaining issues, advancing argument, and enacting critique. Even while it takes an aesthetic form, therefore, it *functions* as journalism, reporting on an issue in a way that exposes and teaches.

TESTIMONY

In that hybrid stance, Colbert would travel to Washington the very next day and testify, along with Arturo Rodriguez, about the AgJobs bill. Colbert, of course, was by no means the first pop-culture figure to testify in a congressional hearing. Just a few months earlier, for example, the actor Kevin Costner appeared before the House Committee on Science and Technology in the wake of the BP oil spill to discuss an environmental technology in which he had heavily invested. A number of other actors and musicians have testified about causes they support, as did Elmo, the Sesame Street puppet, who once spoke to the House Education Appropriation Subcommittee to urge spending on music education.[19] Nor was Colbert the first satirist to testify. A hundred years earlier, Mark Twain spoke on the question of intellectual property and copyright law—testimony that admittedly was less performative, but still interwoven with humor.[20]

Despite precedent, Colbert's testimony was controversial before it even began. The day before, on Fox News, the morning news hosts launched a pre-emptive strike, lamenting that Colbert would be wasting Congress's time and the tax payers' dollars. (In his rebuttal, Colbert assured his viewers that he was paying for all expenses, except drinking water.) And that morning, after Colbert submitted a written version of his testimony—a brief and matter-of-fact summary of his experiences with the "Take Our Jobs" campaign—the Democratic Congressman John Conyers asked him to forgo oral testimony and leave the room. For his part, Colbert refused to go, at first mumbling "no hablo inglés" before noting that he had been invited to testify by the committee's chair and that, unless she revoked that invitation, he would testify as planned. Lofgren insisted that Colbert proceed.

To the chagrin of several of the people in the room, Colbert went off script—or at least traded in the short and serious-toned testimony he had provided in writing for a longer and far more comedic one, which he performed in front of the committee, his fellow witnesses, and the watchful eye of the C-SPAN cameras. As he did with his keynote address at the 2005 White House Correspondents' Dinner, where he mercilessly confronted George W. Bush's ineptitude (with the president sitting just a few chairs away), Colbert challenged not only decorum but also the underlying assumptions of how one is expected to speak within the legislative domain. Like all Colbert performances, the testimony was what I have described as *discursively integrated*, blending voices and modalities—serious and silly, ludicrous and poignant—into an interwoven range of speech genres that would have once been thought to be fundamentally incompatible.[21]

Thus, in full character, Colbert makes a number of purely inane jokes. He laments that his "gastroenterologist Dr. Eichler" has ordered him to eat vegetables and that, "as evidence, I would like to submit a video of my colonoscopy into the congressional record." He insists that "it was the ancient Israelites who built the first food pyramids" and then suggests that his grandfather immigrated to the United States "because he killed a man back in Ireland." After a scripted pause, Colbert turns to the audience and continues, "That's the rumor . . . I don't know if that's true. I'd like to have that stricken from the record." Later, in an exchange with Iowa Republican Steve King, he suggests that the term "corn-packer" is slang for a "gay Iowan." Here Colbert offers the kind of juvenile and often surreal humor that he dabbles in, the quite unserious comedic aesthetic that flows throughout his approach to public affairs, and that critics often focus on in dismissing Colbert's as an illegitimate mode of public speech.

At the same time, Colbert offers several comments that contain his familiar satirical edge—the playful foray into the ridiculous that functions to advance serious critique. He begins by noting that "the obvious answer" to the problem of American farms' dependence on immigrant labor for harvesting fruits and vegetables is "for all of us to stop eating fruits and vegetables. And if you look at the recent obesity statistics, you'll see that many Americans have already started." Familiarly double voiced, Colbert confronts the impossibility (and undesirability) of forgoing fruits and vegetables and thus the necessity of addressing the problem of immigrant labor. His jab at obese Americans further ties the issue to nutrition and public health, adjacent concerns for food justice.

Colbert continues in his satirical vein with the comment that would get the most attention following the testimony. "I don't want a tomato picked by a Mexican," he proclaims. "I want it picked by an American, then sliced by a Guatemalan, and served by a Venezuelan, in a spa where a Chilean gives me a Brazilian." As we will see later, most commentators missed the satirical logic here, Colbert's quite insightful point that the food industry—and indeed, the economy more generally—has become intractably global. Just as Japanese cars are often assembled on American factory floors, so too is the production, distribution, and consumption of food a globally interconnected process, one that restrictive immigration policies—perhaps a wall between the United States and Mexico—could not possibly improve. And again, just as Colbert so eagerly called for his driver "Pablo" to whisk him off the farm, so too here does he note that he'll be eating his American-picked tomato while being pampered in a spa by foreign nationals. Like Murrow before him, Colbert calls our attention to the questions of class that run through the argument—the fundamental problem that affluent Americans too often turn a blind eye to the injustices of a food system that caters to them.

Here Colbert subtly constructs his *ethos*, using irony to develop a standpoint of compassion and a case for action. He continues, with his tongue not quite in cheek, to recall his day in the fields. "After working with these men and women," he says, "picking beans, packing corn, for hours on end, side by side, in the unforgiving sun, I have to say, and I do mean this sincerely, please don't make me do this again! It is really, really hard." While perhaps not a journalistic recounting in the style of Murrow before him, Colbert's testimony does invoke his firsthand knowledge of the daily challenges migrant workers must face. He returns to that point later when Texas Republican Lamar Smith challenges the legitimacy of his testimony. "I know you're an expert comedian, I know you're an expert entertainer," Smith confronts him. "I know you have a great sense of humor, but would you call yourself an expert witness when it comes to farm labor issues?" To that Colbert responds entirely seriously: "I believe I was invited here today by the Congresswoman because I was one of the 16 people who took the United Farm Workers up on the experience of [doing] migrant farmwork for a single day . . . and if," he says, knowing well that none of the congressional representatives in the room had similar firsthand knowledge, "there are other members of the committee that did that, then there's no point in me being here."

Shifting voices between the inane and the satirical, the compassionate and the absurd, Colbert then offers a few quite serious, if brief, arguments about the problem and its potential solutions. First, he addresses the issue in *economic* terms: "This brief experience gave me some small understanding why so few Americans are clamoring to begin a career as a migrant field worker. So, what's the answer? I'm a free market guy. Normally I would leave this to the invisible hand of the market. But the invisible hand of the market has already moved over 84,000 acres of production and over 22,000 farm jobs to Mexico, and shut down over a million acres of U.S. farm land due to a lack of available labor. Because apparently, even the invisible hand doesn't want to pick beans." Here his alleged faith in the invisible hand sets up a critique of free-market economics, a rational-critical suggestion, supported by factual evidence, that government intervention is necessary. From there he suggests a *legal* solution: "Maybe we could offer more visas to the immigrants . . . and this improved legal status might allow immigrants recourse if they're abused. And it just stands to reason to me that if your coworker can't be exploited, then you're less likely to be exploited yourself. And that itself might improve pay and working conditions on these farms . . . Or maybe that's crazy, maybe the easier answer is just to have scientists design vegetables that pick themselves." Again, using humor in the service of argument, Colbert suggests that as long as human labor is required to pick vegetables, then the laborers deserve legal protection and humane working conditions.

Finally, in an exchange with Democratic Congresswoman Judy Chu, a strong advocate for farmworkers' rights, Colbert articulates the issue in explicitly *moral* terms. Chu asks him why, when he could focus on any issue of his choosing, he has spent his time intervening in this one. For the first time in the entire performance, Colbert steps entirely out of character to explain: "I like talking about people who don't have any power . . . one of the least powerful people are migrant workers who come and do our work, but don't have any rights as a result. And yet, we still invite them to come here, and at the same time, ask them to leave. And that's an interesting contradiction to me. And, you know, 'whatsoever you do for the least of my brothers,' and these seem like the least of our brothers . . . migrant workers suffer and have no rights." Referencing a call for justice attributed to Jesus in the New Testament, Colbert invokes his own religious identity (he proudly celebrates his Catholicism) to authorize an argument on behalf of those who cannot speak for themselves.[22] Thus, as did Murrow, Colbert speaks on behalf of "the forgotten people," the ones with the strength to harvest the crops, but not "the strength to influence legislation."

Like his performance on television, Colbert's testimony was equally multilayered, blending crass comedic spectacle, satirical critique, and quite serious argument. Speaking in and out of character, he shifted among the surreal and the sincere, the silly and the sensible. And ultimately, he provided a moral justification for doing so, articulating a sense of responsibility accompanying his position of privilege to work on behalf of those who "have no power." That he would offer such a performance under oath, before a congressional committee, and broadcast live on television, would deeply challenge assumptions of discursive propriety—of how one can, and should, speak both of serious public issues and within the legislative domain.

REACTIONS

Over the next few days, the mainstream news media took up these questions as it grappled with Colbert's efforts to influence legislation, or more specifically his methods. The testimony—although not the television segments that preceded it—was covered by virtually every US television network and most major newspapers, almost all of which provided some kind of interpretive piece seeking to make sense of the event. Often an exercise in border control, the journalistic coverage of Colbert's testimony collectively spoke to a set of tension points that inform wider debates about the shifting boundaries among factual and fictive speech genres, performance, politics, and public voice.

For many, the dominant metaphor was "collision," in all the violence and negativity the term suggests. According to CNN, a funny man and a serious subject "collided . . . today on Capitol Hill."[23] For the *New York Times*, the collision was between "the serious and the absurd."[24] On ABC the hybrid political-insider-turned-television-personality George Stephanopoulos argued that "after blurring for years, the line between politics and entertainment was completely wiped away."[25] The *New Republic* was even more concerned about the collapse of distinctions between entertainment and politics, worrying that Colbert's public presence signified the "valorization of entertainment," which itself necessarily entails the "degradation of politics."[26]

Underlying the widespread concern among journalists and pundits about the collision of the serious and the silly, the political and the entertaining, is a set of normative assumptions about the proper nature of public speech—a conceptual framework that itself is an artifact of an earlier age. As a number of scholars have argued, the distinctions between news and entertainment, politics and art, and journalism and literature are products of the *modern* mind and its inclination toward social rationalization—the allocation of institutions, activities, and modes of speech into clearly differentiated spheres.[27] Thus questions of social justice and the public good were to be addressed within the *political-normative* domain, while the pursuit of the beautiful, the poetic, and the pleasurable was to be contained within *aesthetic-creative* sphere. Journalism and politics were assumed to belong to the former; comedy, art, and literature to the latter.

Of course, those boundaries, and the normative assumptions they entailed, never quite reflected actually existing discursive practices. Journalism and literature have always been overlapping categories, while news has always been, for some, entertaining.[28] So too has the practice of politics never been entirely distinct from public performance. Colbert's testimony sat squarely at the point of tension among these discursive forms. One headline proclaimed, "Now playing on Capitol Hill . . ."—a reference to an apparent collapse of boundaries between comedy and Congress and, more significantly, between play—pleasure—and the sober arena of governance.[29] Similarly, the Associated Press led its coverage with the suggestion that "there are congressional hearings and there are comedy shows, and the twain rarely meet."[30] That is an interesting claim, both invoking a modernist normativity and at the same time ignoring the perhaps postmodern fact that the two do often meet, that *The Daily Show* and *The Colbert Report* regularly cover congressional hearings, more so in some instances than do the so-called real news, and lawmakers often appear on both shows in an attempt to influence the national conversation. Thus *Politico*'s worry that Colbert had turned the "Hill hearing into performance art" seems to elide the unavoidable reality that so much of contemporary politics is a kind of theater—a point that regular viewers of *The Daily Show* and *Colbert* well understand.[31]

This concern for the role of aesthetic performance in the public domain runs throughout the reaction to Colbert's testimony. The *Weekly Standard* bemoaned Colbert's appearance as "empty performance art," a "cringe-inducing, Andy-Kaufmanesque display."[32] The pop conservative pundit Jonah Goldberg took the argument further, suggesting the testimony was symptomatic of "ironic rot"—the "irony or post-irony or ironic post-whatever [that] has been metastasizing through the culture for decades."[33] Equating irony with cancer, the criticism here is based on a misreading of Colbert's journalistic art. Suggesting his performance was "empty" of meaning, critics equate it with the kind of unstable or postmodern irony described by Wayne C. Booth: an irony that defies its own interpretation or reconstruction, that lacks a foundation of conviction.[34] To borrow from Hayden White, such postmodern irony—the play of signs without signifiers—suggests the "foolishness of all linguistic characterizations of reality" and in turn dissolves "all belief in the possibility of positive political actions."[35] Appearing on the dubiously titled segment "Fox News All-Stars," pundit Fred Barnes makes the same mistake. He compares Colbert negatively to other pop culture figures who have testified before Congress. "It's not like when they invite some star in to talk about agriculture or global warming or something," he argues. "*They're* saying what they believe. *This* was an act."[36] Barnes here correctly notes that Colbert was performing an act, but like many others, he fails to recognize that Colbert's irony is quite stable, that although the meaning of his speech rarely lies in his literal words, it ultimately rests on a firm, and quite rational, foundation.

By contrast, a few commentators recognized that the act was simultaneously a form of action. A blogger on NPR.org, for example, rightly locates Colbert within the rich tradition of political satire, that critical art which uses provocation and play in service of democratic dialogue.[37] "The role of a good satirist, from the time of Jonathan Swift until now," the blogger notes, "is to make people see uncomfortable truths as he makes them squirm. On that score, Colbert succeeded."[38] Likewise, an editorial from the *Fort Worth Star-Telegram*, which interestingly was reprinted in a newspaper in the California farming community of Merced, praises "Colbert's strengths as a social commentator" and "his ability to use [his] on-camera persona . . . to find the chase in modern politics and cut directly to it."[39] A columnist for the *Buffalo News* similarly notes the value of Colbert's satirical performance, suggesting he "shined a light in a place where most people are delighted not to look," forcing consideration of "the plight of farmworkers and the realities most of us Americans would rather not face."[40] One hears traces of Murrow here, the suggestion perhaps that Colbert's irony, far from the postmodern indeterminacy of which it was accused, functions in pursuit of the same modernist ideals that motivated Murrow in such a different historical era.

Indeed, with Murrow and his era receding further into the shadows of history, it may take the audacity of Colbert to focus the contemporary corporate media's attention on questions of food justice. Much of the mainstream media's response, however, assumed a defensive stance, ignoring Colbert's argument and instead casting the event as a purely commercial spectacle. Says Greta Van Susteren on Fox News, entirely eliding the substance of Colbert's testimony, "while the nature of the hearing over migrant farmworkers is a deadly serious one, Mr. Colbert's testimony was anything but."[41] Likewise, the *New York Post* offered what it said were the "highlights" of Colbert's testimony, presenting, in bullet form, several of the most inane or ridiculous of Colbert's quips, all of which were severed from their wider rhetorical context.[42]

The emphasis for the *Post* and many other commentators instead fell on Colbert's celebrity, reframing his testimony not as a democratic intervention in an issue of public significance but as a marketing stunt. Colbert, *The New Republic* argued, turned "the Capitol into a ratings opportunity." Denying Colbert any possible motive beyond personal gain, the author insists that his "true cause" is his "own celebrity." Colbert testified not "for the good of the nation" but "to promote himself . . . which is all these people ever do."[43] This accusation reveals what may be the real cynicism in postmodern political discourse, the true absence of, or at least failure to recognize what Frederic Jameson has called "the ulterior motive" or the "satiric impulse" that characterizes more modernist approaches to satire, parody, and indeed public speech more broadly considered.[44]

While few doubted Murrow's intentions, for many Colbert simply *could not* have been interested in the public good. If there is profit to be made, the logic follows, if publicity can serve economic purposes, then private profit must necessarily be the only goal. In this, one hears the abdication of any sense of publicity in the democratic sense—the understanding that public awareness and dialogue are central to democratic practice. Instead, *publicity* is understood entirely through an economic logic—what one could call a neoliberal or consumer-republic frame that equates public speech with private gain and rejects the very concept of democratic dialogue. Even among those who recognize that Colbert brought attention to the issue of migrant labor rights that it certainly would not have otherwise had, the frame is often still economic. Writes the Associated Press, "Colbert's celebrity is a commodity" that Congresswoman Lofgren "sought to leverage."[45]

Amid much of the emphasis on commercial spectacle at the expense of rational-critical substance, a few media voices sought to call attention to Colbert's actual argument—"the truth he spoke," said Keith Olbermann, then still the host of the MSNBC show *Countdown*, "not the truthiness."[46] Similarly on that network, Lawrence O'Donnell celebrated the power of Colbert's appearance to attract cameras to an otherwise obscure congressional subcommittee hearing and the use of that attention to offer the most "eloquent statement on the condition of migrant workers" in the entire hearing.[47] So too did Congresswoman Lofgren herself suggest that "outside the Beltway, people are thinking a point was made, and I think the understanding of farm-worker issues has increased dramatically as a result."[48]

Lofgren's claim about broader public opinion may have been more or less accurate, but on the margins of media discourse, a few voices outside the journalistic and political establishment offered alternative reactions. While much of the mainstream media challenged Colbert's legitimacy and refused to consider the issues in which he was intervening, a few scattered voices sought to engage with and build on his argument. In an opinion piece posted on CNN.com, the evangelical leader Galen Carey, the primary lobbyist for the National Association of Evangelicals, lauded Colbert for, like Murrow before him, focusing "the nation's attention on a very serious issue: the treatment of the hardworking people who produce our nation's food supply." Acknowledging that while some of Colbert's "humor may have been slightly irreverent . . . he did the country a service by highlighting congressional inaction on immigration reform and pointedly referencing the issue's moral dimension." For Carey, Colbert's use of scripture was particularly important, echoing a much older call "to show justice and mercy to those at the very bottom of the social hierarchy." Offering an interpretation of Colbert's testimony radically different from the dominant and dismissive economic frame, Carey suggests Colbert was speaking on behalf of "the civil rights struggle of our day." If "a slightly irreverent comedian can help to prick the nation's conscience and move us to finally rectify this long-standing injustice, then we welcome his intervention."[49]

One finds a similar standpoint even further from the center of media discourse. Writing in the *Muskegon Chronicle*, for example, a local man named Alfred Dabrowski—whose credentials, the paper notes, are that he is "retired from Brunswick Bowling and Billiards" and "has been active in social justice issues for the past 15 years"—uses Colbert's testimony as the launching point to discuss immigration. Dabrowski argues that along with other significant events such as the passing of Arizona's recent immigrant law, "Colbert's testimony . . . remind[s] us there are issues that need to be resolved." That is followed by a thousand-word essay in which he argues for comprehensive immigration reform.[50] Widely dismissed by the mainstream media, the ostensible Fourth Estate entrusted in a democratic system with functioning as a public sphere, Colbert's testimony here resonates at the grassroots level, providing impetus for further engagement. Dabrowski's editorial concludes with a call to action, an invitation for readers of the *Chronicle* to attend a local conference on immigration reform.

On the Legitimacy of Farce

As journalists and pundits struggled to interpret Colbert's testimony, and grassroots activists celebrated it, the *Washington Post* columnist Ruth Marcus well expressed the general confusion. Proclaiming that she is a "huge Colbert fan," Marcus acknowledged the positive attention he could bring to the issue of migrant labor and accepted that irony can play a constructive role in the national political conversation. But she worried that ultimately Colbert's performance before Congress was "farce," and thus, for her, the real question was not "the role of satire in American dialogue" but the "appropriateness of farce at congressional hearings."[51]

The concept of farce provides an intriguing lens through which to consider Colbert's testimony, and indeed the whole of his *Harvest of Shame*. In its most common usage, *farce* suggests something "absurd" and "ridiculous," a posturing tainted by an underlying dishonesty. Thus, as Republican Lamar Smith suggested, if Colbert was pretending, absurdly, to be someone he was not, then the whole thing might indeed be little more than farce, the ridiculous antics of a tone-deaf comedian, and in turn, a degradation of the deliberative political process.

At the same time, though, the term *farce* refers to a specific and rich tradition of comedy. Well describing both Colbert's testimony and his performance in "Fallback Position," farce involves placing characters in incongruous and compromising situations and relying on the actors' improvisational skills to negotiate, often in foolish or lewd fashion, a series of embarrassing pitfalls.[52] Although farce is often unintellectual, provoking belly laughs in place of philosophical reflection, it also can contain satirical edge and encourage "meaningful reflection on the human condition." Indeed, at its core farce is often about victimhood and power: the power of one person over another or of "ideas or misconceptions" over an individual.[53] While we laugh, therefore, at the combination of Colbert's arrogance and ignorance, we are forced to ponder the relations of power he has stumbled on. His farcical intervention in the often-obscured debate over farm labor exposes for us both the victimhood of those who, a half-century after Murrow's exposé, remain exploited and the incompetence of a legislative system that has proved incapable of doing anything about it.

Colbert's *Harvest* thus ultimately asks us to consider the boundaries of acceptable means of political reasoning. It calls on us to recognize that which most in the political and journalistic establishment would have us ignore—that journalism is often spectacle and politics often the empty performance art of which some accused Colbert. In a wider discursive environment in which reason has become a scarce resource, and much political discourse has become farce in the more common usage of the term—the absurd posturing as the reasonable—Colbert's testimony, and his entire engagement with food justice, is a recognition of the unavoidable interweavings of politics and theater, and of journalism and public performance. At the same time, his exploration of the issue—effacing distinctions between the political-normative and the aesthetic-expressive, simultaneously absurd, satirical, and rational-critical—was an attempt to work within this discursively integrated environment in a serious effort to effect some measure of change. Thus Marcus's question is the right one. Is farce appropriate at a congressional hearing? Or more broadly considered, are performative, ironic, and dramaturgical modes of public speech legitimate means for advancing argument and advocating for change? Colbert offered us an experiment in the possibilities of political performance. The blowback it received in the mainstream media suggests it pushed many of us into uncertain territory—using unrecognizable methods to force us to consider our own assumptions, both about the issue of farm labor and about public speech. But that, after all, is the satirist's job.

NOTES

1. Geoffrey Baym, *From Cronkite to Colbert: The Evolution of Broadcast News* (Boulder, CO: Paradigm, 2010).
2. Lynn Schofield Clark, "Religion and Authority in a Remix Culture: How a Late Night TV Host Became an Authority on Religion," in *Religion, Media, & Culture: A Reader*, ed. Gordon Lynch, Jolyon Mitchell, and Anna Strhan (London: Routledge, 2011), 111–21.
3. Keith Beattie, *Documentary Screens: Nonfiction Film and Television* (New York: Palgrave Macmillan, 2004). Although generally credited to Murrow alone, *Harvest* was a team effort by the CBS News staff, including producer David Lowe and executive producer Fred Friendly.
4. Quoted in Robert Gottlieb and Anupama Joshi, *Food Justice* (Cambridge, MA: MIT Press, 2010), 13n1.
5. Gottlieb and Joshi, *Food Justice*.

6. Peter Lee-Wright, *The Documentary Handbook* (New York: Routledge, 2010), 15n6.
7. Reuven Frank, *Out of Thin Air: The Brief Wonderful Life of Network News* (New York: Simon and Schuster, 1991).
8. Baym, *Cronkite to Colbert.*
9. Gottlieb and Joshi, *Food Politics*, 14.
10. Baym, *Cronkite to Colbert.*
11. Gottlieb and Joshi, *Food Politics.*
12. Baym, *Cronkite to Colbert*; see also Geoffrey Baym, "Real News/Fake News: Beyond the News/Entertainment Divide" in *The Routledge Companion to News and Journalism Studies*, ed. Stuart Allan (New York: Routledge, 2009), 374–83.
13. See also Jeffrey P. Jones, *Entertaining Politics: Satiric Television and Political Engagement* (Lanham, MD: Rowman and Littlefield, 2010).
14. See Sophia McClennon, *America According to Colbert: Satire as Public Pedagogy* (New York: Palgrave Macmillan, 2011).
15. Geoffrey Baym, "Stephen Colbert's Parody of the Postmodern" in *Satire TV: Politics and Comedy in the Post-Network Era*, ed. Jonathan Gray, Jeffrey Jones, and Ethan Thompson (New York: New York University Press, 2009), 124–44.
16. Geoffrey Baym, "Representation and the Politics of Play: Stephen Colbert's *Better Know a District*," *Political Communication* 24:4 (2007): 359–76.
17. Gottlieb and Joshi, *Food Politics.*
18. See Amber Day, *Satire and Dissent: Interventions in Contemporary Political Debate* (Bloomington: Indiana University Press, 2011).
19. Debra Bell, "Celebrities Who Have Testified to Congress," *USNEWS.com*, September 24, 2010, http://www.usnews.com/news/slideshows/celebrities-who-have-testified-to-congress.
20. David Corn, "Before Colbert, There Was Twain," *Mother Jones*, September 24, 2010.
21. Baym, *Cronkite to Colbert*; see also Geoffrey Baym, "*The Daily Show*: Discursive Integration and the Reinvention of Political Journalism," *Political Communication* 22:2 (2005): 259–76.
22. Clark, "Religion and Authority in a Remix Culture."
23. *CNN Newsroom*, September 24, 2010.
24. Ashley Parker, "The Whole Truthiness and Nothing But," *New York Times*, September 24, 2010.
25. ABC, "Political Theater: Colbert to Congress," *World News with Diane Sawyer*, September 24, 2010.

26. Leon Wieseltier, "Ghosts," *The New Republic*, October 28, 2010.
27. Baym, *Cronkite to Colbert*; see also Geoffrey Baym, "Serious Comedy: The Expanding Boundaries of Political Discourse" in *Laughing Matters: Humor and American Politics in the Media Age*, ed. Jody Baumgartner and Jonathan Morris (New York: Routledge, 2007), 21–37; Jürgen Habermas, "Modernity—An Incomplete Project," in *The Anti-Aesthetic: Essays on Postmodern Culture*, ed. H. Foster (Seattle: Bay Press, 1983), 3–15; Bruce A. Williams and Michael X. Delli Carpini, *After Broadcast News: Media Regimes, Democracy, and the New Information Environment* (New York: Cambridge University Press, 2011).
28. Doug Underwood, *Journalism and the Novel: Truth and Fiction, 1700–2000* (New York: Cambridge University Press, 2008); Theodore L. Glasser, "Play and the Power of News," *Journalism* 1.1 (2000): 23–29.
29. Jim Jenkins, "Now Playing on Capitol Hill . . . ," *News & Observer* (Raleigh, North Carolina), September 30, 2010.
30. Laurie Kellman, "Colbert Sparks Debate about 'Expert' Celebrities," Associated Press, September 28, 2010.
31. Marin Cogan and Jonathan Allen, "Colbert Turns Hill Hearing into Performance Art," *Politico.com*, September 24, 2010, http://www.politico.com/news/stories/0910/42674.html.
32. Mary Katharine Ham, "Surprise: Colbert Testimony Becomes Side Show Dems Will Regret," *Weekly Standard*, September 24, 2010.
33. Jonah Goldberg, "Cannot Handle the Truthiness?" *Tulsa World* (Oklahoma), October 3, 2010.
34. Wayne C. Booth, *A Rhetoric of Irony* (Chicago: University of Chicago Press, 1975).
35. Hayden White, *Metahistory: The Historical Imagination in Nineteenth-Century Europe* (Baltimore: Johns Hopkins University Press, 1973), 38.
36. Fox News Network, *Special Report with Bret Baier*, September 24, 2010.
37. See Gray, Jones, and Thompson, *Satire TV*.
38. Frank James, "Stephen Colbert Gives 'Truthiness' Jolt on Capitol Hill," *NPR.org*, September 24, 2010, http://www.npr.org/blogs/itsallpolitics/2010/09/24/130106000stephen-colbert-gives-truthiness-jolt-on-capitol-hill.
39. "*Fort Worth Star-Telegram*: Farm Labor Issues No Laughing Matter," *Merced Sun-Star* (California), September 30, 2010.

40. Jeff Simon, "Did Colbert's Comedy Belong in Congress?" *Buffalo News* (New York), September 28, 2010.
41. Fox News Network, *On the Record with Greta Van Susteren*, September 24, 2010.
42. Charles Hurt, "Colbert Shticks It to 'Em At House Hearing," *New York Post*, September 25, 2010.
43. Wieseltier, "Ghosts."
44. Frederic Jameson, *Postmodernism: Or, The Cultural Logic of Late Capitalism* (Durham, NC: Duke University Press, 1991), 17.
45. Kellman, "Colbert Sparks Debate."
46. MSNBC, *Countdown*, September 24, 2010.
47. MSNBC, *The Last Word with Lawrence O'Donnell*, September 27, 2010.
48. Quoted in Ruth Marcus, "Colbert's Circus Tent," *Washington Post*, September 29, 2010.
49. Galen Carey, "Colbert's Reminder: Immigration a Moral Issue," *CNN.com*, September 29, 2010.
50. Alfred Dabrowski, "Learn More about Comprehensive Immigration Reform," *Muskegon Chronicle* (Michigan), October 1, 2010.
51. Marcus, "Colbert's Circus Tent."
52. Kenneth Pickering, *Key Concepts in Drama and Performance* (New York: Palgrave Macmillan, 2010).
53. Norman R. Shapiro, "Farce," in *Comedy: A Geographic and Historical Guide*, ed. Maurice Charney (Westport, CT: Praeger, 2005), 296, 306.

Contributors

Geoffrey Baym is Associate Professor of Media Studies at the University of North Carolina at Greensboro. He is the author of the award-winning *From Cronkite to Colbert: The Evolution of Broadcast News* (Oxford University Press, 2010) and lead editor of *News Parody and Political Satire Across the Globe* (Routledge, 2012). His work exploring the changing styles and standards of public affairs media and political discourse has also appeared in numerous scholarly journals and anthologies.

Mark Canada is Professor of English and Dean of the College of Arts and Sciences at the University of North Carolina at Pembroke, where he teaches courses in American literature. A former newspaper journalist, he is the author of *Literature and Journalism in Antebellum America* (Palgrave, 2011), as well as essays on Edgar Allan Poe, Theodore Dreiser, Rebecca Harding Davis, Thomas Wolfe, and other subjects in *The Southern Literary Journal, American Literary Realism, Journalism History*, and other publications.

John Fenstermaker is Fred L. Standley Professor of English, Emeritus, at Florida State University, where he has served as English Chair and Director, Program in American and Florida Studies. His current scholarship focuses on Ernest Hemingway's life and work between the World Wars, specifically on the Key West years, the author's most varied and prolific period. Author of three books, including, with Richard D. Altick, *The Art of Literary Research*, he most recently has published essays in *Key West Hemingway: A Reassessment* and in *Hemingway: Eight Decades of Criticism*.

Charles Johanningsmeier is the author of *Fiction and the American Literary Marketplace: The Role of Newspaper Syndicates, 1860–1900*, as well as numerous articles about the interactions between periodical readers and serialized fiction in the late nineteenth and early twentieth centuries. He teaches at the University of Nebraska at Omaha.

Elizabeth Lorang is a Research Assistant Professor in the Department of English and Center for Digital Research in the Humanities at the University of Nebraska-Lincoln, where she is the project manager and associate editor of the *Walt Whitman Archive* (http://whitmanarchive.org) and project manager and research associate of *Civil War Washington* (http://civilwardc.org). With Susan Belasco, she edited *Whitman's Poems in Periodicals*, available on the *Whitman Archive*. She is currently at work, with Rebecca Weir, on an electronic scholarly edition of poems published in the *Anglo-African* and *National Anti-Slavery Standard* during the Civil War. Her work has appeared in *Documentary Editing*, the *Mickle Street Review*, *Texas Studies in Literature and Language*, *Victorian Periodicals Review*, and the *Walt Whitman Quarterly Review*.

Carla Mulford teaches early American, Native American, and environmental studies at the Pennsylvania State University, where she has been a faculty member since 1986. The Founding President of the Society of Early Americanists, she has also served on the Executive Committee of the Modern Language Association's Division of American Literature to 1800. She has published nine books and more than sixty articles and chapters in books. Her current preoccupation is Benjamin Franklin, on whom she has planned three monographs. She has completed *Benjamin Franklin and the Ends of Empire* and is about to embark on her new book, *Benjamin Franklin and the Arts of Science*. Examples of the Franklin work have already been published (13 essays), in addition to *The Cambridge Companion to Benjamin Franklin* (2009).

David S. Reynolds is Distinguished Professor of English and American Studies at the CUNY Graduate Center. He is the author of the prize-winning books *Walt Whitman's America*, *Beneath the American Renaissance*, *John Brown, Abolitionist*, and *Waking Giant: America in the Age of Jackson*. His most recent book is *Mightier Than the Sword:* Uncle Tom's Cabin *and the Battle for America*.

Karen Roggenkamp is Associate Professor of English at Texas A&M University-Commerce. She is the author of *Narrating the News: New Journalism and Literary Journalism in Nineteenth-Century American Newspapers and Fiction*. She has published articles on periodical culture, children's literature, and American literature in such journals as *American Periodicals*, *The Lion and the Unicorn*, and *American Literary Realism*.

Andie Tucher, an associate professor at the Columbia University Graduate School of Journalism, has been the director of the Communications PhD program there since its founding in 1998. Her book *Happily Sometimes After: A Story of American Stories*, which explores the intersections of history, memory, storytelling, and the pursuit of happiness in one family's 400-year-long American experience, is forthcoming from the University of Massachusetts Press. She is also the author of *Froth and Scum: Truth, Beauty, Goodness, and the Ax-Murder in America's First Mass Medium* (University of North Carolina Press, 1994), a cultural and social history of the founding of the mass commercial newspaper press in the 1830s and 1840s, which won the Society of American Historians' Allan Nevins Prize. Tucher's articles on aspects of journalism and cultural history have appeared in *Book History*, *Journalism History*, *Cultural Studies*, *Journalism Practice*, the *Journal of Communication Inquiry*, the *Columbia Journalism Review*, *Common-place.org*, and other scholarly and popular publications. Before coming to Columbia, Tucher spent ten years in print and broadcast journalism.

Doug Underwood is Professor of Communication at the University of Washington, where he teaches in the areas of journalism and literature, media and religion, and media ethics and management. He is the author of four books, including *Journalism and the Novel* (2008), *From Yahweh to Yahoo!* (2002), and *When MBAs Rule the Newsroom* (1993). *From Yahweh to Yahoo!* won a 2003 Distinguished Book Award from the Society for the Scientific Study of Religion (SSSR). His latest book, *Chronicling Trauma: Journalists and Writers on Violence and Loss* (University of Illinois Press, 2011), examines the influence of childhood neglect, substance abuse issues, war-time experience, and other traumatic events in the lives and literature of well-known journalist–literary figures. He is a former political and investigative reporter for *The Seattle Times*, the Gannett News Service, and the *Lansing (Mich.) State Journal*.

INDEX

Printed in the United States of America